BEHIND GOD'S BACK:

FINDING HOPE IN HARDSHIP

A MEMOIR

Terry Miller

Developmental editor: Stephen Jarrett, Wemmick Editing
Cover concept: Mary Ellen Trenga and Terry Miller
Cover art and book layout designer: Rainey Opperman-Dermond

All photos are reprinted with permissions as noted in book photo credits.

A portion of "Behind God's Back: Finding Hope in Hardship"
was previously published as "Sticks and Bones"
in *Pittsburgh Quarterly Magazine*, Winter 2015.
Reprinted with permission.

Author's website: terrymmiller.com

Developmental editor's website: wemmickediting.com

Publisher: Hail the Goer Books
Headquarters: Milton, Delaware
Publisher website: htgbooks.com

hail
the
goer
BOOKS

Dot asked me, "Tell me, Terry, where'd you grow up?"

"Arlington Heights," I said. "You know, back in the projects."

Dot sucked in her breath, shook her head, and moaned, "Oh, mercy, child. My, my. Way up there on that hill … behind God's back."

I felt her words. She knew, and she was right.

There were many nights I felt I was growing up behind a long, cold shadow: at the back of God.

ACKNOWLEDGMENTS

Writing a memoir is hard work. Actually, it's heart and gut wrenching, but also more rewarding than I ever could have imagined. None of it would be possible without the kind and loving encouragement of family and friends along this long road.

In 2004, after a national educational forum on "ending welfare as we know it," where I shared, for the first time, some of my personal story of living in poverty and with childhood trauma before an audience of my colleagues, Marge Petruska, an ardent child care advocate, walked up to me and said, "Please tell me you are writing your story!" I thank Marge for igniting the spark in me to begin what has turned out to be a journey home to myself.

Jason Deparle, *New York Times* best-selling author and migration and welfare journalist, the keynote speaker at the event, supported this idea and encouraged me to keep writing. That I did, mostly in fits and starts. But, sixteen years later, I now have a book. Thank you, Jason.

To those who supported me through the years: Marie Hamblett, Elizabeth Beck, Sheila Johnson, Tara Johnson, Janet Horsch, Diane Hernon Chavis, Renny Clark, Emma Liebowicz, and, more recently, Lucia Ellis, I thank you.

A very special thanks to those who slogged their way through the early disjointed, overly explicated, often coffee-stained and doodled-upon drafts of my writing and inspired me keep going: Moe Coleman, Bruce Barron, Kathy McCauley, Jan Beatty, and Jason. Thank you for the magic of your foresight—hearing the story in me before I heard it myself.

To those friends and mentors who served as spiritual anchors as I moved through some of the most difficult aspects of my healing and my writing, keeping me buoyed and away from an open sea of self-doubt: the "home girls," Dr. Abraham Twerski, Suzanne Anderson, Dot Talley, Marijke van Linden, Jodi Butler, and Mary Stokes, I thank you.

A very special thanks to my therapist, Karen Barwick: You continue to help me embrace my truth and my "crackerjack" with open hands and heart.

You recognized and voiced to me that my book was another way "… to be of service to those who are on a path of healing or seeking to do so." This call to service is a prize unto itself.

To other members of my literary village who read and reread the later versions of *Behind God's Back*, providing first impressions, critical insights, and editorial feedback: You drove home my understanding that the book is not really about me. Rather, it is about the larger life lessons that are shared to encourage a collective healing that can take place in the interactive space between the author and the reader. My thanks to those village elders: Maxwell King, Mark Nordenberg, Edie Shapira, Aaron Lauer, Bruce Barron, Gen Davidson, Phyllis Cratty, Carol Trenga, and Cheryl Harding.

To Jolie Williamson: Thank you for joining the tribe at the eleventh hour providing the final, final, final proofreading of the book! Your discerning eye and sharp editing skills strengthened the manuscript and my gifts as a writer. I'm delighted to be reconnected with you.

To Rainey Opperman-Dermond, a talented graphic and industrial designer, with whom I worked professionally for many years: You did not miss a beat, enthusiastically signing onto the project when I asked. Your eloquently clean design of both the interior and cover for the book conveys a simple yet universal truth: that there is hope in hardship. Thank you for bringing your years of experience; your beautifully artistic eye; and your patience, passion, and ability to problem solve in your spirited, open, and kind nature. What a prize you are!

To Stephen Jarrett, whom I owe a debt of gratitude: In 2016, when I determined to roll up my sleeves and really set my heart to writing, Max King said to me "Hire an editor and dig deep." I did. I reached out to Stephen, my stepson, who is a gifted writer, editor, and overall renaissance talent. From the onset of our collaboration, I coined you my "book doula," because without you, *Behind God's Back* would not be. Beyond providing administrative, structural, and technical editorial support, you journeyed with me on an ethereal shuttle between my present and past worlds, gently probing, prodding, and pushing me through intrapersonal veils of mind and spirit, helping me heal my parts and restore my whole. You are a gifted young man with an insightful old soul, and I love you for it.

Finally, to my dear wife, Mary Ellen: What a whirlwind it has been in these years of our togetherness. I have so much to thank you for: being such a smart and discerning early editor, helping me clarify thoughts and untangle storylines; for providing support as I moved through emotional highs and lows as I wrote; for shouting, "Mangia!" and feeding me when I lost track of the time, day, week. For intuitively knowing when I needed a break and inviting me to walk with you and Ollie—our little Buddha. For tolerating my attacking you as soon as your feet hit the floor, coffee in hand, goading you into impromptu wordsmithing sessions before you were fully awake. What a magically intuitive time of day this is. Did I mention, thank you for feeding me? For your belief and spirited insistence that my work is good, my story important, and that it will help others to heal. For intuitively knowing when to offer me a squeeze at the end of especially difficult writing sessions. "Mangia," my love. To eat at the banquet of life with you is a blessing. I so love and appreciate you, and now the world knows, too.

Women of POWER—to all of you: Welcome! And please keep coming back. We need you! To Rosa Davis and all of the team—leadership, staff, donors, community, volunteers – thank you for keeping the light on for all of those who have travelled through POWER's doors and for those who are yet to come.

To my "First State" Recovery Tribe. You know who you are! Thank you for keeping me spiritually sustained, "one day at a time."

TABLE OF CONTENTS

PROLOGUE

In October 1986, I traveled to West Virginia with my friend, colleague, and mentor, Dot. She's someone from whom you will hear a great deal in the pages that follow. Our drive through West Virginia's Allegheny Mountains was breathtaking. Cheat Mountain with its high, rugged, stone-faced ridge stood in stark contrast to the rolling hills ablaze with hues of amber, scarlet, crimson, and auburn that lit our path along Route 33 as we snaked our way into the small town of Elkins. We were directed to our room at the Super 8 Hotel, a place in clear opposition to the majestic landscape we'd just passed through. We pulled our luggage across the littered grounds and into our room with sagging curtains, forced-air wind, and fluorescent sunshine.

"Ah, 'almost heaven,'" Dot quipped with a chuckle.

"Yeah, but 'home sweet home' for now, Dot. I've been thrown out of places worse than this. No frills, no distractions. Just our message, our audience, and us," I said.

The contrast grounded me in reality. Dot and I had been invited to West Virginia to present at a statewide drug and alcohol conference on women and addiction. In 1986, this was still a relatively new field of study and training. We were the featured "content experts," and that rattled me.

Trying to shore-up my self-confidence, I convinced myself that though our work was relatively new, we were sharing important lessons about the unique barriers and challenges women in recovery experience, distinct from their male counterparts. Our presentation would address trauma, motherhood, biological and cultural stigmas, and gender inequalities.

I settled into my room, anxiously reviewing my notes in preparation for our presentation. Dot knocked on the door.

"You ready?" she asked.

"Well," I said, shaking my head and wringing my hands, "today's the day they find out I'm a fraud."

Dot recoiled.

"You need to quit that," she bit. "God don't make junk. In fact, get over here and look in this mirror," she ordered me.

I reluctantly agreed.

She stood behind me, straightening my posture.

"Look into your eyes," she said.

Irritated, I took a deep breath and looked at my face. I zeroed in on a big zit on my cheek, one I wished I had obscured with a little more cover-up.

"I said your eyes, Terry."

Instead, I fixed my gaze on my hair, thinking I had done a pretty decent job cutting my own bangs. I wasn't interested in looking any lower.

"You know why it's so hard to fix on your eyes?" Dot asked. "Cause the eyes are the windows to the soul. The windows to that place inside us that's sacred and holy. When you're feeling unworthy, it's hard to even peek through the windows towards that sacredness. And the eyes aren't even the whole picture. Just a glimpse of it. Still, I want you to look into your eyes now and repeat after me."

"Alright," I shrugged.

Dot stood behind me, put her hands on my shoulders and looked into my eyes.

"C'mon, now," she coaxed.

Breathing shakily, I squared my shoulders and stared right into the center of my eyes.

"There you are. Now repeat after me. 'Terry Miller, one day, you'll be my best friend.'" Dutifully, I repeated Dot's words: "Terry Miller, one day, you'll be my best friend."

I felt ridiculous, because I knew full well that was never going to happen, but I said it anyway. I said the words in the hotel room. We then gave our presentations: earnest and imperfectly delivered gestures that made things—in some small way—better for the women we were there to represent and support.

Now, fast forward about twenty years. I'm trying to parallel park in front of my house, cussing up a blue streak for the neighbors who've hemmed me in. As I start to turn my head on the third cut of the wheels, I catch, for just a second, the reflection of my right eye in the corner of the rear-view mirror. I remember that moment with Dot in the hotel room and dissolve into tears, knowing full well, in that moment—in my soul—that I have become my own best friend.

I don't know when it happened exactly. Nor do I know exactly when I lost my sense of sacredness, my ability to peek through the windows to see myself in my totality. I don't know if I ever really felt my own sacredness as a child. What I do know is that I grew up with an absentee father; a sick, depressed and alcoholic mother; and a colicky little brother. I lived in an atmosphere of hunger, neglect, and abuse. My parents turned their backs on me, and I followed their example—walking away from myself, believing I was unworthy of anything resembling love. Like them, I learned early on that pain could be quelled with an elixir of drugs and alcohol. So that's what I did.

I'm one of the lucky ones, though. In the early 1980s, a moment of grace derailed me from my path of self-destruction, and with the help of a dear friend whom you'll soon hear about, I got clean and sober. Once the fog and malaise of my eighteen-year addiction lifted, however, the years of my accumulated fear, shame, loneliness, and not-enough-ness consumed me. Over time, and with the support of kind and caring friends, professionals, and others, I came to learn that poverty, abuse, neglect, and hunger were not the fundamental traumas in my life. In truth, the core trauma was the fracturing and splitting off of my spirit that happened within me because of those things—the loss of my dreams, my hopes, my desire. My essence.

I have worked hard through all my adult life to heal the physical, emotional, and mental wounds of my past so that I can reclaim my spiritual essence, which I believe is my birthright. I have found that there are many ways into this work. It begins with an honest recognition that the work is necessary, that it is possible, and that I am worthy of it. There's the catch. Because, when I feel unworthy and am riddled with self-doubt and low self-regard, the last thing I want to do is take positive action on my own behalf, especially asking for help.

In one of the darkest hours in my life, when I was emotionally, physically, and spiritually wrecked behind an episode of abuse that I experienced in my recovery, I reached out to Dot for help. In that moment, I did not believe I was worthy of the support, but I knew it was necessary if I wanted to be restored to emotional and spiritual equilibrium.

Asking for (or giving) help never requires perfection. When Dot and I offered our presentation in Elkins, West Virginia, I was speaking to women just like me, riddled with their own self-doubt, fear, and feelings of unworthiness. I can even remember the fluorescent lights in the room that day letting out a persistent, high-pitched whir throughout the presentation, as if to say, "Throw in the towel, Miller. Who do you think you are?" It was yet another bit of imperfection to accept, but that's the whole point, and an unavoidable one, too. We seek and give help in states of imperfection, offering all that we can in the effort to heal ourselves and others. The only "perfection" lies in the heart of the gesture itself, in the impulse to show compassion towards yourself or another person in need.

The practice of letting go has been another important part of my healing: the relinquishing of my attachments to tired and worn-out people, places, things, beliefs, attitudes, and emotions. Restoration via negativa. It's included releasing my grip on habitual negative thinking that I now understand is rooted in my past, a past that always remains ripe for projection into my future and is a main source of my suffering. I used to cling to the remnants of my past as though they were worth something. In some measure, they were, because until I was able to fully embrace those spirit-stripping accounts of myself, I was not able to release them.

An important part of this journey to reclaim my spiritual essence has been to be in service of others. I have found that great personal healing occurs when I turn my attention to the needs of others rather than focusing solely on myself—my needs, my worries, my woe-is-me-ness. To reconnect with my essence, it has been necessary to review my life experiences but not to wallow in them. The best way to not wallow is to be of service to others.

In writing this book, I recount what amounts to my journey home. In the process, I have responded to the cries of my confused young woman, to the tears of my lost and angry adolescent, and to the shuttering of my frightened yet courageous child. By humbly turning and facing every dimension of myself,

I have walked into the prize of my spiritual essence. And, by responding to my own wails of worthiness—my desire to be acknowledged with love, decency, and respect—I have allowed my traumas to inform my story but not to be my story.

I believe that healing takes place in the interactive space between the writer and the reader. It is my hope that some aspect of the account of my life will land in the heart of at least one person. We all are worthy of turning toward, facing, and embracing every aspect of ourselves. I have found that the ultimate prize is the reclamation of our sacredness—our universal and first home.

This small book, then, is my offering to you who are starting or are continuing on your path. You are not alone.

1.

MRS. WELLINGTON'S PARTY

In 1961, Mama found a coveted plot of subsidized housing on Grandview Street in Pittsburgh's Arlington Heights. Without any discussion, she announced to us kids that it was time "to move on and move up." The distance from our then-home in the projects of Arlington Heights to Grandview Street—barely a mile—struck me as an unbridgeable gulf: an expanse not only between the known and unknown, but between the black world and the white world.

When we moved to Grandview Street, I resumed simple routines to comfort myself: collecting pop bottles for refunds, humming soul music I learned from Miss Bessie, and walking back from school with my childhood friends from the projects. But in my new world, even as a seven-year-old girl, I was met with epithets from white classmates, who called me "white chocolate" and "n____-lover" for fraternizing after school with the blacks from the projects, the place I considered my real home.

Even Mama lamented my unwillingness to assimilate. She asked me, in polite and measured terms, to abandon those who had cared for me when she didn't or couldn't do so herself. I had found pockets of compassion in the projects— in Miss Bessie's grits and homemade hot sauce, in stoop-sitting afternoons when mamas braided their daughters' hair and discussed all sorts of things that I didn't understand, in humming along with Mr. Chester's Southern Baptist hymns, and in my best friend Patty Reevers' laughter. Together, these were antidotes to my suffering. Needless to say, the move to Grandview Street was more than a little disorienting to me, a little white girl who got along so well with her black neighbors.

Just before we moved, our upstairs neighbor, Betty Wellington, threw a party. Mama, who suffered frequent dark spells, was in a rare, animated mood and announced to me and my older brother, Eddie, that we were "going to a party!" I squealed with delight when Mama told Eddie to start the bath for me, stage one of preparations for what felt like a distinguished masquerade ball. I couldn't think of the night as bittersweet, a flash of light on the eve of some disorienting change. I was just grateful for Mama's mobilization, for the prospect of us—as a family—experiencing some small measure of contentment.

I was in and out of the tub in a flash as Eddie moped and dragged himself into the bathroom, distressed over his mandated participation. In retrospect, I realize he was attuned to our Mama's highs and lows, intuiting that Mama's cheer would be followed by one of her then-trademark plummets.

"Put your pajamas on. Then come here and let me brush your hair," Mama said.

I was excited because I had a fresh outfit for the party. I had just been given some new-to-me pajamas from Miss Bessie, who lived the next building over. The bottoms were pink with a small white ruffle at the ankle, with a pink-and-white checked top and a bow at the top button. They looked almost new, except for a small blood stain on the right sleeve from when Sharmane, the original owner, had almost sliced off her finger trying to open a tuna can.

"That child bled like a stuck pig," Miss Bessie had told Mama. "Cut that finger straight through to the bone. I thought she was going to lose it. Anyway, Sharmie's grown out of these and if you'd like them for Terry, you're welcome to them."

Mama didn't like taking charity from anyone, but everyone in the projects shared things, so that made it all right. Besides, Miss Bessie and I were close. She had fed me black-eyed peas and collard greens on days I had gone without anything to eat, and when I would show up at her house—inconsolable and crying—she would sing to me and hold me in her family's old rocking chair until I calmed down. Wearing the pajamas made me feel connected with Miss Bessie, her love for me, and my surrogate family next door.

"Hey, Mama. Look. Sharmie's pajamas fit. I like them."

I didn't mind the blood stain on the sleeve. This was my first set of pajamas that came—originally, at least—from a retail store. Mama had made most of my wardrobe from discarded fabric she got on sale from the local five-and-dime. She would walk in and ask for "bolt ends," almost always plaid, sometimes getting them for free. Mama took whatever she could and used butcher's paper to trace and embellish designs for different outfits I needed. Some of these outfits—almost exclusively plaid—were elegant and impressive, revealing just one of her many natural talents. Nonetheless, until Sharmie's PJs arrived, I had been wearing a well-designed but woolen nightgown in the summertime. I had a perpetual rash around my neck and scratch marks on my arms because the fabric was so irritating and uncomfortable. Mama tried to soften the prickly fibers by soaking the pajamas in vinegar, but this only added a sour smell to the irredeemable cloak, which felt to me like some mixture of a straitjacket and a monastic hair shirt.

I smiled broadly at her, modeling the new pajamas.

"Yes, you look splendid, honey. Now stand still," she said.

I stood before the small vanity mirror at Mama's dresser and tried not to make too much of a fuss as she pulled the stiff-toothed brush through my tangled blonde hair. It felt good to be regarded by her.

"Okay, little miss. You're all done. Now it's my turn," she said, laughing. "First, we need some music. Find Billie Holiday and put her on the phonograph."

I did as she said. Mama was on her second highball already and she was letting me put the record on the record player—a rare privilege.

I sorted through the stack of records, wildly swinging the Billie Holiday album in the air.

"This one, Mama?"

"Yes, that's it. Now be careful," she commanded.

"Yes, ma'am," I replied.

Be careful, be careful, be careful, I whispered to myself. I slowly pulled the record out of the album cover, then out of the sleeve, holding only the very ends of the record with my fingers as I tiptoed toward the record player.

"Be mindful not to scratch it," Mama said.

I adjusted the arm, lowered Billie onto the stem, returned the arm until it clicked, and turned on the machine. The turntable began to spin, the record released, and finally it fell down the stack. My hand trembled as I put the needle to the record and the speaker on the little RCA phonograph crackled, a sign of reassurance. Like magic, Billie's voice came through the speaker as she sang "Crazy He Calls Me," and Mama matched Billie's singing every slow, sultry, rhythmic beat of the way, both of their voices hanging in the air— as thick, rich, and velvety as Miss Bessie's homemade chocolate pudding. I knew this was going to be a wonderful night.

❄

With a Winston cigarette burning at her side, Mama sidled up to the vanity mirror with special lights and prepared to apply oils, lotions, powders, and polish to her face—a batch of alluring concoctions I couldn't begin to understand.

Perched on the dresser, I listened closely as Mama explained the art of applying makeup.

"The foundation evens out your skin tone," she explained, "and blush adds color to your cheeks. It's very important to apply it with sweeping upward strokes—always upwards—across your cheekbones so as not to show any makeup lines. Nothing is more unsightly than a woman walking around looking like she has a mask on."

Nothing's worse than a woman with a mask on, I memorized.

"Makeup should enhance a woman's beauty. You understand?"

"Yes, Mama," I said.

"Ready for your next lesson?" she asked.

I nodded.

"Okay, this is the most critical part. We're now going to dress the eyes— applying the eyeliner, mascara, and eye shadow. Special care must always be given to dressing the eyes. *Cosmopolitan* magazine says the eyes are the most attractive feature on women, so it's extremely important to get the dressing just right—too little and you won't get noticed, too much and you look like a clown. We don't want to look like clowns, do we? The idea is to have a subtly dramatic, alluring look."

I repeated the part of her instruction I had actually understood: *Too much and you look like a clown.*

"Now, the most important thing about applying eyeliner and mascara is having a steady but loose hand," she said. "And you know," she added, raising her glass in the air, "there's nothing better to relax your hand than a good stiff whiskey."

With a wink and a laugh to no one in particular, she knocked back the last of her drink.

"Run and make me another one. Then come back and you can help me with my eye shadow."

"Lickety split, Mama?"

"Lickety split," she replied.

I dashed off into the kitchen to make her highball.

Grabbing the bottle from under the kitchen sink, I shouted "Three or four fingers, Mama?"

"Those little fingers of yours? Better make it four, honey. And top her off with the ginger ale."

Unscrewing the cap of the Seagram's 7 bottle, I lowered my nose to get a whiff. The fumes were so strong that they made my eyes water. I carefully poured the dark elixir to the top line in the little shot glass, added ice from the black and gold ice bucket on the sink, and dashed it off with a touch of ginger ale. With the same care I had shown the Billie Holiday record, I walked back into the bedroom, holding the glass with two hands so as not to spill a drop.

"Good job, baby. Now come and help me finish my makeup."

"Can I pick the color?" I asked.

"You can," Mama said, as she swigged down some of her drink, wincing.

Eyeing her glass, she said, "Mmm, really good job, baby."

I smiled.

"I'm thinking about wearing my white shirt this evening, so what color eye shadow do you think I should wear?"

I surveyed the little palette of eye colors—brown, blue, green, white, silver, and pink—and deliberated with grave seriousness, hoping my answer would be the right one, the one that pleased her.

"I think silver and brown, mixed together. Brown for your eyes and silver for the sparkle."

"Good choices," Mama said. "That *will* create the alluring effect we talked about. Start here on the lower lid with the brown. Brush strokes from the inner part of the lid outwards and highlight with the silver on the upper brow using the same method. Use even strokes, inner to outer brow."

She took a long inhale of her Winston and puffed it out.

Leaning into my mother's face, I lightly brushed the sienna dust onto her lower eyelids. But I couldn't contain myself. The soft scent of Oil of Olay on her skin, the Maybelline powder on her face, the shot of Estee Lauder behind her ear, the whiskey ale on her breath—all contained in a fresh cloud of cigarette smoke—made me giggle with such complete abandon that Mama had to finish the job herself.

"You silly little thing," she said, tickling me as I collapsed in laughter, doubling over. "Let's get me dressed."

Mama fetched a large white men's shirt from the closet, one she'd picked up at the Goodwill thrift store. She had thrown padding in the shoulders, added front and back darts to cinch in the waist, and raw-stitched black arrows on the collar tips. The shirt was utterly transformed.

I watched as she slid her long legs into her black slacks and shimmied into the crisp white shirt she'd somehow rendered beautiful. She rolled the sleeves to three-quarter length and added a bright red chiffon scarf around her neck.

"What do you think, honey?" she said.

I was mesmerized.

"You're beautiful, Mama."

She continued to stare into the mirror, unfazed, examining and adjusting herself.

"Earrings or no earrings?" she asked.

"Hmmmm, you decide," I said.

Standing tall at 5'11", turning her head this way and that in the mirror's reflection, she flipped up the back of her shirt collar, threw me a wink, and said, "I'll let my neck carry my elegance this evening."

❄

She polished off the last of her whiskey, applied Kiss Me Red lipstick to her lips, and we were on our way.

❄

Waiting in the dimly lit entryway, we had knocked on the door several times. Eddie, Mama, and I were waiting for Mrs. Wellington to appear. All we

Mama dressed for dancing, circa 1950

had to do was walk upstairs to get to the party, but every aspect of the night felt out of the ordinary—enriched and ceremonial.

Mrs. Wellington opened the door with a smile. She was a large, beautiful woman with skin the color of Tootsie Rolls. She often wore low-slung blouses and tight sweaters that accentuated her large breasts. The men fell all over her. I loved being around her, too, because she was loving, strong, and sassy.

"Oh Marie, I'm so glad you decided to come. And your little ones, too. Welcome," Mrs. Wellington said.

"Terry. Eddie. Your manners, please," Mama prompted.

"Good evening, Mrs. Wellington," Eddie greeted.

"Hi, Miss Betty," I squealed, hugging her around the waist.

"Would you like a soda?" she asked.

"Yes, please. A cherry soda," I said.

"I'll have a root beer, please, Mrs. Wellington," Eddie replied.

"Well, you're both in luck tonight. We're all stocked up. Have a seat over there on the sofa, and I'll be right back with your sodas."

"Marie, the drinks are in the kitchen. Make yourself whatever you'd like," Mrs. Wellington said.

"Thank you, Betty. Don't mind if I do. Eddie, mind your sister and both of you mind your manners."

"Yes, ma'am," we replied in unison. Mama disappeared into the kitchen.

Eddie and I made our way through the crowded, smoke-filled room as a group of men and women swayed to the pulsating bossa nova beat of "The Girl from Ipanema." I plopped down on the gargantuan, red leather sofa, and Eddie sat right beside me.

"Never seen anything like this, Eddie," I said.

Eddie surveyed the crowd.

"Yeah, that Mrs. Wellington sure has some fine stuff for someone living in the projects. And look at all this food," he added, pointing towards the nearby table.

Eddie and I ogled the trays of chips and salsa, chicken wings, greens, potato and bean salads. The things that most caught my eye were the tiny hot dogs wrapped in dough. For us, this was a cornucopia worthy of reverence.

"Eddie, look at those little wieners. How're you supposed to put ketchup on them?"

"You don't, silly. You just plop them in your mouth," he replied.

We laughed.

"I'm taking one," I said.

"No, you're not. Not unless Ma says it's okay. You stay here. I'll go and ask," he said.

"I'll stay right here," I promised.

Eddie was gone for what seemed like forever while I sat there being taunted by the food. I'd had a meal that day, because it was my turn to have one, but I was still aching for one of those little hot dogs. I was sure Mama wouldn't mind me having just one, but I waited anyway.

Looking through the crowd, I spotted Mama in the kitchen. She was talking with two men and Eddie was nowhere in sight. I watched as Mama's hips swayed to the music and I smiled because I could see she was happy. Catching my eye, she tipped her glass in my direction, and I blew a kiss out to her. She grabbed it in the air with her free hand and stuck it in her shirt.

I reached for the tiny hot dog tray and, lifting it in the air, silently asked, "Mama, can I have a hot dog?" Securing the approving nod, I dove in.

"What are you so happy about, little missy?" a man asked me, approaching the couch.

"That's Mama over there dancing, and she said I could have some of these little hot dogs. You ever see anything like this before? I like my hot dogs with ketchup, but I don't see how you put it on with the bread wrapped around it like this. Eddie says you just plop them in your mouth, but who ever heard of eating a hot dog without ketchup? Heinz 57 is my favorite. Mama makes soup out of it sometimes. You think Mrs. Wellington has any ketchup?" I asked.

The man laughed.

"Oh, I bet she does. You go on and ask her when she comes by. But why don't you try some of that chicken over there?" he said.

I had my heart set on the little hot dogs, but my mouth watered at the sight of the chicken legs. Surely Mama wouldn't mind. Around that time, our meals were cobbled together from surplus wartime rations distributed at the old Croatian Center on Carson Street. We would wait in a long line once a month to carry powdered eggs, powdered milk, blocks of government cheese, vats of peanut butter, and—occasionally—a few cans of Spam back to our apartment in Courtyard #7. Toward the latter half of each month, our food ran thin and we would have to ration out meals on a cycle, each of us skipping meals on certain days. Since Mama had diabetes, I sometimes skipped more meals than I should have.

"Let me fix you a plate," the man offered.

Mrs. Wellington came by, and the man said, "Hey, Betty, we need some Heinz 57 over here."

"Coming up," Miss Betty said.

She was gone and back in a flash, handing the man the bottle of Heinz 57. He returned to the big red sofa, offering me a plate set with a chicken leg and a big glob of ketchup.

"Here you go, little miss. Why don't you dip your hot dogs right in there?"

"Thank you," I said.

Reaching out to the platter, I selected several tiny hot dogs and put them on my plate. I dipped one into the ketchup and bit into it.

"Hey, it tastes just like a real hot dog," I said, licking the red sauce from my fingers.

"What's your name?" the man asked.

"Terry," I said. "What's yours?"

"They call me Whitey. 'Cause of my white hair," he said, rustling it to demonstrate.

"I have white hair too," I said.

"Yes, you do. And beautiful white hair at that," he said.

"Yes, that's what a lot of people say. I like my hair," I replied.

"Well, it sure is beautiful. Almost as beautiful as your mama," he said, looking toward the kitchen and shaking his head.

"I helped her get ready for the party. She let me dress her eyes. You know *Cosmo* magazine? It says the eyes are the most important part of a woman's face."

"Really? Well, you did a real fine job, 'cause your mama sure is pretty," he reiterated.

Half listening, I agreed again, but my attention switched to the chicken leg on my plate. Never before had I ever had a full chicken leg for myself. When we did have chicken, Mama and Eddie ate the skin and meat, and I got the meat on the bone and the knuckles. Mama always said the meat closest to the bone was the sweetest, so it should go to the sweetest one in the family.

Whitey left me to enjoy my food, and Eddie finally returned, flustered.

"Where'd you get that chicken? Does Ma know you're eating that?"

"Yeah, a nice man made me a plate. Mama said I could have the little hot dogs, too. Where'd you go?" I asked.

"Ollie Mason's here with his Mom. I was with them," he replied.

"Get some food," I said. "Mama says it's okay. And the chicken is gooooood," I said, drawing out the vowel.

I watched Eddie make his way to the food table and deliberate with trademark stoicism over which items to choose, all while I smacked my lips around the soft chicken meat and licked the grease from my fingers, shamelessly enjoying the food.

Somebody cranked up the music, and "Rock Around the Clock" blared throughout the apartment. Everybody rose to their feet dancing, and I watched as I finished my feast.

I saw Mama dancing off in the corner with several men. She had a drink and cigarette going and she laughed heartily at something one of her admirers had said. Against my will, I was reminded of our trips to the local bar, Stan's Café, where Mama would sometimes dance with older men in exchange for some money or a meal for me and Eddie. The worst part was when she would summon me from the booth where Eddie and I sat, coaxing me to "Give Jimmy a spin." Jimmy, or Jumbo Jim as I disparagingly called him, worked at the butcher's counter in the local food market. I now realize that Jimmy was one of Mama's johns, a "paying customer" and regular of hers. On more than one night, I would endure the stench of Old Spice and bologna on Jimmy's sweaty clothes while he pressed my little head against his hardened crotch during a suffocating slow dance. There was no intervention from the Kachansky family who were eating pizza at the corner table in the backroom or from the owner, Stan, or from Mama laughing with a group of men she drank with in a nearby booth. For me, it was just a momentary nightmare set to the Duprees' "You Belong to Me" and the inescapable evidence of Jimmy and Mama's "nightcap," which I would hear later, long into the night.

Many nights, after Mama and Eddie were asleep, I would creep into the living room where Mama slept, tiptoeing across the cracked linoleum floor to pull a cover over her body and kiss her on the forehead. It was my way of checking to make sure her diabetes wasn't flaring up. If she had a bead of sweat on her forehead and a soft, sour scent in her hair, I would have to keep a close eye on her. If she was breathing easily and not sweating, I could retreat to my bed behind the yellow-striped shower curtain in my and Eddie's bedroom to quietly sing and rock myself to sleep. Sometimes, I would see a wad of bills stuffed in Mama's bra and I felt relief then, not despair, knowing that if Mama didn't drink it up, we would be eating well for a while.

I knew Mama shouldn't drink at Mrs. Wellington's party because of her sugar, but I was still relieved to see her laughing, dancing, and eating.

"Come on, little Miss Terry. Join me in a dance," Whitey said, trying to summon me from the couch.

I looked over in Mama's direction to ask if it would be all right, but I couldn't get her attention. She was obliviously dancing, ordering a man I didn't recognize to make her a drink using the alchemical array of bottles spread across the kitchen table.

Caught in the spirit of the revelry, I agreed to dance with Whitey. Careful not to wipe the chicken grease on my new hand-me-down pajamas, I licked my fingers clean, jumped to my feet, and wiggled to the gyrating beat of "Shake, Rattle and Roll."

Whitey extended his hand, and I put my little mitt into it. I jitterbugged all around and up and down as Whitey pulled me into him and released me in quick sweeping motions. He extended his arm and began to spin me like a top. The next thing I knew, he had me in his arms and was swinging me back and forth between his legs. I giggled uncontrollably. Everyone on the dance floor was laughing and hollering every time he swung me out into the air—higher and higher with each sweeping motion until I was a human pendulum.

A buddy of his was standing a few feet away with outstretched arms and shouted above the music, "Let her fly."

With that request, Whitey swung me low between his legs and, as he brought me forward, released me. I was airborne, heading into a stranger's arms. A cigarette dangled from my "catcher's" smiling lips. Everyone erupted in whoops and hollers. The man turned me around and repeated the exchange, tossing me back into Whitey's arms.

More whoops and hollers followed as Whitey swung me low and released me into the air again.

I felt the sensation of the cool air moving through my freshly washed locks while a mixture of fear and excitement fluttered in my belly.

The reverberating beat of the music pulsed in the air, and dancers laughed as I was lifted higher and higher with each toss. I giggled nervously, but as the men moved further apart to make their tosses even more daring, my laughter turned to nervous tears. I wanted them to stop.

Eddie came back with his plate to check on me and to see what all the excitement was about. He saw my white head fly up into the air and heard the tone of fear in my cries. He dropped his plate on a nearby table.

"Put her down. Put her down right now!" he demanded.

Tugging at Whitey's shirt, he shouted into the stranger's face.

"Give her to me. Put her down now!"

Whitey's buddy, not to be commanded by a little boy, made a dismissive sound and served me up one more time in a show of defiance. With Eddie tugging on his shirt, Whitey almost dropped me to the ground. He held me by a single wrist as I dangled in the air.

Everyone was laughing, but all my senses were blurred by dizziness as I hung and twisted between Whitey's legs.

I spun around, stood on my feet again, and came face to face with Eddie. Seeing him and his look of concern made my eyes well with tears. *You're here,* I thought.

"Come on, Sis, I'm taking you home."

"Okay, Eddie. I'm ready," I whimpered.

Mama wasn't paying any attention to what was unfolding. Probably she had missed the entire episode. She had that familiar five-highball glow about her, and I'm sure things were no longer in focus. Eddie took me by the hand and dragged me over to where she was, seeking permission from a woman he knew was no longer fit to decide much of anything.

Reaching in through the crowd and pulling on her blouse, he resentfully announced, "I'm taking Terry home, Ma. She's tired."

"Oh, and here are my beautiful children. Aren't they beautiful?" she said to those around her.

"That little one sure can dance, Marie," Whitey said. He was latched like a leech to my mother's side.

"Well, of course she can. She takes after her mother," Mama flirted back at him. "All right, Eddie, you take her downstairs if you must. Miss Annie brought some ice cream by today. You've been so well-behaved. Why don't you make a little treat for you and your sister? I'll be down in a little bit."

Pecking us both on the forehead, she sent us on our way. "Go on, babies. Eddie, look after your sister. I'll be down in a little bit. I love you."

Mama with friends at a party

20

"Yes, Mama," we droned, making our way through the crowd and out the door.

We knew that a "little bit" meant forever, or what feels like forever when you're six and nine years old, waiting for your Mama to come home.

2.

MAMA'S AFTER-PARTY,
BUT NOT MINE

Back in our apartment, Eddie headed directly for our bedroom.

"Where you going?" I asked.

"To bed."

"You're supposed to make me an ice cream treat," I said.

He growled at me.

"Change outta your pajamas and put your nightshirt on, and I'll make you a dish," he said, exasperated.

"Chocolate *and* vanilla, please," I said.

"Go," he ordered, half enraged and half endeared.

I was back in a flash, and Eddie had made a nice dish of ice cream for me, as promised.

Despite what had happened with Whitey and the others at the party, we had eaten so much food that day, and for that alone I was grateful.

"I'm going to bed," Eddie said. "Put your dish in the sink when you're done and rinse it out. Ma just got rid of those roaches so she'll pitch a fit if they come back."

Half listening, I nodded while I swirled my chocolate and vanilla ice cream into a creamy soup in my bowl. When I finished, I put my dish in the sink and rinsed it out as instructed.

I was wound up from the sugar and the night's excitement so I decided to stay up and wait for Mama to come in.

I found her transistor radio and turned it on. The static was pretty bad, and I wiggled it toward the window as I had seen her do. In the scratchy background, I heard the radio man announce "Hey There, Lonely Boy" by Ruby and the Romantics. Satisfied with the reception, I plopped down on the couch and rocked myself back and forth to the slow rhythmic beat of Ruby Nash's lonely, lost love.

Within minutes, I was asleep, exhausted from the party, soothed by the words.

❄

Mama finally came home with Whitey in tow. Cracking me on the behind, she woke me with a stir.

"Come on, little miss. It's bedtime," she said, trying to drive me away from the couch where she and Whitey would spend their "nightcap."

"Mama, that hurt," I cried, rubbing my bottom.

"Oh, let her stay up a bit, Marie. She's no bother," Whitey said.

"All right, all right," she said. "You, Mister, go make me a drink. And you, little miss, turn that racket off the radio. Put some real music on the record player," she commanded, her speech garbled.

"Yes, ma'am," Whitey and I said.

Mama cracked me on the butt again and said, "Go!"

I returned to the living room with the little RCA phonograph and s
everal albums.

"Bobby Darin," she ordered, growling, all without an iota of the grace she'd shown just hours earlier. "Put that one on. Then come over here and sing a song with your Mama."

"Which one, Mama?"

"'Splish, Splash.' Put that one on and turn her up," she commanded.

Song number five. I counted the clear ribs as the album spun on the turntable. One, two, three, four, five. I hit it right.

"This is a good one, Mama," I shouted as I jumped on the couch between the two of them.

Mama and Whitey sang aloud, so I wiggled wildly between them, hoping our dancing would mend some of the night's tension.

"Sing it, Mama!" I squealed.

Mama put her arms around me and sang into my face, *"I was a rollin' and a strolling…"*

The smell of whiskey in the air and Mama's happiness made me giddy. I knew Mama didn't really mean to crack me on my bottom. I could see she was happy—dancing and singing and off that old dingy couch that she stuck to like glue. Oh, what a wonderful night this was.

I giggled into her face as she put her hands around my little waist and began to tickle me.

"Reelin' with the feelin'…"

"Mama, stop. You're tickling me. Stop!" I squealed in uncontrollable laughter.

"Movin' and a-groovin'…"

"Mama, please! Stop! It hurts, Mama!" I screamed in hysteria, half giggling, half crying. She had pinned me to the floor.

"Rockin' and a rollin'"

And then she was gone.

I could tell by her eyes that she was unreachable. Though her hold on me was purposeful and fierce and her pitch-perfect voice pierced the air with intention, her eyes were glazed over in a zombie stare, unable to see me. She was possessed.

"Mama, please. No," I pleaded.

But she was too much for me. Once drunk, she was out of control and unstoppable. Her hands were under my nightshirt and in my panties.

She was violating me while Whitey gyrated wildly on the floor, game for whatever unfolded; he had only one thing on his mind.

"Mama, stop," I cried.

"Pushing and a pulling ... "

"Mama, please stop. You're hurting me," I said.

I squealed and wiggled, trying to break her hold on me. But the more I pleaded, the more she groped at me.

"Reelin' with the feelin' ... "

"Eddie, help! Eddie!" I called.

Running into the living room, Eddie hollered over the music, "Stop, Ma!"

"Movin' and a groovin'," * Mama shouted, defiantly, ignoring us both.

"Leave her alone, Ma," Eddie demanded, pushing on and punching her shoulder and back as hard as he could.

Mama and Whitey collapsed in laughter at the sight of Eddie's attempt to rescue me. To them, his concern was comical and futile chivalry.

"Oh, come on, you two. What happened to *my little party girl?*" my mother mocked.

Disgusted, Eddie pulled me away from them and dragged me off into our tiny bedroom. We sat together on the cot, and he rocked me until I settled down and stopped sobbing.

✳

In our shared bedroom was an old wardrobe that Mama had bought from the thrift store. Eddie cleared out the large bottom drawer and fashioned one of Mama's sweaters into a pillow for me.

Handing me a tissue, he said, "Blow."

---

* *Splish Splash* song by Bobby Darin and Murray Kaufman, 1958.
  Copyright by Carlin America, Inc. All rights reserved.

I did.

"Come on, Sis. Get in. You'll be all right in here, and I'll be right here on the cot. Ma won't get to you anymore tonight. I promise," he said.

"You sure, Eddie?" I stammered, looking into the coffin-like drawer. "I'm sure. I'll keep watch," he promised.

We could still hear Mama and Whitey nearby. I climbed inside and Eddie closed the drawer, leaving enough room for me to get some air.

"You all right in there?" he asked.

"Yeah, Eddie," I said.

"You'll be all right, Sis. Just go to sleep."

In this cramped crib, I sang quietly and rocked myself to sleep.

❄

In the early morning, Mama made her way into our bedroom. Eddie was asleep on the cot, and somehow—even through her whiskey sour blur— Mama spotted a tuft of my blonde hair draped over the edge of the makeshift crib.

Tugging on the brass pulls, she opened the drawer and stirred me from my sleep. I climbed out, wiping the sleep from my eyes. She pulled me onto her lap.

She was crying.

I looked at her closely. Her hair was matted, her clothes wrinkled, her breath sour and smelling of vomit. Those dramatic, alluring eyes we had taken such care to dress were leaking mascara down her face. *Too much and you look like a clown*, I remembered. *Nothing's worse than a woman with a mask on.*

"What is it, Mama?" I asked. "Are you sick? Do you need your medicine? I'll get it, Mama. Don't cry."

Everything in my world was disintegrating, Mama included. My few friends from the projects hadn't made it to Mrs. Wellington's party, perhaps knowing the mayhem that would unfold there or knowing we were about to leave anyway. The people I had encountered there instead, men like Whitey, were more like ghouls to me, part of the grotesque tapestry I had observed while inverted, disoriented, dangling by a single wrist between Whitey's and a stranger's legs. I wanted to see my friends, to walk just one building over to knock on the door and see Patty Reevers or Miss Bessie, but it was too late. In my brother I saw—at just nine years old—a boy prematurely sobered by the dysfunction around us, robbed of hope, functioning as our stand-in caretaker.

✳

Hearing her apologies the night after the party, I put my arms around Mama's neck and began to rock her, feeling my own frailness and her vulnerability.

"Don't be sad, Mama. Please," I pleaded. "It'll be all right. I promise."

Mama continued to cry—deep, hot, heaving tears that rose up out of the swell of her belly.

I drew myself up in her lap, threw my arms around her neck, and leaned my head into her sweaty, disheveled face. The beautiful mask we had constructed together in front of the vanity mirror had been reduced to synthetic clown smears. Her weakness was transparent for both of us to see. Feeling her chest throbbing against mine, I coaxed her, "Let's sing, Mama. It'll help us."

3

PEACHES

Mama sat outside in her folding chair, sipping on her third highball, and I leaned up against the old incline railway wall next to our flat. It was the last remnant of the old St. Clair Incline that had been one of some twenty inclines in Pittsburgh at the beginning of the 20th century. This one ran up along 22nd and Josephine Streets, depositing its load right there on Grandview Street, our new home. The incline was built in the 1880s and transported mill workers and freight from the South Side below. It had been torn down in 1935, and the only thing remaining of the operation was a red brick wall that ran almost half the block of Grandview Street. The kids I met referred to the wooded area below as "the Inky," and the wall where my mother and I sat was called the Inky Wall.

That night, as the sun was going down, I sat on the side of the wall looking over treetops and taking in the generous view of the city below. There was a cement foundation pad at the base of the wall that accommodated my butt just right. Mill workers were dumping slag in the valley, and we sat there in silence, watching the sky light up in brilliant shades of orange and gold. It looked as though the sun was trying to rise up out of the smoke-hazed sky.

I loved looking down on the city from the rooftop in the back of our "new" apartment. It became one of my nightly rituals. Tiny lights in the distant buildings twinkled like little stars. The old Gulf Building—the highest building in Pittsburgh at the time—featured an architectural "crown," lit to forecast the next day's weather (blue for sun, red for rain). That night it shined blue, predicting a sunny day to come. Polka-dotted lights ran along Carson Street on Pittsburgh's South Side, where the Jones and Laughlin steel mill reigned.

Living on top of that hill, we absorbed a lot of the soot that drifted from the mill. Depending on how the wind was blowing, clean clothes hanging out on the line sometimes had to be rewashed before they even got on our backs. Still, Mama used to tell us to never complain about the mill soot.

"It's a good thing," she said. "It keeps the economy going. Means men are working and that's good for all of us."

I didn't know what any of that meant—only that I was coughing a lot and having to rewash clothes I hadn't even worn yet, as though we lived at the base of an active volcano.

Mama sipped her Seven and Seven out of her favorite highball glass and told me we needed to talk. She said that my best friend, Patty Reevers, had moved to Cleveland and our old neighbors from the projects, Bessie and Chester, had moved on, too. I knew what she was getting at.

"Now you know Patty is gone from those projects. And now you don't have any excuse to go back there like you do, thinking I don't know about it. Miss Bessie and Chester are gone too. Everybody's finding their way to a better life. Just like us," she said.

She inhaled her Winston 100, already red- and bleary-eyed from her drink.

I sat there sinking, staring, fighting back tears. *What better life?* I wondered. I couldn't help but privately compare their love for me with Mama's love. I was left with her version.

I watched silently as crucibles of molten steel traveled across the Hot Metal Bridge to the furnace on the other side, stacks all ablaze and setting the sky aglow. I wished I could be carried off into that light, too. I didn't want to be where I was. I didn't want to be alive anymore.

The siren went off at the fire station atop Eccles Street and shocked me back into the moment. With tears welling up in my eyes, surrounded by fires on the horizon and periphery, I turned to express a futile protest against Mama's news about Patty, Miss Bessie, and my other friends. As I did, my heart sank to see that Mama now was gone.

Without a word or sound, she had vanished into the night. She had the habit of delivering bad news when she drank, leaving me to absorb the impact alone and without knowing if it was true or not.

I sat there on the Inky Wall, staring down into the abyss below me. It was about a forty-foot drop, and I wondered if anyone would miss me if I just leaned forward into the darkness and plummeted into the rocks below.

My head was numb and racing at the same time. My daddy had left long ago, and Eddie was spending more and more time at his place. Everyone was slipping off into the night without a word or even the slightest echo of a goodbye. I wondered if I could do the same.

A rare photo of Mama and Daddy together, 1951

Alone in the chill of the night, I shifted over into Mama's seat. It was still warm where she had sat. I claimed her seat quickly, absorbing the residue of her presence: atoms and molecules of heat still in motion.

Dazed, I reached into the ashtray for Mama's half-smoked Winston and lifted it to my mouth. I had never smoked before, but that night I sucked the last bit of smoke out of her cigarette and flicked the butt into the night air as though I had been smoking all my life. It blended perfectly with the soot, the fire, and the smoke around me.

On the stoop sat Mama's Seven and Seven. I lifted it to my nose. It smelled strong, overwhelming, and inviting. I slugged it down hard and fast like I had seen the men do at Stan's Café. The gesture reminded me of war films in which medics speedily applied a tourniquet to a shrapnel wound and remedied the pain by making it invisible, cloaked, and smothered. A blast of heat from the highball rose up in my belly, and I felt at peace with the fire that rose out of the stacks at the mill. I choked. My eyes watered. My head raced. In the swell of my belly, the initial rush of fire cooled to a soft glow and a sense of calm washed over me.

Within minutes, like magic, my loneliness and fear were replaced with a feeling of well-being. The void that had consumed me just moments earlier was replaced with a tranquility and serenity I had never before experienced in my eight short years of life. Woozy, I relaxed and settled into this new-found pleasure.

I looked at the empty tumbler and noted to myself: *This has magic.*

And in that blink of an eye, I had found my new best friend, a concoction with mysterious powers that made me think *maybe, just maybe, I can make it here.*

I wandered back into the apartment, where Mama was passed out on the couch as usual. I took the afghan and covered her as I had done hundreds of times before, kissing her on her forehead.

Pushing the shower curtain around my bed, I crawled in without a sound. Eddie was sound asleep beside me. The sip of that magic tonic had soothed me, and for the first time I could remember, I didn't need to rock myself to sleep.

✳

Just after Christmas that year, Daddy called Mama and asked for Eddie to come and visit him for the holiday. He didn't want me, but Mama insisted that I go along.

A rare visit with my daddy, 1959

"You're going," Mama said. "That's that!"

My daddy, who, for most of my eight years had been a rare, fleeting presence in my life, had a condition known as Charcot-Marie-Tooth, which Mama described as "a disease in his legs and feet that makes it hard for him to walk." What registered with me, though, was the conspicuous metal braces he wore on his legs. The sight of them made me and my friend Patty Reevers compare him to Frankenstein. This was an apt comparison for a man who was, to me, an anomaly: a wounded creature who made no effort to mask his disdain for his only daughter.

My daddy's mama had passed around this time, but he still shared the family apartment with his sister, my Aunt Marilyn, in Bellevue, northwest of Pittsburgh. She never married and she cared for my daddy and his sick legs.

She fussed and doted over Eddie when we arrived that evening. My presence was tolerated. I contented myself with the small bowl of Christmas ribbon candy that sat in the center of the coffee table. No one was yelling at me for trying some, so I dove in. Still, I couldn't help but notice a nasty smell in the air.

"What's that smell?" I finally asked.

"It's still the New Year, so we're having pork and sauerkraut for supper," Marilyn reported. "Come to the table. It's ready to eat."

We went into the small dining room, where we all squeezed around a little table that Marilyn had set for dinner. I saw potatoes and meat on the table, and my mouth began to water, but the pungent sauerkraut smell hung in the air, and I didn't like it. We had never eaten sauerkraut before, and I instantly hated the smell. I had my eye on the big bowl of mashed potatoes.

"Are they real potatoes?" I asked. "Or did they come out of the box like at home?"

"No, they're real potatoes," Marilyn said, annoyed.

That's all I needed to hear.

Marilyn served me a plate with pork, sauerkraut, and mashed potatoes.

"More potatoes, please," I said.

"You eat that plate," my daddy said.

"May I have some butter?" I asked.

Marilyn shoved it in my direction. I reached out as far as I could to grab the butter tray. Using my fork, I made a little well in my mashed potatoes, then put a big glob of butter in the middle of them. I smashed it all together and was ready to dive in.

"Eddie, you say grace," Daddy instructed.

I put my fork down on the table, bowed my head, placed my hands at my heart, then made the sign of the cross. Eddie recited the prayer.

"In the name of the Father, the Son, and the Holy Ghost, Amen. Bless us, O Lord, for thy gifts which we are about to receive through thy bounty, through Christ our Lord, Amen."

I quickly made my sign of the cross and dove into my mashed potatoes.

When I was done with the potatoes, I started on the pork. We didn't have real meat very often, and the pleasure of the feast at Mrs. Wellington's party had been lessened by the memory of Mama and Whitey tormenting me. In fact, every time I had heard the melody of Bobby Darin's "Splish, Splash" since then, I felt nauseous and wanted to leave the room.

The pork was tender and juicy and fell apart as I tried to stick my fork into it. After several attempts, I just went for it with my fingers. I lifted the juicy meat to my mouth, but I immediately rejected it because it had been cooked with that sauerkraut. It tasted ruined to me. Foul.

I tried to brush the cabbage off with my finger.

"Eat your dinner, girl," Daddy said.

"I don't like it. It tastes spoiled," I said.

"I don't care how it tastes. You're going to eat it or sit there until you do," he said.

Lowering my head, I thought to myself, *I'm not eating it.* It was bad enough to be with him and my aunt—to be so openly unwanted—but I wouldn't have my meal ruined (a real meal for once) by eating something so rotten and putrid. It was more than I could stand.

Daddy rose out of his chair laboriously, the metal of his braces creaking as he did. He waddled over and hovered above my seat at the table.

"That mother of yours is always complaining that you don't have enough food to eat, but when I put it right in front of you, you refuse it. I'm not having it. Eat your dinner."

He lifted and then slammed the plate in front of me.

Tears welled up in my eyes and I lowered my head, twirling the disgusting sauerkraut on the end of my fork.

I'm not eating it and he can't make me, I thought, committing with as much resolve as I could muster. I would not be humiliated again.

Daddy's fist came down on the table with a bang.

"Eat it, damn it!" he yelled.

"I don't want to. It smells bad. I'm not eating it!" I screamed.

Grabbing my arm with one hand and the edge of the table with the other to steady himself, he leaned in and said, "Oh, you're going to eat it."

I squirmed to release myself, but he had a firm hold on me.

Daddy had a few drinks in him by then. This emboldened him—just like it did Mama.

"Let me go!" I screamed, "I'm not eating. I hate it!" I yelled right back at him.

"You sassing me, girl?" he asked. "That's it! Marilyn, get my strap and get me a rope," he ordered.

Eddie stared at Daddy, stunned and mute.

Aunt Marilyn, accustomed to obeying him, did exactly as he said, fetching the strap and rope from another room. It strikes me now that he had those objects readily accessible in a designated spot, the way other people keep their wallet and keys on a tray.

Eddie continued to watch Daddy, wide-eyed, trying to understand if this was an idle threat. What little intervening power he had with Mama was futile around my father. When he drank, my father was a beast who terrified both of us.

Holding me down in my seat, Daddy ordered Marilyn to take Eddie out of the house.

Marilyn was flustered, but she reached for her purse sitting on the window sill. She slung it on her arm and took Eddie by her other free hand. Eddie passed by me with tears in his eyes.

"Eddie," I cried.

He tried to pause as they walked towards the door, but Marilyn goaded him forward with force.

The door slammed shut, and they were gone.

Daddy steadied himself against the table and struggled to get the ropes around me.

I squirmed against him and the ropes. I knew if I could free myself he'd never catch me with those sick, decrepit legs of his.

But he was too big, too long, too strong. He roped me down tightly—across my chest, around my waist, binding my feet and hands to the chair, too.

"*Now* let's see if you're ready to eat your dinner, girl," he said, smirking.

"I can't breathe, Daddy. I can't breathe," I said, hyperventilating. "Please stop. I'll eat it. I'll eat it," I pleaded.

"Damn straight you'll eat it, you little bitch. Disrespect me here," he yelled in my face. "Little bitch. Just like your mother."

He leaned down to my eye level and interrogated me with his eyes. But then something changed—lightened—in his expression. A dawning awareness.

"You a little whore like her too?" he asked.

Struggling in my seat, I twisted and turned to try to free myself, but I was too small and weak against the ropes.

He began unbuttoning his pants.

"Daddy, stop," I gasped. "Daddy, please, I'll eat it."

Thump-thump ... thump-thump ...

A glittery white snow begins to fall.

A Lucky Strike cigarette pack rustled in his shirt pocket.

Sauerkraut-soaked, tobacco fingers shoved down my throat.

Thump-thump … thump-thump …

Glittery snow everywhere.

A greasy VO5 mop in my face.

Rows of tiny pink and green flowers on the wallpaper.

The water-stained, cracked ceiling.

Thump-thump … thump-thump …

Aqua Velva in my nose.

A clock strikes two tones.

Glittery snow everywhere in my mind.

Pushing, pulling, pushing, pulling.

Grunting.

Groaning.

Thump-thump … thump-thump.

Blizzard conditions blind everything, and I am gone.

❄

Excerpt of letter from Mama to Eddie

In the County Court of Allegheny County, Pennsylvania

COMMONWEALTH

Marie L. Young

vs.

Edward E. Young

No. 2092 19 55

Y-49329

TO THE HONORABLE THE JUDGES OF SAID COURT:

The Petition of _____ Marie L. Young _____ respectfully shows:

That on the _____ 6th _____ day of _____ October _____, 1955, the above named defendant at the above number, was ordered to pay your petitioner the sum of _____

Twenty-eight ($28.00) Dollars per week

with which order he has failed to comply, so that now he is in arrears to the extent of _____

Current arrearages _____ Due December 6th, 1955 _____ $ 224.00

Old arrearages _____ $ _____

TOTAL - - $ 224.00

Petitioner _____

Mrs Marie L Young

ALLEGHENY COUNTY, ss:

The above named petitioner, being duly sworn, deposes and says that the foregoing petition is true and correct to the best of (his her) knowledge, information and belief.

Sworn and subscribed this _____ 7th _____

day of _____ December _____, 19 55

David B Roberts
Clerk of County Court

Adona J Green
Deputy

Mrs Marie L Young

And now, to-wit, _____ December 7th, _____, 19 56, the foregoing petition having been presented in open Court, upon consideration thereof, a rule is granted on said _____ Deft. _____ to show cause why the prayer of the petitioner should not be granted. Returnable the _____ 4th _____ day of _____ January _____, 19 56, at 9:30 o'clock A. M.

Kaufman
Judge

ATTACHMENT

And now, to-wit, _____, 19 ___, the foregoing petition having been presented in open Court, upon consideration thereof, an attachment is directed to issue forthwith as prayed for.

_____
Judge

Court arrears notice seeking payments from Daddy for child support

He never wanted me, my daddy. Just as soon as I was born, he left. Mama petitioned the courts for payments, $28 a month, but he never made them.

I didn't know why he didn't want me. Why he never asked for me. Never paid me any mind. He was just a speck of my life, except for that night.

That night he wanted me, though.

He had a great deal he wanted to share with me that night.

Things fathers should never share with their little girls.

"Peaches," he called me from then on.

❄

A big box arrived at our apartment on Grandview Street a few weeks after New Year's. I remember that it was extremely cold. We were out the day it came because Mama wanted to buy some end-of-season fabric that was on sale downtown. While we were gone, the water main in the apartment building froze and broke wide open, soaking the big box and freezing it to the hallway floor.

When we arrived home that evening, the door to the building was frozen shut.

Eddie pushed the door back and forth, creating an opening big enough to get his hands inside. Fortunately, the ice chipper was outside, so he finagled it through the opening and chipped away while swinging the door back and forth. Eventually there was enough room for us to get inside.

That's when we saw the malformed, frozen box.

"Look, Mama," I squealed. "There's a big package in here, with me and Eddie's name on it."

"Let me open the apartment door," Mama said, agitated. "The whole apartment is probably flooded."

Squeezing by me, Mama entered our apartment and was relieved to find no water damage inside. She sighed.

"Who's it from, Eddie?" I asked, barely able to contain myself. We had never received a special delivery.

"Get inside," he directed. "It's dark, and I can't see just yet."

Sliding on the ice, I crashed to the hallway floor, bruising my hip.

"It's frozen to the floor, Eddie. How are we going to get it inside?" I asked with anticipation.

"Get inside, so I can see," he said, frustrated with me now.

I went in as Eddie chipped away at the base of the box with the ice scraper, trying to release our prize from the frozen floor. The big box still was wet on the bottom so it shredded apart as Eddie worked to release it.

Inspecting the top corner of the box, Eddie reported, "It's from Daddy."

My heart sank, though I'm not sure what I had expected instead—some good luck, maybe, or some show of divine mercy that I'd heard the nuns talk about.

I looked to confirm that my name was on the box alongside Eddie's, but I couldn't imagine that there was anything in there for me. *He hates me,* I thought. *And I hate him back.*

Lightheaded, I retreated to the couch and began to rock myself.

Thump-thump … thump-thump. I was remembering our last "meeting."

Eddie continued to work on the box. In a growl of frustration, he jabbed the ice scraper into the top of it to create an opening, then tore it open ravenously.

Inside, he found some shirts and pants for him, a miniature train set that he had asked for at Christmas, and a King James Bible that Daddy said he should have since he was now an altar boy at St. Henry's Church. Eddie thumbed through his Bible, smiling. He was elated. He loved my daddy, and Daddy loved him.

Eddie, at age eight, with Daddy

41

Eddie, at age twelve, with Daddy

Rocking and singing to myself, I kept an eye on the door and watched tearfully as Eddie pulled all his treasures out of the box, ecstatic over his cache of gifts.

I sang lightly to myself.

Jingle bells, jingle bells, jingle all the way. Oh, what fun it is to ride in a one-horse open sleigh, hey!

"Hey," Eddie said, "There's something else in here, but it's stuck to the floor."

Curious, I went over to the door.

"It's black and soft," he said. "Some kind of stuffed animal."

Eddie climbed inside the big box, half disappearing, and worked to free its contents.

"I think this is for you, Sis," he said. "It looks like a duck or something."

Finally, he fell backwards with a thud. The box tumbled over as he released a stuffed black swan from the bottom of the box.

"Yeah, this must be for you," he said, proudly resurfacing with the prize in his hands. He was waiting for me to acknowledge his herculean feat.

But I had never seen anything like that swan. It was the biggest stuffed animal I had ever encountered. A beautiful black swan that was wet and frozen on the bottom, as though it had been fetched from a dark and murky lake.

"There's a note on it," Eddie said.

"What does it say?" I asked.

"To Peaches, from Daddy," Eddie said.

With a twist in my belly and a soft snow now falling in my head, I took the swan from Eddie and placed it by the floor heater to thaw out.

42

I walked away while it pooled water on the floor. On the couch, I rocked myself. Looking at the enormous, beautiful, soggy black swan, a part of me wanted to embrace it and a part of me wanted to tear it to pieces. Later that night, once it had thawed and dried, I leaned my head against it in sorrowful commiseration.

My head was clouded. The snow started falling around me as it had in his kitchen. Rocking in place, I sang another Christmas song. The season's idyllic lyrics were a balm, an escape route.

4.

FINDING GOLD IN THE RUINS

I woke on our couch at 5 a.m. and squinted at the cracked ceiling to see if the watermark and peeling plaster had changed. Only a week earlier, Donna, our upstairs neighbor, had fallen asleep in her bathtub with the water running. That day, I had been asleep on the couch. In an instant, I was gasping for breath under a flood of dirty water, plaster, gypsum, and lath board. It was a supernatural deluge. Already anxious taking care of Mama, I then began playing the role of chief building inspector, reporting to Dan the fix-it man any issues I found with the flat that we rented on Grandview Street. There were many issues.

This morning, though, I judged that the watermark and bubbling plaster had not changed since Dan's repairs. From behind the shower curtain that surrounded my bed, I breathed a sigh of relief. I used extra caution not to rouse Mama as I made my way from the bed to the kitchen. As quietly as I could, I washed the dishes in the sink, including the coffee pot, my real point of focus. At age nine, I couldn't start my day without it. I was hooked on the stuff. Like alcohol's magic, coffee had acquired an almost romantic allure for me. I loved everything about its mobilizing power.

Sliding a cigarette out of Mama's pack of Winston's and snatching the matches from the stove, I climbed out onto the back-porch roof to greet the day and took in the view of the city from my perch. The shift change was beginning at Jones and Laughlin Steel again, and the mill workers made their way along Carson Street like ants. I puffed on a cigarette I snagged from Mama's pack and assessed from the golden pink hue of the horizon that it would be a beautiful day. The coffee pot began to gurgle, a sign that the first perk was about to erupt. The sweet bouquet of coffee burst through the window. I flicked my cigarette into the air and climbed back inside to make my "cup a Joe," as Mama called it. I slugged it down quickly then dashed into the bathroom, where I swished my toothbrush across my mouth, jumped into my swimsuit, crept through the bedroom again, and made my way outside. I had work to do this morning and I wanted to get to it before anyone woke up.

I parked my Radio Flyer wagon in the hallway behind the door. It was my most prized possession. On a recent trip to the Goodwill store, Mama had bought the wagon for me.

"What on earth do you want with that thing?" Mama had asked. "It's beat up and the front wheel is all twisted. It's not safe and you can't ride in it," she said.

"I'll have Dan fix the wheel. And besides, I don't want to ride in it. I just want to carry things in it."

"Like what?" she asked, perturbed.

"Well, I could use it to haul our laundry from the backyard, for one. Or I could use it to fetch Mrs. Pritchard's groceries," I said, carefully making my case.

Mama had already picked up a few shirts and a wall clock for the kitchen, but none of that was as dear as the wagon. I could see Mama doing the math in her head, but I interjected before she could complete all the sums.

"Mama, I have 32 cents to put toward it."

Plopping down on the floor of the thrift store, I kicked off my right shoe, removed my soiled sock, and peeled a quarter, one nickel and two pennies from my foot.

"Where did you get that?" Mama asked.

"Running Mrs. Mellon's laundry up from the back for her and helping Johnny Roof shovel coal in their coal cellar yesterday," I said.

After just about a year on Grandview Street, I had discovered ways to get out of the house and engage with the new world around me. I had figured out ways to make a little bit of money for me, Mama, and Eddie, spending as much time as possible outside in the sunlight and fresh air. Anything was better than staying in the quagmire of our little apartment, where Mama's diabetes and drinking dictated everything.

"So, these jobs you're doing. *That's* how those socks got so grimy," she snipped.

"Yes, Mama. May I please get the wagon?"

Mama reached into her bra and pulled out two damp one-dollar bills. Exasperated, she gave me a look and tossed her shirts and wall clock into the wagon.

"Go on now," she said.

With great delight, I marched toward the checkout lane, pulling my wobbly, rusty, and squeaky prize behind me.

Dan did try to fix the front wheel later, but even after he oiled it up pretty well, it still wobbled and made a racket. I didn't mind. I had already accepted that I was an invisible person whose circumstances would, no doubt, make me visible. Best to embrace that, I thought, and to accept life's minor embarrassments. *I'd rather be outside in the fresh air announcing my every move with a squealing wagon than cowering in our apartment,* I thought.

After my morning coffee, I carried the wagon outside so as not to wake anyone. Once outside, I made my way to "the Fort," barefoot and pulling my wagon behind me. I hoped the pickings would be good. The Fort Playground was just one block up the street from our flat. I loved the fact that it was so close and I especially loved being the only person there early in the day. I pretended it was my own backyard, and most summer mornings, it was. I was almost always the first one at the pool and in the park.

The older boys and girls in the neighborhood partied in the park on summer evenings—smoking cigarettes, drinking alcohol, playing poker, and making out. I would hang out at the swimming pool as long as Mama allowed—usually until the street lights came on, but if she had a little drink in her, she let the curfew fly.

I loved hanging around the older kids. They didn't seem to mind me much, and they even sent me on errands to buy things for them from the park store— pop, cigarettes, frozen candy bars, soft pretzels. I'd fetch whatever they wanted and it usually won me the prize of a few cents and sometimes a nickel—decent compensation for a "runner" like me.

Systematically, I moved through the grass, searching for pop bottles, bottle caps, and Mallo Cup coupons. First, I moved up the grassy slopes along Fort Hill, then along the swimming pool fence. This was an especially lucrative spot where the boys played poker under the locust trees and often left their pop bottles lodged into the tiny hexagons of the wire fence. I swept around the borders of the pool, loading my Radio Flyer with the fruits of my labor. Before making my way to the gutters around the swing sets and basketball courts, I sat on the bleachers at the pool, taking in the quiet and magical calm of the early morning and the placid surface of the water.

When we first moved from the projects to Grandview Street, I took to the water immediately; it was my daily sanctuary. I felt safe in the water. Just standing in front of a crystal blue pool of water calmed me. If I went there early enough, especially on a Sunday before the pool opened, I could sit and listen to the water swishing gently around the pool and hear nothing else.

Before leaving the pool area, I poked around the big, green trash barrel to see if any visiting families had left bottles there. Sure enough, I found three Coke bottles. *Six cents. Not bad*, I thought. Into the wagon they went. A trip around the gutters at the basketball court brought even more treasures— five bottles in all.

This is a good morning, I thought.

I wondered if I could even buy some soft penny pretzels for myself with the cash I would get for the bottles. I hadn't even been to the Oak Tree yet.

Pulling my rickety wagon, already nearly full with bottles, I headed across the small, unkempt baseball field toward the Oak Tree. There was another green trash can along the way. Looking inside, I saw something shiny below the candy wrappers, empty cigarette packs, and discarded sno-cone cups. A couple of buzzing wasps were interested in what was down there too (a reservoir of sucrose, I'm sure), but I went for it, anyway. I dove headfirst into the can, steadying myself with one hand while rummaging with the other. I plucked two Pepsi bottles out of the festering pool of syrup and water at the bottom of the can, pleased with myself and my find.

The old Oak Tree spread its glorious branches on the other side of Fort Hill, behind the local "rec center." This was where the older boys—guys who were actually old enough to drink legally—met to play poker. On hot summer days, everyone wanted to be under the cool shade of the old Oak Tree. It was prime turf. The younger guys played cards there too and necked with their girlfriends. But when Charlie Pritchard, Bucky Eubenthal, and Greg Zugich entered the park, the younger guys gathered up their cigarettes, lighters, cards, and women, and headed without a word of protest to the fence along the pool. Surrendering that spot was a respect thing, and no one asked any questions.

These older guys held court under the Oak Tree every night, telling stories, carving their names into the trunk, playing cards, drinking liquor, and making out with their girlfriends. It was the drinking that I was focused on, because these guys drank the hard stuff and they cut it with Canada Dry ginger ale that came in quart bottles. That's what I was after, of course. If the partying was hard the night before, I would start collecting a little before the sun came out—a nocturnal scrounger. It meant I could count on five or six bottles easily. This morning the prize was four quart-sized bottles and six Coke bottles. Thirty-two cents just from the Oak Tree alone.

By then, my little Radio Flyer was overloaded and nearly impossible to pull. It continued to announce its presence everywhere I went with a loud mechanical squawk. With two hands, I dragged the wobbly cart to the water fountain, where I washed every bottle and did the math to see what prize my tow would bring. All told—seven Canada Dry ginger ale bottles, 11 Coke bottles, 13 Pepsi bottles, two Frescas, five Hires root beers, five Seven-Ups, and one RC Cola. As I loaded the clean bottles back into the wagon, I did the math, and, if was right, my morning's work would fetch me $1.09. In my mind, I was a nine-year-old sultan.

The sun started hitting the rooftops of the houses on Eccles Street. I guessed it was close to 7 a.m. by then, and I knew that Harry Joe, the owner of the Fort Hill candy store, would be unloading pop cases from the Pepsi-Cola truck, cleaning the meat slicer, shaving ice for sno-cones, and replenishing the penny candy case, readying himself for a busy day at the store.

Pulling my wagon behind me, I circled back to the pool, down Fort Hill, up Sterling Street and into the alley and the old garage that Harry Joe had turned into his store. I was drying two of the bottles against my swimsuit when I heard Harry Joe's voice through the sliding glass window where kids ordered their treats.

"How'd you make out today, kiddo?" he asked.

"If my math is right, I made a dollar nine cents," I said proudly.

He stepped away from the meat slicer where he was working to give me his full attention. He patted the sweat off of his forehead with the bottom of his apron.

"Well, let's check your arithmetic," he said.

I loaded the clean bottles two by two on the counter of the window, and Harry Joe counted as we went along. I never thought that Harry Joe would try to rip me off, but there was a tenacity to what I did each morning, an attachment to and story about each and every item I fetched, so I always triple-checked the value of my haul before I handed over what I'd found.

"Well, looks like you got it right again," he said.

I couldn't have been more pleased as Harry Joe fetched a fresh dollar bill, one nickel and four pennies from the register and handed them to me.

"Thank you very much," I said, securing the money in my tight, sweaty fist and reaching for my wagon to head home.

"Here you go, kiddo," Harry Joe said. He stuck his head and hand through the window to give me a frozen Black Cow sucker, which he knew was one of my favorite treats.

"Thank you, Harry Joe."

"Go on home now," he said. "I know you have some more work and arithmetic to do. Keep going."

He was right. I took the shortcut across the baseball field and down the hill.

The sun was up, but there was still a chill to the air and the cool dew on the grass along the third-base line felt wonderful on my bare feet. At home plate, I turned to look at the tracks my wagon had left. It pleased me somehow to see the pattern of my wagon and pigeon-toed tracks etched in the grass. Evidence that I existed. Nothing wrong with being a little conspicuous.

When I arrived back home, I was surprised to find Mama still asleep. I quietly rummaged through the top drawer of our shared dresser. There I found the

Band-Aid tin buried in my underwear, just where I had put it last. This was my secret bank, my safe. I opened it and dumped out the money I had collected earlier in the week. With the day's draw included, I had accumulated $4.51.

I was giddy with excitement and whispered to myself, *We're going to have treats today.*

Opening the fridge, I found a half-used tin of Spam and the last of a block of Army surplus cheese that we had gotten in the food line that week. I began to cook the greasy meat and cheese, the smell of which made me sick to my stomach, but it was all there was to eat. The smell woke Mama. She asked if there was any coffee.

"Yes, ma'am," I said and fixed a cup for her.

"So, you're making breakfast?" she yawned.

"Yes," I said.

"There enough to go around?"

"There's enough for you and Eddie," I said, knowing Mama needed to eat because of her sugar. "I'm not really hungry today, Mama."

A heavy silence fell in the room, disturbed only by the eventual sizzling and spattering of the greasy Spam as it heated up. I stirred away at it, adding chunks of cheese, pretending it was the stellar culinary creation that it wasn't. I wished Mama would say something. I wished she would offer me some of her food or just some kind of consolation. But if she didn't eat any food, it would send her blood sugar flying, and that could mean another trip to the emergency room, a trip we couldn't afford.

"Harry Joe gave me a frozen Black Cow that I put in the freezer for us to share later," I said.

"Harry Joe? Have you been up to the playground already?" she asked.

"Yes, Mama. I took my wagon and I've been collecting pop bottles this week. And guess what?" I teased.

I ran to the bedroom dresser, pulled out the Band-Aid tin, and brought it back to her.

"Look how much I found, Mama. Four dollars and fifty-one cents."

I was seeking something from her: a wry smile, a single word of validation.

Mama looked at the money and then at me. Taking a deep breath, she turned her gaze out the kitchen window, sipping her coffee. By this time in my life, I had become accustomed to her long silences. I wondered what she must be thinking. Likely wondering how we had gotten into such a mess, with husband and daddy long gone. No education, no job, no money, no food, and no family to speak of who was willing to help.

"We can get some chipped ham from Isaly's deli," I said. "Maybe some vegetables and real potatoes, too. Maybe even a can of the Planters peanuts that you like so much, Mama."

I had become the cheerleader of our motley squad, always trying to keep Mama's spirits buoyed. I was coming around to the idea that maybe things could be okay here on Grandview Street next to the park, where I could make my rounds in the morning—poking through the grass with sticks and grazing for pop bottles that won me some momentary peace of mind, some purpose. Through my morning work, Mama, Eddie, and I would have another meal and another day together, and that prize felt like more than enough to me.

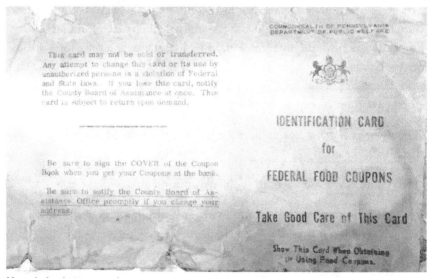

Mama's food stamp card

I sat there with Mama while she stared out at the rising sun, drinking her coffee and wincing with each sip. I realized that for her, the morning was a kind of torture. The dawn of a new day that I relished as my time to live, explore, and thrive was, for her, an excruciating repetition of suffering. I kept talking to her about what we would do with the money, all the good food we would have for the upcoming week, and how we wouldn't have to worry, at least for a few days. But I was just white noise, straining to fill the space between me and Mama's unbearable silence.

5

DONNIE: MOTHER CHILD

It was our third year at Grandview Street, and I had adjusted to the odd rhythm of our solitary life there. Mama's drinking waxed and waned in cadence with her depression and our need for food and other resources. Sometimes Mama's best deal for getting food into the house was to make her usual rounds at Stan's Café in the Heights or Tambellini's on the South Side to see what she could get for dancing with the men there. Since she took Eddie and me along with her, she was assured of getting a meal for all of us on the spot. This was ostensibly a good thing, but it made for late nights for me. A late night meant a ride home with one of her johns, but also a long night for me as the curtain around my bed did little to keep out the sounds of "lovemaking," no matter how much I sang to myself, afraid to fall asleep out of fear that Mama's men would make a visit to my bed, too.

On the flip side of her escapades was a deep depression that was her constant companion. She was either "up" with the drink or "down" in its aftermath: hungover and despondent. Eddie was increasingly absent, spending more time with his best friend, Richard, or with Daddy. I took responsibility for managing our little apartment, tending to Mama's sugar and her darkness.

When the summer of '65 circled around, I was ready for it. Two days before Memorial Day, I sat along the fence at the swimming pool at the Fort and watched as Mr. Timko, the pool supervisor, put the water in and tested chemicals to get the chlorine levels right. Even now, the smell of chlorine stirs a visceral, euphoric recollection within me. In the days leading up to the opening of the pool, the lifeguards would arrive to go over pool schedules and divvy up their space in the guards' locker room. Mike Ford, the head lifeguard from the previous summer, had returned, and I couldn't have been more pleased. He was the first one to take a shining to me and had taught me how to swim and dive. A new guard, Annie, had joined the team too. She was slim, with waist-length blonde hair that she wore in a long braid.

Together, she and Mike took me under their wings and prepared me for swimming and diving competitions. They gave me access to the pool in between the designated teen and family swim periods so I could practice my strokes and diving with total focus, alone in what was, to me, a magical sanctuary. That swimming pool was the one place where I felt safe. Mike and Annie were truly my "life guards," protectors of a sacred space that was necessary for my survival.

Eddie and Terry

In late July of that summer, Mama went off to the hospital, and I was told to stay with our upstairs neighbors while she was gone. I was concerned because when Mama went to the hospital, I always went with her, usually in the back of a police paddy wagon when her sugar was out of control. These were the days before emergency response services—pioneered at the Freedom House in Pittsburgh's Hill District—were available for people like her. Before then, if you needed to get to the hospital, you called the police and they came in a paddy wagon and threw you in the back with no equipment and no ride-along. In its crudeness, it might as well have been a pioneer wagon. I recall being tossed around in the back of those wagons on more than one occasion when Mama got sick with her sugar. Still, I was so thankful that we had a phone and that the police actually came. Sometimes, if they were out on other calls, the wait for the police seemed interminable.

Four days passed after Mama went to the hospital in the police wagon, and no one told me why she had gone. I was supposed to stay with our neighbors, Bucky and Charlotte, but I spent my time making my rounds: collecting bottles at the park in the morning, practicing at the pool during the day, and finally "relaxing" in our apartment at night, rocking myself to sleep on the couch. Charlotte checked in on me occasionally, but for the most part, she left me alone. When I asked about Mama, she told me only that she was fine and would be home soon.

On the morning of the sixth day, I lay in the sun on our stoop, soaking in the warmth of the morning rays while I waited for Paul, the pretzel man, to come. It was a Tuesday morning, and Paul turned up on the corner of Grandview and Sterling Streets at around nine-thirty with his bag of warm nickel and penny pretzels. I was a regular customer, and this morning would be no different. Sitting on the stoop in my flip flops, I had my five pennies ready, and though Paul always tried to get me to buy the one big nickel pretzel, I always went for the five penny ones. I knew I was getting more for my money. They also were much more fun to eat. I called them "bologna fingers."

On this particular morning, Paul arrived on schedule, and I ran to collect my prize.

"Morning, Miss Terry."

He brushed the sweat off his forehead with the fabric of his shirt.

"Hi, Paul. Here are my pennies."

"I suppose I'm not gonna talk you into a nickel pretzel today."

"No. I want five penny ones, please. May I pick?" I asked.

"Go on, now," he said, opening the paper bag. "I respect a customer who knows what she wants."

Diving into the large bag of warm pretzels, I fished around for just the right selections. Soft and fat, not too crispy on the tops and bottoms, not too much salt. Paul opened a small paper bag for me, and after finding the right ones, I dumped them into my sack.

Satisfied with my choices, I counted my five pennies into Mr. Paul's hand and headed back to my stoop.

"Thank you, Mr. Paul. I think Mama's coming home from the hospital today and she will be happy to have some pretzels," I yelled over my shoulder.

"Those are for her, huh?" he asked, with a look of muted despair.

I nodded cheerfully.

"Good!" he shouted, feigning enthusiasm. "Well, you have a nice day, Miss Terry."

Sitting on the stoop, I peered into the bag to see which pretzels I would eat. I figured Mama wouldn't mind if I had three of them myself. I sorted through the bag, appraising each pretzel, leaving the two plumpest ones for her. Chewing off the bottoms of the others, I pushed my fingers into the warm dough of each one. "One, two, three bologna fingers," I sang to myself as I wiggled them in the sunlight and danced about.

Just as I bit into the one on my index finger, I saw a taxicab arrive at the corner. This was a rare sight in those days. We no longer lived in the projects, where cabs never dared to drive. Even so, a taxi was almost never seen on Grandview Street either. I watched with interest as it slowed down, nearing our flat. Mama sat in the back seat and appeared to be holding something. I was filled with excitement as the cab came to a stop. Mama reached over the seat to give the driver some money, then he hopped out.

"Hey there, kiddo," the driver said, rubbing the top of my head.

He opened the door for Mama, who emerged with a blanket in her arms.

"Mama!" I squealed, and grabbed her around the waist.

"Hi, honey," she said in a weary and shallow voice. "Come along inside," she continued, practically stumbling. "I have something very special to tell you."

I heard sounds coming from the blanket that Mama was carrying and I realized that there was a baby inside.

I opened the door to the flat, and Mama went immediately to the couch, opening the blanket where there lay the sweetest, prettiest little baby I had ever seen.

"This," Mama said, "is your little brother."

I sat down on the couch, looking at Mama in disbelief and then at the baby. I put my baby finger out, and his little hand grabbed onto it.

"Where'd he come from?" I asked.

"Well, let's just say an angel brought him to us," she said.

"Can I hold him, Mama?" I asked.

"Sit up here on the couch and be still."

I did as she instructed, and she put him into my arms.

"It's important to support his head, so make sure your arm is always in a good place to keep his neck and head supported."

I shifted my arm to cradle the baby's head, and it felt so good to hold him in my arms. When he started to fuss, Mama reached into a bag and pulled out a bottle of milk.

"Here you go," she said. "You feed him."

I lowered the bottle, and the baby sucked on the nipple and squeezed my baby finger as he did. About halfway through the bottle, Mama took him into her arms and tapped rhythmically on his back.

"This is how you burp the baby after he eats," she said. "And with some luck, he will go to sleep once he's done eating."

Sure enough, the baby settled into a deep, tranquil sleep after his feeding. I was mesmerized. I couldn't believe that Mama had brought a baby home from the hospital and that I now had a baby brother.

"You keep an eye on him," she said in an exhausted whisper.

"Yes, Mama."

I curled up on the floor and peered into the baby's sleeping face. He was the most beautiful thing I had ever seen. I put my hand on his little back and patted him gently, as she had done. I figured Mama wouldn't mind. I could not believe my good fortune. First, I had penny pretzels for me and Mama, and now Mama was home with my new baby brother.

I didn't understand where the baby came from and I really didn't care. All I knew was that we now had a little family again. I looked into our one bedroom adjacent to the living room and saw that Mama was out like a light. I left the baby for only a moment to make sure she was okay.

"Mama, are you sleeping? Do you need anything?" I whispered.

"I'm good, honey. You look after baby while I rest. Can you do that for me?" she asked.

"I can, Mama," I replied in a hushed tone. Pulling a sheet over her, I kissed her on the head to make sure her sugar was okay. Noticing that there wasn't an acidic, salty taste on her forehead, I knew she only needed to sleep and recover.

I went back to the baby and put a pillow on either side of him so he wouldn't roll anywhere. I sat there on the floor with my head resting on the pillow, staring at my new baby brother, feeling that I would never take an eye off of him—that I would protect him forever. I watched intently as his little body slumbered before me and I could not believe there could be a day more wonderful than this one.

Nor could I know that this was the day I would become responsible for the care and well-being of this child. I was already a "parentified" child, placed in the impossible state of being responsible for my mother's happiness and health. Somewhere along the line, our roles had become reversed. Instead of her modeling appropriate behavior for me, I was doing the modeling. Instead of receiving a sense of emotional security from her, I was expected to be her emotional base. As a result, I didn't know much of the world beyond my immediate family and interpreted our warped reality as, in many ways, *the* definitive reality. And though our roles were reversed, I still depended on my mother for my survival and for a sense of connection. The child welfare folks had already been sniffing around us. What I feared most was that they would split us up. I had few choices other than to comply and fulfill her needs.

This, of course, meant that my own physical and emotional needs went completely underground. My response was to work harder at taking care of Mama, hoping it would keep the government people at bay. I also wished that Mama would notice and appreciate my effort. This never happened, at least not in my young life, because you can't be both the most important person in the family *and* the least important person in the family. Pushed to those two extremes simultaneously, I felt overworked and exhausted yet unseen due to the insidious, neglectful "acts of omission" of Mama and Daddy. I existed only in a functional role and in my private experiences of loneliness and pain.

Of course, all I really knew then was that I had a brand-new baby brother and loved him dearly. Mama told me his name was Donnie, and I loved his name too. For the rest of the summer, I spent my days learning how to feed, burp, bathe, dress, change, cradle, and rock him and put him to bed. That was pretty much the extent of my actions, because little babies (I learned) don't do much beyond eating, puking, pooping, and sleeping. I did my job, and I knew Mama was pleased. I couldn't take my eyes off of him. He smelled so good and had the biggest brown eyes with mile-long lashes. We didn't have a baby stroller, so this meant that I had to stay pretty close to home. Swimming went by the wayside for the rest of the summer, but I didn't mind, because I loved being with Donnie.

Mama seemed fine with me looking after him. Somewhere around three weeks after he was with us, she let me watch him on my own. Mama had run out to the market, by way of Stan's Café, and after some time she made it home with a six-pack and some food and milk for the baby. I had done a good job because the baby was asleep on the shared bed when she returned. We both tiptoed through the bedroom and into the kitchen and unpacked the groceries together.

"There's a surprise in there for you," she said, smiling like a giddy teenager. Sure enough, there was an ice cream sandwich. "Yes," I squealed in a hushed tone. Mama and I giggled as she popped open an Iron City beer that fizzed all over the place. We tiptoed again through the bedroom and into the living room, closing the glass door behind us.

"Here you go, Terry. Have a sip of the good stuff. You've earned it tonight."

She offered me her beer.

Little did she know that I had long been sneaking sips of beer and draining her leftover highballs. This was the first time Mama directly offered me a drink, and I gladly accepted it. I glowed with a sense of approval and initiation. I was ten years old.

Something shifted between us that night. I felt on more equal footing with her somehow. Maybe I felt that by offering me a sip of her beer, Mama was telling me I was more like an adult. I certainly felt that way caring for a baby— her baby. I also felt her sense of relief. She knew that yet again her daughter would bear her burdens, the consequences of her wayward actions. Ceding the lion's share of responsibility to me had boosted her mood, and for this titanic inheritance I was compensated with an ice cream sandwich, a smattering of shared laughter, and a sip of warm beer.

Heading off to school that fall was difficult for me. I didn't want to leave Donnie, but I also had to go to school. I was ten years old and heading into fifth grade at St. Henry's Catholic Grade School. Amazingly, considering the disheveled state of the rest of her life, Mama insisted that I attend a Catholic school, which did not charge tuition at that time—only a fee for books, which we often could not afford. I was now on the second floor of our school, where the fifth through eighth grades were housed.

Me and Donnie, 1966

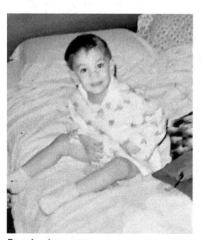

Donnie at age one

I was set to be in Miss Bryant's fifth-grade class, but we came to learn that she had a family crisis and would not be back to teach. This created quite a fuss in the school, and Sister Juliana, the principal, tried to figure out how to cover the class. We heard through the grapevine that Sister Constance, the sixth-grade nun, was going to teach us instead. By everyone's word, Sister Constance was "crazy." I had already observed her manic lectures when she was a substitute teacher in my fourth-grade geography class.

She had a tendency to digress from, say, discussions of the islands of Southeast Asia to share sudden and apocalyptic premonitions.

During my fourth-grade year, for instance, there had been an earthquake in Alaska, and she obsessed over the event, linking it with the Apostles' Creed. She would tell us about the magnitude of the earthquake, the number of people killed, and the floods that followed the cataclysm, then launch into her conclusion that this was God's wrath visited upon the earth for our collective wickedness and sins, for which we all must pray for His forgiveness. She would then make us kneel at our desks and recite the Apostles' Creed. Over and over again, she would say, "Repeat after me: I believe in God, the Father Almighty, creator of heaven and earth. I believe in Jesus Christ, God's only Son, our Lord, who was conceived by the Holy Spirit, born of the Virgin Mary, suffered under Pontius Pilate, was crucified, died, and was buried ... He is seated at the right hand of the Father, and he will come again to judge the living and the dead ..."

"This is His judgment day," she would say. "Repeat after me. I believe in God, the Father Almighty ..."

Bespectacled, old, and wrinkly under her crisp white habit and flowing robes, a yellow-stained hanky in one hand and the large cross of Jesus Christ in her other, she railed at us to "repent for [our] sins and repeat after me...I believe." Joey Alferi, our self-appointed instigator, would poke at Sister Constance, reminding her that this was a geography class. But his taunts were only met with fury as she flailed about, swinging rosary beads and thumping on her desk.

"Sinners, repeat after me ... I believe in the Holy Spirit, the holy Catholic Church, the communion of saints, the forgiveness of sins ..." and on and on. One day she worked herself into such a state that Emily Ewing ran out of class to get Sister Juliana to come and calm her down.

Needless to say, I was quite pleased when I learned that Sister Elenora, my fourth-grade teacher, was going to take Miss Bryant's class until they found a new instructor. I don't know why, but Sister Elenora always went out of her way to be kind to me. She knew that my family didn't have any money because I was always behind on paying the book bill, a debtor at age ten. And she knew that there was no father in my home and that ours was the only family in the school without one. None of that seemed to matter to her. She invited me to help after school with cleaning the chalkboard and erasers and she picked me to be one of the flower girls for the May devotion to the Blessed Mother Mary.

I didn't understand the source of her kindness, but I needed it and could, in fact, thank God for it.

I remember clearly that first day of fifth grade. Sister Elenora was positioned outside the school where the fifth-graders convened. The sun was out and, as usual, all the students stood two abreast in alphabetical order. The bell clanged and we all stood at attention to say the Pledge of Allegiance. Kevin Zigler, my classmate, fidgeted with his clothes and necktie. After that, we began our procession into St. Henry's: first grade, then second, then third, and so on. As I entered the building, a part of me wished I was at home with the new baby, but a bigger part of me felt a sense of excitement as we walked through the door and then immediately up the steps to the second floor. I was now on the floor with the big kids, and Sister Elenora was going to teach us, at least for a while, so I felt like I was going to be all right.

When we arrived at the second-floor landing, we proceeded into the hallway, where there stood the most beautiful statue of the Blessed Mother with baby Jesus in her arms. I had seen the statue before but now I felt as though I was seeing it for the first time. I felt a sense of solidarity with Mary. Both of us had cared for a special child whose appearance was unexplainable and immaculate. The Blessed Mother was dressed in a beautiful blue robe with gold trim and a soft pale pink undergarment. On her head sat a seven-pointed, bejeweled crown under which she wore a white veil with a ribbon of gold trim. In her arms she held the infant baby Jesus, adorned in a simple white robe and also with a crown on his head. Both of their faces appeared calm and peaceful. As I walked by, I reached out and touched Mother Mary's blue robe. I thought about how we had learned that she was favored by God to become the mother of Jesus and that by a miracle of the Holy Spirit, she bore baby Jesus in a stable in Bethlehem. I then thought about Mama and how, by magic, one day she had shown up with my baby brother. I looked at how lovingly the Blessed Mother looked at baby Jesus. I thought to myself, *That's how I look at Donnie. I love him that much, too.*

Being on this new floor with the older kids, in a higher grade, and caretaking for Donnie, I felt like I had grown up. Looking into the soft and caring eyes of the Blessed Mother, I felt connected to her. I thought I was full of sin, though. I knew my body was soiled by my own family (both my mother and father). I knew, through the violently shouted words of Sister Theodosia, that "Jesus died on the cross for my sins!" Though I was only ten, I knew full well the burden of carrying Christ's cross and I bore the emotional and physical scars to prove it. But as I passed this beautiful image of Mary with her baby, I felt that maybe not everything in me was bad if I was acting like this sacred woman, caring for a child I regarded as lovingly as she regarded baby Jesus. With the start of each school day, I felt a sense of serenity and reassurance each time I passed the Blessed Mother and baby Jesus on our way to class. I made a habit of touching her robe every day on my way to class. It was my gesture of solidarity.

As the school term continued, Mama, Donnie, and I found our rhythm at home, too. Eddie was spending more and more time out of the house, and though I missed him, I was increasingly angry with him. I wanted him to pitch in more and help me manage things, but he just didn't have it in him anymore. He was always leaving, never saying goodbye, and clearly resented Mama. I expressed my anger toward him when we would play hand games like thumb wrestling together. I would either get too rough or taunt him when he lost. In truth, my longing for his companionship outweighed any bitterness I felt. I just wanted my brother back.

As for Mama, her sugar, drinking, and dark moods continued to give me fits. Constantly sorting out who was going to eat each day, how much, and when completely overwhelmed me. I knew that Donnie needed to eat, but when Mama's sugar was out of whack, I had to be sure she got what she needed, too. I don't know who had put the welfare folks on our track, but we were on their radar by then, and I never knew when they would show up. Trying to keep on top of things was a constant worry. I feared more than anything that we would be separated, that our family would dissolve.

Then again, having the welfare on our tails was a good thing in certain ways. For one thing, Mama stopped carousing as much. She settled into mostly seeing just one of her johns, a guy named Bill. He came like clockwork on Friday nights around 7 p.m. Dressed in a nice suit, tie, and silver watch, he always came toting two bottles of whiskey, Seagram's 7 Crown, plus potato chips, dip, and Klondike bars for us kids. We didn't socialize much with Bill, but he was an unexpected godsend. Out of all of Mama's "man friends," I liked Bill the most. I wasn't a kid anymore, but like anyone else who goes hungry on a regular basis, I enjoyed knowing treats were coming on Friday nights. And though the sounds they made at night kept me awake and unnerved me, I never feared that Bill would come to my bed. He really seemed to like Mama, and I knew that every Saturday morning, much-needed money would be on the coffee table or stuffed in Mama's bra to help get us through the week.

Friday nights with Mama, Donnie, and Bill, who took this photo

The moment I got home from school, I would scoop Donnie out of his crib, throw him on my hip, and go about the business of feeding, changing, or playing with him, whatever he or Mama needed. As we both grew a little older, Mama allowed me to take him out and about. Eventually, the only place I didn't go with Donnie was to school.

One summer day around the time he was three or so, we were heading up to the park. Walking along Eccles Street, we came to my classmate Alan Korbel's

Me and Donnie

66

grandma's house. She lived across from the ballfield. And just like at my grandma's house—a house I visited less and less frequently—she had hostas growing along the side of her house.

"Hi, Mrs. Korbel. Hi, Mrs. Muller," I said, greeting them and waving as they chatted on the porch.

"Hi, Terry. How's that little one doing?" Mrs. Korbel asked.

"Oh, he's good. We're just heading to the pool."

"Good, sweetie. Well, have a nice time," she said.

As we passed the porch, I slowed our pace so we could pop the heads of the hostas that hadn't yet bloomed.

With Donnie on my left hip, I stooped down and popped a purple bud. Coaching Donnie, I leaned him into the plants, took his forefinger and thumb and said "press." He did, but his little fingers couldn't quite get a pop out of the bud. I pressed another bud, and he heard it pop and laughed. As I leaned him into the plants for another round, I heard Mrs. Muller ask Mrs. Korbel, "She always has that child with her. Is that her little boy?"

A swell of hot feelings came over me, and I immediately felt that I had done something wrong. I listened for Mrs. Korbel's response.

"Honestly, I don't know. I think it's her brother, but you're right. I never see the mother with the child. Only this one. Who knows? It's all very sad."

Donnie was getting the hang of popping the buds and he laughed into my face as he successfully popped another one. I repeated Mrs. Korbel's response in my head: "*It's all very sad.*" I felt observed by the two women—a target of sorts—so I rushed us to the park to avoid the feeling. Donnie howled when I started to run, because I was taking him away from our new game with the hostas. But his crying quickly turned into laughing as he was distracted by the joy ride, bumping up and down on my hip as we ran. I felt the cruel irony in his growing sense of euphoria. He was ecstatic and oblivious while I ran as fast as I could—in a state of exhaustion and despair—just to get us to the park, to some neutral, communal space where we could catch our breath and be inconspicuous again.

At the park, I leaned up against the swimming pool fence with Donnie at my side and tried to understand why I felt as though I had done something wrong when I hadn't. I felt embarrassed and ashamed about our family being talked about so disparagingly. And along with my bruised sense of pride, I was afraid that they would be the ones to call the child welfare folks and break us all apart.

I sat there on that sunny day surrounded by the sounds of children's laughter and the splashing of water with the pungent scent of chlorine filling my nostrils. Donnie sat at my side, entertaining himself with a caterpillar he had discovered. I thought about how long I had contended with Mama's dark moods and with the darkness she had created in our lives. *It's all very sad*, I heard Mrs. Korbel saying.

By the time I was a teenager, I was doing all I could to ease Mama's burdens, but a darkness weighed on her permanently, some immovable sense of dread. I felt it had something to do with some issues between her and her mama, or maybe between her and Daddy, but she never said. I knew only that everyone just seemed to go away. It seemed that everyone in our family had disappeared, forsaken us. There was a time when I was very young when we were included in the family. I know this because there was a picture of me in Mama's arms at one of the Stubna family reunions. This would be my maternal grandmother's family, but the Grandinettis were there too—my grandpap's family. Some fifty members of our family were in the photo: aunts, uncles, cousins, grandparents, and great-grandparents—an extensive and exhaustive cast of loved ones. Everyone except my daddy. But Mama, Eddie, and I were there. Loved, or so the picture suggested.

❄

By age four or five, like the difference between night and day, we were living in the projects, and no one from the family ever came around again. They rarely came to see us on Grandview Street. The whole cast had virtually disappeared.

Eddie was gone now too. Daddy finally got his way and had Eddie sent to seminary to become a priest. He did his first year of high school at South High on the South Side, but he struggled. Going from a small parochial grade school to a large inner-city high school, with kids coming from all over the city, just didn't work for Eddie. He was a ragged, weepy, shaky mess from ninth grade on.

Stubna Family Reunion, 1957

Mama pushed at him and encouraged him to buck up and try to fit in, but Eddie just didn't have it in him. His grades slid and he retreated into himself, spending hours either at St. Henry's Church with his only friend, Richard, or holed up in his cell of a room, practicing saying Mass. Daddy called for him many weekends, and, after so many years fighting with him about visitations and unpaid child support, Mama gave up and just let him go. Daddy took advantage of her lack of fight to get Eddie enrolled in seminary, commencing his sophomore year. I don't know when it actually happened, but something turned in him, and the chivalrous boy who came to my rescue when we were kids was gone.

I sat at the pool with Donnie, gazing at the merriment around us, but I also felt the grasp of Mama's ghosts upon my soul—all the withered secrets she had heaped inside me. Later in my life, I would show a photo of myself at this age to my friend Dot. She sucked in through her teeth, shook her head, and said, "Girl, the light is gone outta your eyes."

❄

During that time, like Mama, I had learned that a drink helped to keep ghosts at bay, and it was not long before I was ratcheting up—smoking pot and popping pills to help me get through my days.

Me and Donnie–lights out

As with most children, growing into adolescence was a difficult for me. I had a love-hate relationship with my changing body. I was curious about its transformation—and Mama was of no assistance—but also afraid of it. Already having been violated by both of my parents and having survived inappropriate groping by Mama's male friends, I loathed the catcalls, fondling, and ogling of older boys and men. Mama didn't see any problem with it, and, when she had a few drinks in her, which was often, she poked at my body and said I had just what men are looking for.

"You need to get out of those jeans and flannel shirts if you want to land yourself a man!" she would say.

She was probably right, but I wasn't remotely interested in "landing a man." In fact, I had taken to sneaking Eddie's shirts out of the laundry and hiding them in the hallway to wear to school. It really pissed him off because I would lie and say I didn't know where they had disappeared to. I was in a public high school by then, with no dress code, and Eddie's shirts were perfect for covering the silhouette of my blossoming womanhood.

Though I aimed at inconspicuousness, these maneuvers didn't always keep me out of harm's way. Older boys in the neighborhood had me in their scopes. Soon they were stalking me or taunting me when I was home alone with Donnie. In those early adolescent years, I would find myself forced into cars by guys with the prize of their stiffening manhood shoved down my throat.

I thought back to my second-grade teacher, Sister Theodosia, and how she would say in catechism class how baby Jesus "died on the cross for *my* sins." With all the things that had happened to me, I believed I was damaged, rotten inside and out, and that this was just the additional price I had to pay for being so bad.

Mama's sugar flares, drinking, and dark moods persisted, and though I was angry at her, I also wished that I could somehow fix or relieve her. Trips to the hospital became more frequent, and it was all I could do to keep up with things. Bennies, black beauties, dexies, and other drugs all helped to keep me ahead of my studies while I remained responsible for Donnie's and Mama's care. Meanwhile, pot and booze kept at bay my most unspeakable memories and the reality of my life. I imagined every bend of the elbow to lift a joint, a drink, or a pill to my mouth as a magic wand casting out my problems, aiding to numb the wounds that swelled within me. It got the job done for a while, but I would soon come to realize that there aren't enough drugs or drinks on this planet to heal a sickness of the soul—though it didn't stop me from trying.

6.

LANDING A MAN

Mom sat in plaid shorts and a white tank-top, eyes obscured under the brim of a frayed straw hat she had bought at the Goodwill store. She was facing the city, catching the last of the sun's warm rays. I was moving about the flat, fixing a meal for Donnie and cleaning up the living room. Our apartment and the hallway doors were open, and I heard Mama talking with someone outside.

"You boys moving in downstairs?" she asked.

I peeked outside. She was speaking with a guy, short in stature but built like a tank, dressed in jeans and a T-shirt with a square of smokes, Lucky's, in his pocket.

"Yes, we are," said the man.

"I'm Jerry, and this is Fran, Paul, and Marcia."

"Nice to meet you. I'm Marie," Mom replied.

Jerry had a six-pack in his hand.

"Let's get this started off right. Would you like a beer, Marie?" Jerry asked.

"Well, yes, I would," Mama replied, with the lilt of flirtation in her voice. "I think we're all going to get along just fine."

Jerry sat on the stoop, and he and Mama talked up a blue streak while Marcia, Paul, and Fran carried furniture down the steps into their new apartment. I was done with my chores and wanted to go and meet my friends without Donnie in tow. I didn't want to go outside while Jerry was sitting there on the stoop. I peeked out the door from time to time to see if he was gone yet, but he had a beer in one hand and a cigarette in the other, and it didn't appear that he was moving anytime soon.

Donnie finished his supper, and I did the dishes. When I made my way back to the front room, I could see that Jerry was gone, no longer staking out the place.

"I'm heading out, Mom. Donnie's fed and the dishes are done."

Mom had slugged down two beers while talking with Jerry, but she already had a fresh one in her hand.

"So, these guys moving in downstairs are college students, Terry. From Carnegie Institute," she gushed. She hadn't yet discovered that one of the new arrivals was a woman. "Real nice fellas, and I think you should go on down there some time and welcome them to the neighborhood."

"I'm going to the park to meet Sandy. What time do I have to be home?" I asked.

"You know what time. Ten o'clock. Don't come rolling in after that," she snipped.

I shrugged and made my way out the door. Mama was already lit, and I knew she wouldn't be awake when I came home, so even at 16 years old, I knew it didn't matter what time I returned.

I met Sandy and Greg at the monkey bars, and we put our money together to see how much booze we could buy. We had enough for a bottle of wine, two six-packs, and a standard kickback for Charlie, our runner. Charlie was 21, and he ran to get alcohol for us kids. We met him in the alley by the pool to make the exchange. With our take in hand, we made our way down to the end of South Side Park, where kids went to party. It was a quiet, almost serene night.

Sandy and Greg were an item. They had been dating for some time, and I expected that they would marry one day. Greg popped open a beer for Sandy and one for himself as I cracked the seal on the Thunderbird. It was a bottle of "wine" that tasted god-awful, as pungent in smell and taste as gasoline, but it got the job done for the buck. I later learned that the original owners and marketers of Thunderbird specifically targeted ghetto dwellers (now euphemistically called "inner-city residents") and the drink became most popular among homeless alcoholics.

Before long, Sandy and Greg were making out. I thought it odd that they were fine with me hanging out with them when we all knew that they would

74

be going at it. We didn't discuss it, but I suspect my presence ensured that Greg would only hit a double at most. I didn't mind. I leaned up against a tree—bottle in one hand, cigarette in the other—and through the guttural moans of their make-out session, I listened to the hum of the train below. I watched the sun set through the polluted Pittsburgh air and pondered what Mama had said about our new neighbors and how I should welcome them to the neighborhood.

The next day I called Sandy.

"So, listen," I said, "these guys moved into the apartment downstairs, and my mom said I should go down and meet them."

Sandy didn't respond. She just listened.

"You wanna go? They go to Carnegie Institute, and she was drinking with one of them and said they're nice guys. I'm thinking about it but I don't want to go by myself. What do you say?" I asked.

Sandy thought about it for a minute.

"I'm supposed to meet Greg," she said, "but what the hell. Let's do it."

"Great. Come by at six and we'll check it out," I said.

At exactly six o'clock, Sandy knocked on our open door.

"Hi, Sandy," Mama yelled, emerging from another room. "How is your mother doing?"

"Oh, she's doing well, Mrs. Young. She says to tell you hello."

"Well, make sure you give her my best," Mama said. "What are you two up to tonight?"

"We're going to go and meet the guys downstairs," I began, and before I could finish what I was saying, Mama squealed.

"That's great! They're college boys, you know, and just like I always tell Terry, you either gotta learn a good skill or land yourself a good man, and I think these guys are a real opportunity for you two."

I was embarrassed that Mama had said that out loud. It was bad enough she said it to me on a regular basis, but it embarrassed me that she would say it to Sandy, too, who already had a boyfriend.

Mama was on her second highball and now she was fussing with Sandy's blouse.

"Sandy, you have such a sweet figure, and this blouse is fetching. I think, though, that if we put a little cinch at the waist, it will accentuate your curvy body and those sweet breasts of yours."

Sandy smiled nervously and shot me a glance. I saw the discomfort in her face, but I felt glued to the ground. My heart was beating hard in my chest and my head filled with falling snow as everything unfolded in slow motion.

I watched as Mama put her hands around Sandy's waist and the small of her back. She leaned into Sandy and popped the top button on her blouse.

Laughing, she said, "Oh, Sandy, no wonder the boys are so drawn to you."

Thump, thump.

Thump, thump.

I broke through the floating white haze in my mind and snatched Sandy from my mother's hands.

"Stop, Mama. Just stop!" I yelled. "Sandy looks fine. And we're leaving now."

"What's your problem, little miss? Don't you dare take that tone with me!" Mama shouted. "And is that what you're wearing?" she continued with a disapproving scowl. "You look more like a boy than a girl. How on earth do you think you're going to land a man dressing in jeans and T-shirts? You can stand to at least put a little makeup on," she huffed.

Too much and you look like a clown, I thought. I watched her clumsily reach for and then sip her highball.

"Come on, Sandy. Let's get outta here."

Mortified by my mother's behavior, I apologized to Sandy outside our apartment. "Sorry about that," I said. "She didn't mean any harm."

76

Standing at the top of the steps with a quick wind blowing through her long, silky, almost-black hair, Sandy adjusted and rebuttoned her blouse.

"It's okay, Terry," she said, sounding slightly irritated as she rummaged through her purse for her hairbrush. Her hand was trembling.

What if I had left to go to the bathroom? What if I had tended to Donnie? I wondered. *What would have happened if I hadn't stood right there? If I hadn't intervened?*

This incident further confirmed my fear about bringing friends to the house. My collection of friends was small already, so when we got together, I always insisted that we meet at their place, the park, or Isaly's deli on Arlington Avenue. My house was the last resort—used only out of absolute necessity.

I never knew what state Mama would be in and I knew that if she had downed a drink or two, all bets were off. She could be unhinged and lewd and excuse it all in the aftermath as a byproduct of the booze.

The snow in my head began to clear as I tried to shake off my embarrassment and shame. I hoped that Sandy was telling me the truth—that she really was okay—but I could tell that she was rattled.

"You still wanna do this?" I asked.

"Yeah, let's go see what all the fuss is about," Sandy said, her face still flushed.

Even then I understood that I could not undo what had happened. Those few moments between Sandy and my mother would stay with her forever, and with me, too.

The wind whipped around outside as we made our way downstairs to the new tenants' apartment. I wished for nothing more than to be invisible, to be carried away by that same merciful wind. But I was stuck there and charged with making "the right impression."

We arrived at the door of the lower flat.

"Ready?" I asked.

"Yep. Let's do this," Sandy said.

We both took a gulp of air.

Inside we could hear the sound of boisterous laughter through the driving bongo beat of Santana's "Black Magic Woman."

"Good taste in music," I said, trying to lighten our mood.

"Yeah, and I think I'm getting a whiff of reefer through the door," Sandy said.

We both giggled.

"Here goes," I said, as I knocked on the door.

We waited while the partying carried on.

I knocked again, but still no response.

"Maybe we should go," I said.

I wonder now what would have happened if we had just left after the first knock or if Sandy and I had decided to do something utterly simple that night. Maybe just a walk somewhere, accompanied by the wind—two friends who trusted each other, who wanted to share their thoughts, dreams, and frustrations, and who didn't need to explore the "opportunity" that awaited them.

"Look there," Sandy said.

I turned to the door and through a crack of the reed shade covering the window on the door, I saw a face peering out at us.

I waved.

"You Jerry?" I mouthed.

The man on the other side of the glass laughed, pulled the shade aside, and smiled at us. He held up his other hand, which contained a beer and a joint.

"You in?" he mouthed.

Smiling, we both gave an enthusiastic thumbs-up.

The door swung open, and there stood Jerry: dark curly hair, buff as all get out, handsome, and engulfed in an asphyxiating plume of fragranced smoke that filled my lungs and head with a dizzying sensation. I sucked in a deep breath of marijuana smoke as I stepped into the kitchen.

"Let's get you fired up properly," he said, passing me an alligator clip that held a half-smoked joint.

Without the slightest hesitation, I hit the joint.

Wow, I thought to myself, *I have never felt this good.*

And as quickly as the shame, guilt, and embarrassment had consumed me when my mother groped Sandy, it dissolved instantly with my second toke of that joint.

Jerry pointed us in the direction of the booze and disappeared to dance in the living room with a group of moccasin- and denim-clad guys and gals singing "Black Magic Woman."

I made my way over to the kitchen sink, where there was a keg of beer icing down.

"I'm Paul," said a handsome guy with a moppish Peter Tork hairdo. I wondered for half a second if he was *the* Peter Tork, but I determined that he was much cuter than the Nordic-looking bass player of the Monkees.

"And this is my girl, Marcia," he said, tugging at the arm of a slender, dark-skinned woman with long black hair.

"We live here with Fran. He's out on the back porch somewhere," Paul said, smiling.

My attention was on Marcia, who cast a sensuous glance in my direction while pouring a beer from the tap. I don't think I had ever seen such a beautiful woman. She was mesmerizing. Her deep, olive-colored skin was flawless, and her perfectly almond-shaped eyes were alluring. Lifting the glass in my direction, she invited me for a drink.

"I'm Marcia," she said, pouring me a beer. "I'm not Paul's girl. I'm not anyone's girl, actually," she said with a laugh.

"I understand," I said, though I really didn't.

All I knew was that this gorgeous woman with a soft Indian accent and the faintest scent of coconut oil about her was raising a glass of beer with me, saluting some unspoken acknowledgment of our female solidarity. The lyrics of Helen Reddy's "I Am Woman" pulsated through my mind, even though it was not a concept I understood, let alone embraced. But at that moment, with an enchanting woman at my side, I felt I really could "roar."

Marcia passed me the joint.

"You live around here?" she asked.

"Actually, I live right upstairs," I said, inhaling. "My mother said I should meet the 'nice college boys' who moved in downstairs." I laughed a little.

Taking my hand, Marcia led me into the living room where the guys were playing poker, swilling beers, and smoking weed.

"I'm guessing she would not approve of all this," she said.

I hit the joint again and looked around.

"You'd be surprised," I said. "This is pretty tame."

To the right of the living room, I noticed a dark, windowless room lit only by a soft purple glow of infrared lights. I saw rows of branches hanging upside down from wires that ran the length of the room.

"Those are Fran's prized possessions," Marcia said. "He's been growing pot since he was twelve years old. You, my dear, are smoking some of the best shit in the county."

"I am smoking some of the best shit in the country," I repeated, amused.

Marcia laughed.

"Sinsemilla," she tutored. "Fran has perfected this process of growing pot so the female plants are allowed to blossom without pollen from the male plant. Wish we could figure that out too. Either way, you get these beautiful flowery blossoms with no seeds and a perfect high. Smooth, isn't it?" she asked.

"Yeah, it's smooth all right. And no paranoia," I said. "I like that."

"That's right, baby," Marcia said.

The silky, tropical fragrance of the sinsemilla was intoxicating and made me acutely aware of my surroundings. Santana rocked on, and I swear I could hear every lick he played, every soft beat of the bongos, every shimmer of the cymbals that sent chills up my spine as I swayed to the rhythmic wave of the keyboard.

I am home, I thought to myself.

I lost track of Sandy, but then I heard her laughing from somewhere else in the apartment. I assumed she was doing all right.

Marcia took me by the hand and led me into the bedroom to the left of the living room. There, another group of people—mostly men—sat in a circle, passing around a pipe and bong, talking about the Kent State killings: four students who had been gunned down by National Guardsmen in 1970. They argued about the newly imposed draft system that would send some of them to fight in a war that they all opposed. Tempers flared and pipes flamed as their discussion fought to eclipse Santana's screaming licks.

Out on the back porch, another group of guys sat around drinking beer and debating constitutional law, summer internships, and whether the Steelers would bounce back from their dismal 1969 season (1 win, 13 losses). Their next season hinged on the success or failure of their number-one draft pick, Louisiana native Terry Bradshaw.

As I moved through a bedroom that consisted of two beanbags and a single mattress tucked in the corner of the room, someone passed a pipe to me. I hit it and passed it along.

Marcia went into the living room, sitting on Paul's lap with legs and arms draped around him. She said she wasn't Paul's girl, but from the looks of it, she was. I tried to mask my disappointment.

In the small bathroom off the bedroom, Jerry sat cross-legged on the lid of the commode, his legs folded up under him.

"You want a hit?" he asked.

As I walked into the pink and white ceramic-tiled bathroom, I saw my friend Sandy sitting on the edge of the tub with a guy who was tapping another keg.

"Oh, yeah," I said.

"This is Fran," Jerry said. "He lives here with Paul and Marcia," he informed me.

"Hey, Fran," I said. "Dude, this is some awesome reefer."

"Yeah, this batch came from the Allegheny National Forest," Fran explained, with an almost clinical air. "I've been planting all around the region, and this is some of my best stuff." He explained how the soil in the National Forest has a good organic base and how he added nutrients to it—bone meal, sweet lime, and phosphate that generated the fragrant bloom.

I stood in the bathroom hitting the joint, drinking a beer, nodding enthusiastically at Fran's remarks.

Fran got another bag of ice from the freezer and dumped it into the tub.

"Come on," Fran said to Sandy. "Let's go check out the view." The two of them headed out to the back porch.

Our flat is at the most upper right corner of this photo where the tall lights are standing.

View of Pittsburgh from the back porch, 2016

I moved to the edge of the tub and topped off my brew.

"So, Marie is your mom?" Jerry asked.

"Yeah," I said.

"She and I had a real nice chat yesterday," he said. "And she sure was right about you."

A nauseous feeling welled up in my belly and I felt the snow begin to fall again in my head.

"Is that right?" I asked.

"Yeah, girl. You are a looker," he said.

I let the comment pass, reaching for the joint.

"Come on now, don't be that way," Jerry said.

Untangling his legs, he came over to the keg to pour himself another beer.

I stood to make my way out to the porch.

Jerry leaned into me.

"Your mom said you're looking for a new beau," he said with an intentionally salacious tone.

Another wave of nausea rose in my stomach. Nervous, I didn't know what to say. Without consent, he wrapped one of his finely chiseled arms around my waist and pulled me into him.

My heart racing, I froze.

Suddenly someone in the bedroom blasted Janice Joplin's "Me and Bobby McGee," and Jerry flew out of the bathroom to join the rest of the gang singing into imaginary microphones. "*Busted flat in Baton Rouge, waiting for a train,*" they bellowed, off key.

I stood alone in the bathroom and sucked in air. *What else did Mama say to him?* I wondered, drifting off into a dope-induced dissociative state while the spot where Jerry had touched my waist flared with discomfort, as if I'd been scalded.

From above, through a soft snow, I saw images of my drunken Mama putting her hands on me in a way mothers should never touch their children. I saw me and Donnie hiding in our secret places. I saw myself being pushed into the arms of drunken men or made to dance with them in exchange for a quarter dropped in my pocket that would—in time—bring the prize of a meal. I saw the local miscreant, Bobby Graham, pulling me into his car and pushing my face down on his dick.

In a trance, I hit the joint again, but even Fran's "perfected" marijuana failed to ward off the deep dysphoria that came over me.

Why did Mama do these things? Am I like her? Am I going to be like her, live like her? Am I a whore? I must be if these things keep happening to me. Men wanting my body? I hate my body. I wish I was invisible.

I slugged down another drink at the bathtub bar in an ill attempt to quell my pain. I was alone in the bathroom as the party raged: high-decibel anthems of faux-liberation, all of it incapable of easing my pain.

❄

In the weeks that followed, Mama had another episode with her diabetes that put her in the hospital for a spell. As usual, I managed things at home.

I got Donnie to school, made sure he was fed and tended too, and stayed on top of the bills and apartment. Mrs. Pritchard, who lived a few doors down, offered to keep an eye on Donnie until I got home from school every day. This was a big help, though it did little to lessen my anguish. To deal with that, I turned more and more to drinking and other drugs.

Jerry pursued me, and though I was confused about my feelings towards him, I didn't know how to say no to his advances. I didn't know "no" was a choice. Six years my senior, and a burly hulk of a man, he was an intimidating sight to me. The reptilian part of my brain went into survival mode, considering it safer to go along rather than to have things possibly turn ugly. We became an item. We did not date, per se, because we always ran with the whole crowd. Basically, that meant that we partied at the lower flat on Grandview Street. Mama could not have been more pleased that I had landed a college man, and Donnie wondered what had happened to the constant eye and care of his older sister.

One evening, during one of the parties, Jerry took me by the hand and led me downstairs to the basement. Behind the steps, there was a small crawl space. He guided me up the steps and into the cramped, damp opening. He followed.

Without a word, he leaned into me, opened my belt buckle, and fumbled to get my pants open and unzipped. He unzipped his jeans and produced his hardness.

With labored breath, and a soft snow falling in my head, I was pressed against the mildewed sandstone wall as Jerry thrust himself into me. Sucking my breath in hard, I cried quietly as my flesh ripped and his muscular hands groped my breasts. It was over in minutes, though to me it seemed interminable.

Numb, I put myself back together.

With a wink, Jerry whispered in my ear, "You're mine now, Terry Teenie."

And that was that. I was his. Like my father, he had branded me with a nickname, an imposed pet name. It was the very opposite of what couples my age and older were starting to experience, deciding on their terms of endearment for each other—"sweetheart," "baby," "sugar," etc., using these words reciprocally out of a sense of connection, out of a desire to greet each other every day with a gentle and sincere diminutive.

From the outside looking in, people thought we were the perfect couple. Even before finishing college, Jerry had a good job as an electrician. I had finished high school and, at Mama's constant urging that "you need to get a good skill in case you can't land a good man," I had enrolled in the Connelley Skill Learning Center, a trade school. Founded in 1930 and named for Clifford B. Connelley, a pattern maker, engineer, and consulting supervisor of Pittsburgh's Industrial Schools, the school provided vocational training for low-income students so they could begin work immediately after graduation. I enrolled in the clerical program to keep my shorthand and typing skills sharp. The instructor was Miss McKinley, a West Virginian with a sweet drawl and a kind and welcoming demeanor. My skill level was already pretty high, but with her gentle encouragement, I worked hard and improved.

Clifford B. Connelley Trade School, Hill District, circa 1973

As a part of the training, we learned advanced clerical and filing skills and how to run a mimeograph and ditto machine. We also practiced how to write a resume and perform well in interviews, including how to dress and engage in verbal and nonverbal communication. As we neared the end of the training program, Miss McKinley shared that human resource representatives from local companies would be coming to do mock interviews with us. A handful of us were selected to participate in the practice interviews. I landed one of the spots with Koppers Company, then a Fortune 500 company.

I recall the day of the interview. Because Miss McKinley was so kind and encouraging toward me, I wanted to do well—almost entirely for her. I had already been working part-time at a summer program at a local Baptist church, and with the small pay that I received, I purchased a white blouse, blue skirt, nylons, and a pair of shoes at the then-thriving Kaufmann's department store.

On the morning of the interview, I curled my hair and put on makeup, which I normally went without. As I looked into the lit mirror and applied eye shadow to my lids, I thought back to the time I had applied makeup to Mama's face and the fallout of the evening that followed. My eyes froze into a distant and familiar stare, and a sick feeling grew in my belly as I stroked the powder over my own eyes. The next thing I remember is being on the bus to school, dressed for my interview with Miss Bernice Austin from the Human Resources Department of Koppers Company.

Miss Austin was a tall, beautiful African-American woman dressed in a plaid suit, short jacket, long skirt, navy blue pumps with a gold buckle, and gold jewelry. I was taken by her presence. There was something very powerful about her, and, at the same time, her eyes were kind and reassuring. In the interview, I fielded questions about my typing and shorthand speed and accuracy; my telephone, mimeograph, ditto machine and record keeping skills; and how I would assist my supervisor with planning meetings and correspondence. The mock interview was over in about 20 minutes. Both Miss McKinley and Miss Austin led the class in a discussion about how I did. Even though the comments were generally positive, I wanted to disappear. At the end of the class, Miss Austin came and shook my hand and thanked me for participating.

"I think Terry is someone special," Miss McKinley said, and Miss Austin nodded in agreement.

The very next day, Miss Austin called and offered me a job at Koppers Company.

I started in the mail room, but over the years, even as my addiction progressed, I would "fall up the ladder," eventually working my way up to a position in the office of the division president.

I began my tenure with Koppers Company in the fall of 1973. Jerry and I had settled into a routine of daily partying by then and when we weren't with his friends, we were doing "house projects" and spending time with his family—mother, father, brother, and sisters. I didn't mind this so much because Jerry's family were nice and kind to me. It didn't hurt that they all drank, too. At that point, as long as I had a drink, joint, or some other chemical in my system, I could get through anything.

I moved in with Jerry when I turned 18. Mama, who had pushed me into his arms, was now less pleased with him and unmistakably pissed with me. The time leading up to the move was wrought with tension. Mama sensed it was coming and picked fights with me, perhaps trying to get under my skin. She certainly was not giving me any incentive to stay with her. Donnie didn't understand what was going on with all the bickering between me and Mama. I felt guilty and conflicted about leaving him, but I left anyway. Jerry kept saying to me that I was 18 and an adult now and I could leave. So, I did.

In some way, something good came out of it. Though she didn't say as much, Mama was impressed by my enrollment in the Connelley Skill Learning Center clerical program. When I started the program, I brought home a brochure that outlined the different training and trade programs they offered, and sure enough, Mama gave it a look for herself.

At different points in her life, Mama's welfare caseworker would give her information about where to take classes to earn her GED (General Educational Development) certificate, which is the equivalent of a high-school diploma. Despite her interest, Mama's health, dark moods, and drinking always seemed to sabotage her efforts. Around the time I completed the Connelley program and started my job at Koppers Company, Mama had an appointment with her welfare caseworker and asked about Connelley. Her caseworker encouraged her to take the GED exam, which would qualify her for Connelley's skill training programs.

One day, when I went by the apartment to pick up the last of my clothes, Mama asked, in a detached way, how the job was going.

"Pretty cool, I guess. I mean, it's a mail room, so nothing too exciting, but the people seem pretty nice."

"Oh, that's good. You know there is a medical transcriptionist training program at Connelley," Mama said.

"Yeah, I know. I got to know some of the girls taking those classes when we were on class breaks. It seemed like a pretty intense program," I replied.

"Yeah, well, I'm going to sit for my GED. The caseworker's going to help with that paperwork. Then I was thinking I might go for that program."

"That's great, Ma. I think you should," I said, as I shoved clothes into a shopping bag.

"The brochure says the program covers basic medical terminology, but then there are classes in everything else. Anatomy, the digestive and reproductive systems, pulmonary medicine, neurology, pathology, and radiology." She had clearly memorized the brochure's contents. Knowing her, my guess is that she had read it front to back twenty or more times.

"Yeah, intense, like I said. But it seems like you know what you'd be getting into."

"Yeah, well, with you gone now, too," she said, in a tone of resignation.

"If it means anything to you, I really think you can do it and you should go for it," I said, as enthusiastically as I could muster.

"Well, maybe," she said.

"Do it, Mama," I said, more sternly. "It's time you gave yourself something. Do it."

I gathered up my things, kissed her cheek, and headed out the door.

In the days and months that followed, Mama sat for and passed her GED exam. She then applied to the medical transcriptionist program and was accepted. This brought about a lightness in Mama, as she now had something that gave her purpose, focus, and even some hope. When I dropped in to see her and Donnie in the subsequent months, I would find her studying for her classes, flashcards strewn around the apartment. She would even ask me to help her with what she called "rapid flashcard drills." This involved my giving her a term and her rapidly shooting back the spelling and definition of the term, breaking each one down by prefix, suffix, and root, identifying the system it was a part of, with descriptive words associated with diagnoses, prognoses, and treatments. I helped her develop creative, original acronyms to memorize the terms.

I was impressed and glad to see that Mama had found something meaningful in her life, but her drinking was still in the mix. There was clear and even disturbing tension in the apartment between her and Donnie. I felt it was related to my leaving, and this only served to fuel my guilt and deepen my pull towards drugs and alcohol.

Either way, a small light had gone on in Mama's eyes. Mine were clearly dimming.

Jerry and I rented a flat in the city for a short time, drinking and doing drugs daily. We lived right across the street from a bar, which was ideal for us because when we ran out of "hooch," which happened often, we knew we were set until 2 a.m., when the bar closed. Jerry could always just go to the bar, but I was still underage.

One night, Jerry left the apartment for a booze run. I already had a few drinks in me and was grateful that I had some reefer and cigarettes, because I didn't know when he would get back. Sometimes he would stay at the bar until closing. Sometimes later. In the apartment, we had a big coconut candle that someone had given us at Christmas. It was an oversized novelty candle housed in a large coconut shell, with three wicks in it.

Once he left, I slung the candle in a crocheted plant holder and hooked it to the light fixture in the middle of our bare living room. I put Carole King's "Tapestry" on the hi-fi, lit the wicks, turned off the lights, and spun the candle around and around then let it go. Sitting on the floor, I fired up a joint and crooned along with Carole to "I Feel the Earth Move Under My Feet."

In the darkened room, the spinning candle threw shadows on the walls of its roped holder. Under the euphoric influence of Fran's pot, I felt the sensation of riding on a carousel.

I sat there singing and thinking about Mama and Donnie. My move out of the flat had been hard on both of them. I had always been there to care for them, and I was Donnie's sister-mom. From diaper changes, potty training, cooking, helping with homework, and fending off bullies, I was his caretaker. From the time he was born, I hitched him up on my hip and schlepped him wherever I went. And then there was Mama, who seemed to have no one else in the world but me. I still didn't know what was between her and her family, but it was serious enough that they rarely came around, and I knew that they didn't really want to see us when we visited. Mama relied on me for her physical and emotional well-being, and for so long I had complied in trying to set her right. I forced my own needs underground so I could properly care for the two of them, but this did little for me in return.

I sat on the floor of my and Jerry's bare apartment, stoned and riding a musical carousel with Carole King. Feeling sorrow and remorse for having abandoned Mama and Donnie, I cried through the lyrics of her *So Far Away*.

Drifting into a dreamlike state, I thought about my brother Eddie. In 1970 he had disappeared into the world of junior seminarians, training to be a religious leader. He showed up from time to time for brief and awkward visits with Mama. Donnie was always excited to see his older brother, and that was good, but by this time I had let go of him. I made the best of our time together, but emotionally I was disengaged, fueled by my drug and alcohol use.

Then, sometime in 1972, I was shocked to learn that Eddie had enlisted to serve in Vietnam. The war was in full swing by then and a topic of heated discussion among Jerry and his friends. The draft, a mandatory "order of call" to military service, went live in late 1969; men born between 1944 and 1950 were entered into lotteries to determine their order to serve in the military. Jerry and his friends protested against the war. Well, I don't recall that they actually went to any protests. They just drank, smoked dope, and bitched about it.

It made absolutely no sense to me that Eddie would enlist, unless he was going to serve the troops as a chaplain. It was the only thing that made sense.

I dragged on a cigarette, tearing up. News coverage of the war at that time was nonstop. I was aware enough to know that tens of thousands of soldiers had already died, killed in action in Laos, Cambodia, and North and South Vietnam. Though Eddie and I had lost the connection we had as children, he was still my brother, and I feared that his service would be the death of him.

I held that thought and contemplated Jerry's fate. While tens of thousands died in Vietnam, tens of thousands of other American men were dodging the draft and heading to Canada. Jerry planned to be among them. His draft number had been called, and he refused to serve. Initially, he planned to get shit-faced drunk and somehow break his foot so he would be rejected when he showed up for his call to duty. But at the last minute, he chickened out. He told me he would go to Canada instead.

The haunting melody of Carole King's "Tapestry" reached me through this litany of thoughts. Her tapestry unfolded in bits and pieces and, though not defined, it embodied a creative sense of wonder about it.

I sighed. I realized that an entire hour had passed.

Another hour passed, and still no word.

I sat on the floor, completely disillusioned and depressed. At that point, I *needed* a drink, and there was no denying it. Reflecting on my life at only eighteen years old, I was convinced it was over. For the first time, I uttered to myself the words, "I am an alcoholic," and knew it was an absolute truth.

The candlelight settled and flickered softly in the middle of the room, and the phonograph skipped repeatedly at the end of the record. I sat there alone in my shame, feeling trapped, with no means of escape. My mind was obsessed with the next drink, and my body compulsively craved it. But I was all out. The "only one more drink" eluded me.

In a hypnotic state, I turned off the phonograph and I walked to the candle, dousing the wick with my fingertips. The bite of the heat in the darkened room roused me to the bleak and lonely truth of the unraveling of my own tapestry.

I went to bed, and when Jerry finally stumbled in, I pretended to be asleep. Even this reminded me of how I had feigned sleep when my mother came into my and Eddie's room as children. Closing my eyes like shutters. A goodbye to myself and the world.

Something happened to me that night, in the heart of my isolation. I was only eighteen, but I knew I was in trouble, not just with alcohol, but with Jerry, too. It was clear to me that I needed help, but I didn't know what help was or how to get it. Still, the mere realization was a step: an acknowledgment of my crisis.

I'm grateful that Jerry decided to stay out that night, to drink too much, to not give a damn about me. Alone on the floor, unable to numb myself with alcohol, without any human consolation other than Carole King's warbling voice, I was forced to reckon with myself—with the rawness of my predicament.

7

JACK

On a sunny day in May 1979, Jack strolled into the office at Koppers Company around 8:30 a.m. He was humming a tune and gave me a wink as he sauntered by.

"Hey there, Mr. Rose," I smiled back at him.

Jack disappeared into his office, and in a few minutes, I heard him mumbling, "Aw, shit! How the hell did I do that?"

I let it go because I didn't work for Jack. His secretary, Miss Kniss, was in the president's office delivering coffee to the management team, which assembled there every morning to shoot the breeze before starting the day. Joe, the shoe-shine man, came by and spit-shined everyone's shoes, and Miss Kniss served up coffee and pastries purchased from Kuntz's Bakery on Smithfield Street.

Marge Kniss had worked for Koppers Company for over thirty years. She was the secretary to the president of the company's iron and steel division, Bob Wilson, and the vice president, Jack Rose. Marge was a petite, almost frail-looking woman with blue eyes and soft, sandy blonde hair. Even if she hadn't gone out of her way to tell me so, it would have been obvious that she had attended (and relished) "charm school." She was very proper. She sat upright with her back always one full inch away from the back of her chair, always in a dress cut just below the knee, and she folded her hands neatly in her lap with her feet crossed at the ankle. And though she walked with the slightest bounce in her step, you knew that she could balance a book on her head as she went, probably while offering a tutorial on silverware etiquette.

Miss Kniss was all business. She took her post very seriously and had been rewarded with the highest clerical position in the entire division. She was a consummate professional with excellent shorthand, typing, and proofreading skills. And she performed every task personally, professionally, and efficiently. She was my tutor, in effect, and I learned quickly.

When she bounced out of Mr. Wilson's office that morning, I said, "Marge, I think Mr. Rose might need your assistance. He's mumbling about something in his office."

"Hmmm," she said. She grabbed her pen and steno pad and bobbed past my desk into Mr. Rose's office.

"Oh, there you are," Jack shouted from his desk. "Take care of these for me. Somehow, I tore a hole in them."

In a moment's time, Marge reappeared in the clerical bullpen, carrying her pen, steno pad, and Mr. Rose's damaged pants. Marge strolled over to her desk, unfazed, and pulled a sewing kit from her desk to begin stitching Jack's pants.

I've seen just about everything now, I thought.

I loved Jack, and he and I had done some heavy partying over the years, but I was blown away. He was in his office without his trousers.

I could hardly believe it, but Marge sat there straight as a poker, sewing his britches, exuding the sense that trouser repair was standard procedure covered in charm school.

Jack rolled out of his office in his Cornell Carnelian red-and-white striped boxer shorts whistling "Hey There, Georgy Girl," and by then I was officially mortified.

Stopping at my desk, he leaned into me, singing, "Hey there, Terry girl," and gave me a knowing wink.

I could smell the fresh scent of booze on his breath, and even though Jack and I had shared more than a few drinks together, I was incredulous. Even so, I couldn't help but hum along with him as he bopped me on the head with a rolled-up newspaper and danced a pantsless foxtrot into Mr. Wilson's office. He's doomed, I thought.

"Hey, Bob! Harry! How are you fellas doing?" Jack asked, bounding into the office.

Almost immediately, the door slammed shut, and Marge and I stared at each other as we craned our necks, trying to make out the yelling going on inside the office.

Embarrassed and nervous, Marge moved her hands nimbly to complete her mending task. She knotted the last stitch and bit the end of the thread.

Marge neatly folded the pants at the crease and draped them over the back of her desk chair. Harry, our financial officer, came out to retrieve them and told Marge to call for a car to come around to the back of the building. Harry then disappeared back into Mr. Wilson's office.

Marge called the chauffeur and busied herself with a proofreading task.

I sat at my desk, moving papers around and trying to look busy, but I was completely preoccupied. On one hand, I thought Jack's behavior was bizarre, but on the other hand, I found it quite funny—comically brazen and self-destructive. For this last reason, I felt an odd sense of relief. I had done some awfully self-destructive shit as a result of my drinking, but never anything like that. I thought to myself, *I'll never get that bad, and if I do, I'll quit!*

After some quiet, murmured conversation, Mr. Wilson's office door opened and Jack emerged—fully clothed—with both Harry and Mr. Wilson at his side. It was obvious that both Jack and Bob had been crying. The two men supported Jack as they walked through the bullpen area. I didn't know if he was unstable just from drunkenness or from the intensity of their conversation. Probably both.

Mr. Wilson gave Marge a grave look.

"Marge, gather up Jack's things in the office and get Mrs. Rose on the phone for me."

I looked at Jack as they walked by my desk. He sheepishly glanced down in my direction, and I lifted my hand from a pile of papers to wave to him. A faint smile came across my face—maybe because the moment was, for both of us, so intensely, imperfectly, unmistakably human. I wondered where they were taking him and wondered if Mr. Wilson had fired him. Watching Jack escorted out of the office, I knew my drinking was as bad as his, and the only thing I had going for me was the pure "luck" that my own addiction to drugs and alcohol had not shown up on the job yet. It had been "contained."

Around this time, I was doing human resources training at Koppers, and we were told that Jack would be out of the office for 28 days. By this time, I had received the Employee Assistance Program (EAP) training in drug and alcohol abuse and I knew that the Gateway Rehabilitation program lasted 28 days. I quickly surmised that they had sent him off to rehab.

In the time that Jack was gone, I thought of him often, usually when I drank alone at the house Jerry and I shared. I still hadn't left Jerry, though his emotional brutality and our shared dysfunction weren't lost on me. Going through Employee Assistance Program training that year had confirmed what I had long known. I was an alcoholic. My damning responses to the "Are You an Alcoholic?" questionnaire—which I never turned in, of course—blew away any veneer of composure.

Moving my thoughts to Jack, I wondered how he was getting on, if he was staying sober, if I would ever see him again. The rehabilitation facility was a mystery, too. I wondered if it was an idyllic, life-affirming sanctuary or a clinical, cold sanatorium that left him no other option but to face himself. Either way, I hoped it was a place where Jack would find real help and support.

Jack came back to work at the end of August that year, just before our quarterly board meeting. Mr. Wilson had called us all into his office on the day before his return and told us he would be back the next day.

"Jack's doing really well," Mr. Wilson said. "And we're happy that he'll be back with the team tomorrow. There'll be no party," he said, scanning our faces, "just business as usual."

Leaving the office that day, I promised myself that I would not drink that night and that I would be sober the next day when Jack arrived. I wanted to honor his efforts for at least one special day.

After work, I hopped on the trolley heading to my and Jerry's home in Castle Shannon, originally an Irish-settled mining town and now a southern suburb of Pittsburgh. I felt good about my resolution. I even considered what I would wear for the occasion: a blue jumpsuit with a white blouse that

Jack liked. I would polish my shoes and curl my hair too. I assured myself I could step up for him.

And yet, in the 45-minute trolley ride home and the five-minute trek up the hill to the new house that Jerry and I shared, my thinking changed entirely. The reality of where I was headed for the night, back into that house with Jerry, eclipsed any short-lived resolve. *Maybe*, I thought, *I'll just smoke a joint, but I won't have a drink. It's the alcohol that gets me in trouble, but I can smoke a joint and get my clothes ready for work.*

I got into the house and changed my clothes. I put on dinner because Jerry expected a hot meal when he came home, though I never knew when that would be. It could be eight, ten, midnight, or even later. But *whenever* it was, he expected a hot meal to materialize.

I fired up a joint and pulled some leftovers out of the fridge to warm on the stove. There were two beers there, and I thought I could have just one, and that would be it.

With a sweet marijuana bloom surrounding me, I sat at the kitchen counter and lit a smoke as I downed a Rolling Rock beer. Without a thought, I went for the second beer, too, and after having gulped that down, I went to the downstairs game room and filled a pitcher from the keg in the refrigerator. Before I knew it, I was wasted, alone, and full of shame and remorse that I couldn't stop myself from drinking.

Jerry used to say, "First you take the drink, then the drink takes you." We would laugh at that statement, holding hands as we stepped together off the metaphorical cliff. We would nod, raise our glasses, and gulp down our drinks. Recovering alcoholics say it this way: "One drink is too much, and a thousand is not enough." And that was the real truth. Restlessness and insatiability followed even a single sip. It was never the last drink that got me in trouble, but always the first one.

Jerry rolled in at some point that night, and a hot meal was waiting for him. I was loaded and feeling pretty miserable about myself and my life, but this was nothing out of the ordinary. He was indifferent, only inconvenienced by the fact that I had drunk both of the Rolling Rocks, which forced him to lumber downstairs to the keg.

I made it to work the next day, supported only by the influence of some "uppers." I had popped a few amphetamines to get going and slugged down a coffee to finish the job. I rolled out the door, confident that the drugs would kick in by the time I got to the office. They did.

Jack came in around eight-thirty that morning. He looked wonderful, illuminated. He must have spent some time in a tropical location, because his skin was tanned. Against his shock of silver hair, I noticed his crystal blue eyes and perfectly straight, white teeth. I also noticed his outfit: a blue and white seersucker suit in which he looked absolutely stunning.

I was anxious—due in some measure to the drugs kicking in—but also because I was so curious about what I would see in Jack. How would he be? What would it be like for him at work or at business lunches without drinking? How would he be at the company picnics where he and I usually posted ourselves at the keg, pouring one for others and two for us? How would he be at board meetings, or *after* the board meetings, when the alcohol really flowed?

I had learned at the EAP training that an admission of alcoholism and "going for help" meant a whole lot more than just going to rehab for 28 days and offering a reconciliatory speech to friends and family. It meant a life without alcohol, a complete 180-degree turn. Going to recovery meetings and staying sober "a day at a time" was the real mission.

Jack went into the kitchen area across from my desk to make himself a cup of coffee. Flashing a smile, he turned to greet me.

"Good morning, Terry. It's good to see you," he said.

Shakily, I rose from my desk to give him a hug.

"Hi, Jack. It's good to have you back," I said.

He smelled of cologne.

"It's good to be back," he said.

Then he did something I didn't expect, a gentle gesture I had never seen from him before. He stepped back and held my shoulders at arm's length, looked me square in the eye, and asked, "How are you doing, Terry?"

I couldn't hold his gaze. Between the hangover, amphetamines, and nerves, I was shot and emanated shame. Trembling, I felt Jack look directly into the depths of my hollowness. I managed to sputter, "Fine, Jack. I'm just fine," but he instantly knew it was a lie.

"Well, good, Terry," he said, in a defeated kind of way. "I really am so glad to see you."

For the next two and a half years, I kept a close eye on Jack. He was changing. He came into the office every day with a smile on his face and a cup of coffee in his hand. At company functions, as I drank and took drugs, Jack remained sober and seemed genuinely happy and at peace with himself.

His eyes had changed, too. Where they once were red, bloodshot, and lifeless, they now shined with beautiful clarity. He was alive, joyful, *and sober,* and for the life of me I didn't know how he was doing it. I spied on him, actually, secretly appraising and admiring his change, but also watched for any crack— for the inevitable moment when he would trip up and drink again. I skeptically observed his process, glad for what he had experienced, but couldn't believe anyone could truly stay sober.

Then, in the spring of 1981, I took a call that came in to Mr. Wilson's office. It was Jack, and I patched him through. After speaking with him, Mr. Wilson came out to the bullpen to tell us that Jack's wife, Mary, had passed away suddenly that morning due to a brain aneurysm. We were instructed to wait to learn about the arrangements. Mr. Wilson asked Miss Kniss to come into his office to draft an announcement to send to all Koppers Company staff. I was to work with Mr. Smith on drafting an obituary. Marge and I both grabbed our pens and steno pads and went to work at our respective stations.

In the face of Jack's tragedy, I could only think, *This is it. This is the moment Jack drinks again. This is the moment he unhinges, reverts, implodes. And how couldn't he?*

In the days that followed, Marge and I fielded questions about where the service would be held, if donations were being requested and for what organizations, if it was appropriate to send food and flowers to the family, and so on. Marge was having a hard time holding it together, as Jack had been her boss for almost ten years. Over that time, she had become close to Jack's wife and his three daughters.

On the day of the service, I dressed in a black suit and a crisp white shirt. I curled my hair and polished my shoes. I wanted to look my best, but before leaving the house, I rolled a joint and took it with me. Barb, who worked in our international division, was picking me up to drive us to the service, and I knew she would be all right with me smoking a joint. I couldn't imagine doing the funeral straight and I knew if I took a drink, I would reek of booze. Barb picked me up, and I fired up the joint, offering her a hit. She refused, obviously put off by my offer, and that suited me just fine.

I imagined what a wretched scene it would be. I predicted Jack would arrive at Westminster Church with a belly full of booze. I simply couldn't imagine Jack remaining sober after suddenly losing his wife of so many years. Though it was obvious that Jack had changed for the better, I just knew, because he drank like me, that he would be drunk. Excusably drunk.

I filed into the church with the other guests to the sound of a soloist singing "All Things Bright and Beautiful." The church was a sea of black suits and women clutching handkerchiefs. Barb and I sat somewhere in the middle of the crowd, and from my seat I could see that four long pews in the front had been reserved for family members. Through a reefer fog, I heard the organ dive into a deep tone and then commence the chords of "Abide with Me" as the family began to file into the first pews. I watched the front of the church through the bobbing heads of peering penguins, all waiting to see Jack and his daughters arrive. In my drug-induced state, the family procession seemed to go on forever, with family members filling in the fourth row from the front, then the third, then the second, and finally the first row.

Just as the organist struck the final chord, I lurched forward to see Jack enter from a side entrance of the church, walking tall with every inch of his 6' 3" frame, upright and composed. In his outstretched arms, he embraced his three beautiful, grief-stricken daughters, escorting them to their place in the front row of the church.

The organ music ceased, and through a hum of sobs and blowing of noses, I heard the minister's droning voice reading vaguely familiar scriptures and speaking of God's power over death, the "communion of saints," and belief in the resurrection to "life everlasting."

Images appeared in my mind of elderly Sister Constance, my sixth-grade teacher, who in her demented state had recited those words of the Apostles' Creed in every class. As the minister buzzed on, excerpts of the creed ran through my head, ingrained from hundreds of mandated repetitions.

I reflected on this word *resurrection* and considered what I was witnessing. Here was Jack, a drunk like me, but he was sober. Had he been resurrected? *I* could not make it into the church that day without a drug in me and yet there was Jack, contending with perhaps the greatest tragedy of his life— the sudden loss of his wife—and consoling his grieving daughters with dignity, sober as a judge. Perhaps he really was reborn. He was undeniably happy and calm at work, even at company parties and picnics where the drinking was heavy. I had watched him like a hawk for signs of distress, but he always had a cup of coffee or soda in his hand and the drinking of others didn't seem to bother him.

I continued to drink and take drugs. It had become more and more difficult for me to look Jack in the eye. He could see right through me—through my lies, despair, and hopelessness. He always asked how I was, and I always lied. I saw his newfound ease and lightness in sobriety, but I could not comprehend it. My shame and self-loathing kept me from asking.

As I sat stoned in the pew that day, I was ashamed of my weeks of sleuthing and observation—of my expectation that Jack would drink in his time of grief and loss. Perhaps a part of me had even rooted for his plummet.

I joined the choir of mourners, quietly weeping into a handkerchief. But my tears were not for Jack, his daughters, and their loss. My tears were for me. For the loss of my innocence, the loss of my "self," and the resulting emptiness and despair that consumed me. I had clung in desperation to alcohol, but my dependence only reinforced my sense of unworthiness.

On the ride home from the funeral with Barb, the spring air felt somehow nauseating to me, embodying an inaccessible vivacity that I both wanted and resented. It reminded me of how my mother had looked out the kitchen window when I was a child, staring at life as though it was something encroaching and foreign.

✳

Through a drunken fog, I glanced at the clock on the kitchen wall. It was around 2 a.m.

Phone in my hand, I heard the voice on the other end of the line say, "If you'd like, I can come over to talk with you some more, Terry. I'm really glad you called and I want you to know that I am here for you."

Is this Jerry? I thought. *No, it doesn't sound like him.*

I looked out the window and saw that it was snowing. Jerry's truck was in the driveway, but there was no sign of him anywhere. *Who am I even talking to?*

I lit a cigarette.

The man continued to talk to me.

"It's a really big step to reach out and ask for help," he said.

A little more alert, I realized that the man on the other end of the phone was Jack. Panic shot through me.

"Yeah," I stammered, "organizing" a few random objects on the kitchen table. "I'm okay. Really, I'm fine."

"Tell me what you have there, Terry. I think I should come over so we can continue this talk in person," he said.

"No, I'll be all right, Jack. Thank you, though," I said. "All good."

"All right, then, but please tell me what you have there. I won't get off the phone until I know you have flushed the drugs. You're not alone," Jack said. "And you don't have to live like this anymore."

With that statement, I completely lost it. I realized that I was coming out of a blackout. I must have called Jack and asked for help in the midst of a half-conscious haze.

"Terry, my dear, if I can get sober, I know you can," he said. "You just can't do it alone. You don't have to be alone anymore. Really," he said, more gently.

Sobbing now, I couldn't find any words. My throat constricted. No one in my life had ever spoken so kindly to me or handed me that kind of hope.

Maybe that's because no one really knew the kind of pain I was in. I had never articulated it, nor shared the depth of it with anyone. But here was Jack, someone I admired, who used to drink the way I did. He was a widower still in mourning, offering to drive to my house in the dead of the night through rapidly falling snow. To help me.

Crying and sputtering, I said, "Jack, I don't remember calling you. I'm so embarrassed. I'm so sorry to have bothered you. I should go."

Jack sounded panicked.

"No, no, Terry, you're not bothering me. You did the right thing. Stay on the line with me, please," he pleaded. "If you don't remember, Terry, you told me you have a lot of drugs there. You told me you were going to take them. Tell me what you have, and let's get rid of them, okay?"

I looked around the kitchen counter. In my blackout, I must have pulled out all my stashes. There were baggies of pot, amphetamines, some downers, a few poppers, and a small amount of cocaine. There was also a pot of Irish stew I had started for Jerry, but I had left it on the burner while I was blacked out. It had transformed into a calcified, burnt, inedible mass. Fitting, I thought.

"Yeah, there are drugs here," I said, with some defiance.

"Okay, can you flush them?" he asked.

Between the tears, fear, and the effect of the dope and booze I had already taken, I really didn't know what to say.

"Yes, I can," I finally agreed, unable to wage any protest.

I gathered up *most* of the drugs and stumbled into the bathroom. There I stood over the commode, emptied the contents of the baggies into the toilet, and flushed them away.

"That's good, Terry," Jack said.

"Do you want me to come over, so we can continue to talk?" he asked.

I was so embarrassed and dumbfounded that I really couldn't process his offer.

"How about we talk tomorrow at work?" I asked.

"That's fine, Terry. What's important is that you did the right thing tonight. I know it took a lot of courage to pick up the phone and make this call," he said. "Rest now, and we'll talk in the morning. Please call again if you need to. I'm here for you. Anytime."

"Thank you, Jack," I said, crying into the phone, still more humiliated than consoled.

I hung up the phone, went back to the bathroom, and threw some cold water on my face. I looked into the mirror and gazed for a brief moment into my bloodshot eyes.

Courage. What courage? You have none, I thought.

When I awoke the next morning, I had a throbbing headache, and fear shot through me like I had never experienced before.

What the hell happened last night?

I showered and dressed as quietly as possible. Jerry, who came in at some point in the early morning, stumbled around the house getting ready for work. I packed a lunch for him and headed to work. I don't remember if we even spoke a word to each other.

Just a month earlier, I had been promoted to an HR position and had my own office next to Mr. Wilson's corner suite. That morning, on Tuesday, November 3, 1981, I sat quietly at my desk as the men congregated next door. Miss Kniss bounced back and forth with coffee and doughnuts, her steno pad in hand at all times.

At about 8:30 a.m., Jack came into my office. Without a word, he removed my coat from the back of my office door, reached for my hand, and put my coat on me. We then walked in silence to the main office of a recovery program in downtown Pittsburgh. Back then it was located on Fourth Avenue, in the old Engineers' Society building, a place with which I was very familiar, and where I had done a good deal of my drinking.

Once we went inside, we had a cup of really bad coffee, and Jack picked up some recovery literature and the organization's basic text. His treat. He even made a donation to the office on our way out. Outside, the wind was strong, and snow was starting to fall.

Unfazed, he led us to Point State Park, where we found, then sat together on, a freezing cold bench. With our breath and speech visible during a brewing snowstorm, Jack told me his story.

Today, I tell people that Jack's candor in relaying the effects of alcoholism on his personal life made me feel like I was hearing the English language for the first time. He told me how his drinking made him feel about himself and how it had impacted his sense of self-respect. Brushing snow from his eyes, he told me about missing his daughter's piano recital because of his drinking and how he absorbed the family's collective embarrassment and disappointment that night. How their disgust required no verbal articulation, because it was readable on his daughter's and wife's faces. He told me about feeling that same sense of shame when he emerged from a blackout in New York City just minutes before a meeting with some of Koppers' most important clients from Turkey. He even told me about his blackouts *in Turkey*—emphasizing the nature of his addiction. According to him, his addiction was a mobile condition that traveled with him to every corner of the world. In Turkey, it had rendered him a kind of "invisible man," an amnesiac who couldn't even identify himself coherently in an unfamiliar environment. His drinking, he said, was an unshakable leech that dragged his sense of self-worth down to nil on a near-daily basis.

And yet, as he offered me his own litany of past failings—both of us laughing a little at the relentless weather—he spoke to me in the language of one alcoholic to another. Simply knowing that a man who had sunk to similar depths had found the sobriety and fortitude to live with dignity and to communicate it shamelessly gave me an immediate sense of hope.

When I had started at Koppers as a teenager, I looked around at the other employees and deemed them responsible and intelligent professionals. I had thought to myself, *They have something I want.* Ironically, hearing Jack's story—the story of a man with a sterling reputation who had fallen and risen, phoenix-like, out of almost certain destitution—made me feel again that, *He has something I want.* What he had was strength and peace, and it was a bulletproof version of what I had witnessed in the church during his wife's funeral. In other words, Jack had been tested and proven under the most brutal circumstances. His recovery wasn't an abstraction or a platitude; it had been forged through honest, conscious effort. I didn't know what he had, I just knew I wanted it.

8

BRIDGES TO CROSS

As quickly and furiously as the snow fell, I determined that with Jack's support, I would go to Gateway Rehabilitation Center for its 28-day recovery program. He reassured me that our health insurance plan would cover the cost and he felt confident that Mr. Wilson, our boss, would support my decision. Work was the least of my worries, really. What I anguished over more was how I would tell Jerry that I was going to rehab. I recognized immediately that this defining decision would release me from his hold. Still, I shuddered at the thought of even having the discussion with him.

"Before you speak to Jerry, let's make sure there is a bed available for you. You don't want to have that conversation first and then not have a treatment slot," Jack said.

That made sense to me, but I was quite surprised when we returned to the office and Jack asked me to step into his suite so we could make the call to Gateway together. No nonsense and no delays.

"It's important that you are on the line to say that you are willing and ready to go to treatment. This is your decision and you need to own it," he said.

I began to shake visibly as Jack dialed the phone. I considered that Jerry might actually hurt me if I tried to go. I considered backing out on my promise to avoid all the discomfort that would follow in exchange for the discomfort I already knew.

Then my mind harkened back to something Jack had said to me. He said that he would rather go through life sober, knowing he was an alcoholic, than go through life drunk while straining to convince himself that he was not. I understood perfectly what he was saying, as only another alcoholic can.

Jack and I waited as the intake specialist checked the treatment calendar.

Seeing that I was nervous and overwhelmed, Jack reassured me, "Listen, the hardest part is done, Terry. You've already asked for help. It's a big deal to stop carrying that burden by yourself. You are not alone anymore. We just have to take it one step at a time."

I nodded my head in agreement, but inside, my addiction was already dissuading me. *This is a mistake. Jerry is not going to go for this. This will not fly. You can't leave for 28 days and live in some secluded compound. What the fuck are you thinking?*

Sensing my inner conflict, Jack weighed in.

"Terry, there is never a good time to go to treatment. Your mind will give you a million reasons not to go. That's your disease telling you that you don't have a disease! And yet you said you identify with most of the things I shared with you, right?"

"Right," I said.

"Well, as our French counterparts say, *voilà*! If you are identifying with me, and I'm an alcoholic, then you must be an alcoholic! Kind of an undeniable parallel there."

"I know. I'm just scared."

"Who wouldn't be? Look," he started to say.

Jill, the perky admissions specialist popped back on the line.

"Mr. Rose. Terry. We will have a bed available on Friday, November 6. Terry, may I put your name in for this treatment slot?" she asked.

"Please do. I'll be there," I said.

Jack rose from his desk, stood behind me, putting both of his hands on my shoulders, and kissed me on the head. I reached for his hand and nodded. He exited the room so I could continue the call.

Jill explained to me that we would have to complete a pre-intake screening that would lay the groundwork for a personalized treatment plan. Though Jill's chirpy voice annoyed me, I detected her underlying kindness and understanding. In the hour that followed, we discussed my drinking and drug history, the types and duration of my use, my previous treatment history (none), my underlying mental and emotional problems, employment condition, family life, legal issues, and health coverage. Finally, we discussed transportation arrangements to get me to treatment. The pre-intake screening was the start of what I will call now my "shadow exam," a thorough unearthing and perusing of everything in my psyche that I didn't want to confront.

I explained to Jill as euphemistically as possible that I did not think my husband was going to support me in this decision. (Yes, Jerry and I did eventually marry in the late 1970s. It was an uneventful, booze-induced "tying of the knot" notarized in a sterile magistrate's office downtown). Jill, with trademark cheer, encouraged me to use my support network. *I don't have one*, I thought to myself. She encouraged me to go to recovery group meetings, get phone numbers of the people there, and use them.

"Okay then," I said, numbly.

We completed the call, and I sat there in Jack's office, stymied by my conflicting feelings of despair and hope. I knew I was doing the right thing for myself, but it was a hard and alien thing to do. I was most terrified by practical concern number one: how this would play out with Jerry.

I walked out of Jack's office and went to mine, where I found Jack highlighting meetings on a list.

"So, first things first," he said, pushing a glass of water my way. "I'm going to take you to a wonderful meeting tonight and tomorrow night. And what's our plan for Thursday night? Guess what? *Another* wonderful meeting. Then, it's off to Gateway on Friday."

Jack was being a little playful with me, smiling at the juxtaposition of my stress and his sobriety as he worked to fill my time, second by second, with all the enthusiastic vigilance of a helicopter mom until I walked through the doors of Gateway. In truth, I treasured his care for me: the highlighting of the meetings, the glass of water I began to drink. To see a person you respect strike the pause button on his or her own life just to make you a priority, even fleetingly, is a life-changing gesture.

"I'm scared to tell Jerry about this. He's going to flip the fuck out."

"You know what? On your way home after work, just tell him. Tell him that you need to do this for yourself and you hope he can support you. Tell him that either way, you are going to do it. Keep it simple. Tell him you're going to treatment on Friday and between now and then you will be going to some recovery meetings. That's the plan. That's what happening. Tell him to expect that. You hope he'll be a part of your treatment experience. Leave it at that. Anything else leaves wiggle room. Room for him to manipulate you, so don't even offer that space."

I sighed. I wished I could convince Jack to tell Jerry directly, but it was my responsibility. My cross to bear.

"I'll come for you at six-thirty tonight for the meeting," he said. "Step one, right?"

Jerry picked me up from Koppers, and I did exactly what Jack suggested. I told him that I was an alcoholic and that I was going to get help at Gateway Rehab. I told him about my talk with Jack and how he had been sober for over two years and that he was helping me and that I wanted him, Jerry, to support me, too.

As expected, the conversation with Jerry escalated quickly. From the driver's seat of his red Ford pickup, he angrily yelled that I was not an alcoholic and he defiantly questioned whether I thought *he* was an alcoholic, too. He asked if I was trying to ruin our marriage. He reminded me that I was nothing without him.

"How stupid are you? Really, Terry," he winced, looking at me in disbelief and launching into a maniacal laugh that accompanied his fury. It frightened me.

The first time I had heard him laugh like this was early on in our relationship. Over beers, he and a friend were reminiscing about a time when, as teens, they had caught some stray cats and tortured them. They laughed and laughed, hollowly and heartlessly, indifferent to my reaction to their brutality. I was horrified. In retrospect, I should have run like hell. Instead, I succumbed to the trappings of a relationship with a man who, in outward appearance, seemed perfect. Internally, within the confines of our new, outwardly beautiful suburban home, I felt confined, worthless, and alone. Drinking and drugs allowed me to play the part of the happy little wife, but nothing was further from the truth.

Jerry ranted about Gateway and addiction, and I wilted under his rage. I sat there numb, letting him fume.

By the end of his tirade, he was practically panting. He collected himself and, in a flourish of resignation, said, "If people feed you shit and you're stupid enough to eat it, so be it. Fuck it!"

I wondered where all of that volcanic energy had been resting for the past couple of years. Dormant, stifled by booze, erupting in bouts of reckless anger just like the one I'd witnessed.

On the outside, our lives looked normal, even happy. Jerry's work was very important to him, and he was a valued employee at his job. A union tradesman, he stood in good favor whether working in the shop or in the field. Family—his family—was extremely important to him. In fact, we spent every free moment with his family—his mother and father, sisters and brothers, nieces and nephews. They supported one another and worked on family and home projects together. It was really special in many ways. And I was sincerely welcomed into his family, growing to love them over the years. In the world of outward appearances, it all looked perfect: Jerry and I, the all-American, upwardly mobile suburban couple of a large and loving family. There was truth in that, but there also was a significant catch. At every single family gathering, the booze flowed abundantly and freely, and everyone partook. What on many nights started off looking like an American fairytale-family episode of "Ozzie and Harriet" eventually dissolved into drunken, reckless, angry, and verbally abusive scenes from "Shameless."

Back in the truck, Jerry's ranting came back into my field of awareness. Demeaned and berated, I could hardly wage a response to his verbal attacks. The heavy artillery was lodged. He clearly resented me for wanting to take even a single step out of our quagmire. I wondered if he was afraid. Numb with a soft snow swirling in my head, I watched him from the passenger seat as we headed home, counting the minutes until the meeting with Jack.

In a daze, I reflected on a memory from earlier in the year. In February 1981, I had first tried to talk with Jerry about our drinking and how it was affecting our marriage. Even then, some sliver of me knew I needed help, and I knew that our marriage was hanging by a thread. I thought maybe Jerry would be open to trying therapy with me to help the marriage.

He did not take that well. He shoved me against the kitchen cabinets, my head smacking off a door. Leaning into me, he said, "There is nothing wrong with our drinking or our marriage." Out of breath, he added, "And remember where you come from. You were just a little shit. A tramp in the streets. Terry Teenie, remember? I took you out of there and I can put you right back."

The "bitch" was implied.

I remembered this episode with such clarity because it was a turning point in my addiction. After this interaction, my depression took hold more deeply, and whatever modicum of control I had regarding my drinking and drug use dissipated. From that point on, I used with complete abandon, without regard for the impact on my work, my marriage, or my life. A switch flipped in me, and I wished for death. The occasional, romanticized idea of suicide was now at the forefront of my mind, and I thought of it in more concrete terms: the physical implements or substances required to make it happen, painlessly or otherwise. My newfound preoccupation with death coincided with my growing fascination with female writers and poets who committed suicide. Sylvia Plath, the iconic poet who wrote vividly about death and suicide, especially captured my attention. I studied her works of poetry and journals and read *The Bell Jar,* the only book that details her descent (with some fictional liberties) into mental illness. She used her writing as a platform to interrogate the intimate details of her everyday life.

In a journal entry from 1959, she wrote, "Very depressed today. Unable to write a thing. Menacing Gods. I feel outcast on a cold star, unable to feel anything but an awful numbness." Though not a writer at that time, I identified with her "awful numbness," simultaneously feeling everything and nothing at all.

In "Lady Lazarus," Plath wrote, "Death is an art, like anything else. I do it exceptionally well." Actually, her third attempt led to her demise. Upon learning that her husband, Ted Hughes, was having an affair, she put out bread and milk in her children's bedroom, closed and sealed the door with tape and rags, then fired up the oven and stuck her head inside.

The fact that Plath was just thirty years old when she finally managed to get the job done seduced me. I had always believed that I would dead by thirty. I actually thought I would be lucky if I even made it until then. Reading

114

Plath's work, I felt that I could relate to her, and this proved an antidote to my own melancholy. Jerry's verbal and belittling abuse pushed me deeper into my addiction, and I began to hoard a mixture of pills—amphetamines, barbiturates, and even some amyl nitrate that I felt could help me get the job done.

As I entertained thoughts of suicide and forged my secret relationships with Plath, Virginia Woolf, Mary Sexton, and others, a mysterious power rose in me. I felt contained within a boundary that I was creating for myself. I felt safe with them. We were isolated bearers of an endangered language; when I read, we could convene and commiserate. No one, not even Jerry, could get to me. I was the sole member of this secret society that gave me an odd comfort and internal peace.

On the drive home from work that night, Jerry unloaded his vitriol as much as possible, but he didn't hit me or even threaten to do so, though I thought he might. Looking back, I can't help but wonder if his restraint was related to the fact that months earlier at a house party, I had walked in on him in a compromising situation. We never discussed it. I had simply left, shaking my head and smiling to myself. Believe me, I had my own indiscretions. Addiction and abuse can take you there. Even so, at that time, I believe he had felt something: perhaps a grain of guilt that I believe impeded him from interfering in my desire to get help at Gateway. It was as if we entered into a non-verbal joint contract of absolution. Forgiving reckless behavior on the one hand and deciding to leave it behind on the other. Whatever the case, I was able, by some miracle, to leverage the situation to do the one thing I most needed to do to save my life. A far better choice than downing the pills I had stashed to end it.

When we finally got home from the drive, Jerry slammed his lighter on the table.

"And where do you think you're going to get the money to pay for rehab? If you think I'm going to give you one nickel, you're out of your mind," he said.

I feared Jerry, but I also knew I had Jack in my corner. I thought to myself, *Push, shame, bite, and demean as much as you'd like.* It didn't matter. I was going to rehab.

I left the house to go to my first meeting with Jack. When I returned later that evening, Jerry was still out, God knows where. Probably he was nursing the terrible wounds I'd inflicted through my desire to heal myself.

The next three days were the longest in my life. They began the next morning, when Jack and I went into Mr. Wilson's office at Koppers Company to tell him that I was going to rehab.

Jack spoke on my behalf at first, and Mr. Wilson nodded, appearing unsurprised.

"Do this for you, Terry. Not for Jack. Not for me. Not to save your marriage. Do this for you. Because you deserve to be happy and sober. Just look at Jack. He's doing great, and you will too."

I held back my distress as much as I could, clearly on the verge of tears.

"Look," he said, "Jean is working on the insurance coverage. Today and tomorrow, just spend some time wrapping up our visas for the guys on the Ankara contract. After that, Jean will pick up any outstanding work while you are away. Does that sound good?" he asked.

I nodded in agreement and stood to leave his office. Mr. Wilson rose and reached out to give me a hug.

"As far as the others in our office are concerned, you are out on a 'medical' leave. That's the beginning and end of it. That's all they need to know, and I'll take care of communicating that to them. You get yourself ready to go in the meantime. I'm sure you feel overwhelmed right now, but this is actually an exciting step for you. Focus on you, and we will all be here for you when you get back."

I could only manage to say "thank you" as I fought back tears and left to do my remaining work.

I spent the next two days doing as Mr. Wilson and Jack directed. I worked to complete my international projects, then prepared my outstanding projects to pass along to Jean. I kept my head down and worked away, trying to make Jean's "inheritance" as clear-cut and prepared as possible. Chalk it up to the work ethic I'd developed while collecting bottles at the Fort Playground, but I felt tremendously guilty for leaving, for passing off what was "mine" to someone who had held up her part of the bargain. Regardless, it had to happen. It was one of many lessons in humility and letting go that I would learn.

Over the next two days, after getting home from work, I packed some things, then waited for Jack to come and pick me up for a meeting. Though we drove to work together in the morning, Jerry didn't speak with me much except to poke at me verbally, claiming I was being "brainwashed by program people." On the two evenings when I came home from my meetings, Jerry was seated in the kitchen, smoking and drinking. He spat his bitterness and anger at me, and though his voice was slurred and blunted, his words jabbed at my heart with the heat of a hot poker.

"You know, I always thought you were stupid, but you really are letting this guy take you for a ride. Does he have something on you? How are you gonna get there, huh? You're not taking my truck. And how do you think this is going to play out when you come back? Have you thought that through?"

I stared off as Jerry jabbered at me. Then an image of Jack came into my mind. I saw him walking into church on the day of his wife's funeral. I remembered it vividly, seeing Jack wrap his arms lovingly around the shoulders of his three daughters, summoning all his strength to comfort and console them rather than himself. Just as they leaned on him that day, I leaned on him on my path to Gateway. In a blank state, I mustered a response to Jerry.

"I'm going to Gateway tomorrow. That's all I know. And you're going to take me, or I'll take a cab. Or I'll call Jack, who already has offered to take me. But, either way, I'm going. There are family sessions, and I hope you'll come. But even if you don't, I'm going."

Jerry muttered some profanity-laced retort I can't even remember. I cried as I went to my room to finish packing. My mind was jumbled with competing thoughts: *Maybe he's right. But Jack and Mr. Wilson say to do this. And I deserve to be happy.*

Exhausted, I finished packing and curled up in the recliner. I closed my eyes, but didn't sleep all night.

In the morning, I put on a pot of coffee, packed a lunch for Jerry, and showered before he woke. He got up, showered, dressed, and came into the kitchen for coffee. We didn't even speak to each other. Margie, at Jack's request, had typed up the directions to Gateway for me, and they sat on the coffee bar. Jerry lit a cigarette, sipped his coffee and looked over the directions. He folded them and shoved them in his shirt pocket along with his cigarettes.

"Let's go. I don't want to be late for work," he said.

We drove to Gateway in silence. I fixed my gaze out the passenger-side window, welcoming the quiet. When we arrived at the facility, Jerry came inside with me. When the intake specialist welcomed us, she asked if he would like to stay for the admission process. He declined, saying he had to get to work.

Jerry and I exchanged an awkward embrace. I told him I'd be in touch when I could. He nodded bitterly, turned, and walked out the door.

In the next few hours, I went through a rigorous admission process. I completed a psychosocial evaluation replete with questions about co-occurring disorders (depression, they concluded). Next, I received a medical evaluation, attended orientation, and finally went to my room, where my bags were searched and I met my roommate, Phyllis. Phyllis was a rough- and ragged-looking woman of about 50, suffering from malnutrition. She was ghostlike in appearance: bleached skin, bulging eyes, and hair as wiry as her disposition. I noticed her yellow, tobacco-stained fingers and teeth, between which she chomped a filterless Camel. She was coming off booze and a combination of Tuinal, phenobarbital, and Valium, all prescribed by her doctors, but what I most remember is that she smoked almost ceaselessly. It was her first day out of detox and in the general population. *What a welcome*, I thought.

Typically, one's roommate would take the newcomer to the next scheduled activity of the day, but since Phyllis was new to the general treatment population, Carol from across the hall appeared and took me to lunch instead. Later, we were assigned to the same therapy group, led by my designated therapist, Suzanne Anderson. Carol was entering her third week of treatment, and she was kind and enthusiastic about her recovery program. She spouted a number of recovery slogans: *One day at a time. That's all you have to do. Quit just for today. Don't let yourself get too Hungry, Angry, Lonely, or Tired— HALT—or you'll be setting yourself up for a drink.*

I was appreciative, but overwhelmed. I wanted *her* to halt. She gushed about Suzanne, and I nodded as affably as one can nod in validation of praise heaped upon a person you haven't yet met.

"She's amazing. You're going to love her, I promise! I am learning things about myself that I never knew, and I'm really starting to believe I can stay clean and sober. She's awesome!"

I would find out soon enough what all the fuss was about. Following lunch in the cafeteria, I learned that everyone had a "job" at Gateway, and mine was going to be "Milk Maid." This means I was charged with doling out glasses of white or chocolate milk and juice from the machines in the kitchen at mealtime. A slight demotion (and adjustment) from my work at Koppers, but so be it. I liked having work to do.

After I was introduced to some other members of the rehab community, Carol ushered me to my first therapy group with the celebrated Suzanne Anderson. I took a seat in the circle next to Carol, and she introduced me to some of the others. Long before she entered the room, Suzanne's presence was felt. In the hall, I heard a woman with a deep voice talking and laughing with a colleague. It was her laughter that caught me, like a deep-toned wind chime with a noble sound ringing through the hall and then rising like bubbles, spilling through the hallway and into the therapy room.

Still laughing and flashing a wonderful smile, Suzanne entered the room. She was tall and lean and dressed in jeans and a Mali mud cloth top. The lower top had a white background with bold black symbols painted on it. The overshirt was reversed, featuring a black background with white markings that appeared to be hand-painted. I wondered what language or secrets the emblems held.

Still chuckling to herself and settling in her seat, Suzanne clucked with a smile, "Okay, everyone. It's good to see you. Let's get started. We have a new group member today. Let's all welcome Terry to the group."

I nodded.

The group ran for two hours. For the first portion of the meeting, I was asked to share why and how I came to treatment. Group members chimed in when I hit upon something that they identified with. Most important to me in this first session was that some people in the group provided real moral support to me, saying that coming to treatment was the best and hardest thing they ever did for themselves. They encouraged me not to "leave before my miracle happens" and they reminded me it was just a day-at-a-time process. I made a mental note of a few of the members who predictably rolled their eyes in response to the encouraging words of the "recovery rooters."

As much as I struggled with my own cynicism, I determined that I should keep my distance from them. I was there to change, not to intellectualize or quip or be "right" about the complexity of something that, in certain ways, was and is quite simple. Oddly, I thought, Suzanne said virtually nothing during the group, giving each of us ample time to share.

"Okay, that's it for today. Turn in your second-step assignments. The next session will be held in the cafeteria. Our time together will involve paint, so dress accordingly," she said, laughing to herself.

I rose from my seat to leave.

"Terry, before you go, let's arrange a time for a one-on-one appointment. Have a good night, everyone. Dr. Twerski is scheduled to give a talk this evening at seven. What am I going to say about that?" she queried the group.

"Be on time! Seven *sharp!*" they droned.

"There you go," she said, laughing as we shuffled out of the group room. Carol walked alongside me, prattling in my ear about how wonderful Suzanne was and giving instructions for the next part of the day. Still shaking off the booze and drugs, I listened as best as I could with my half-baked brain and wondered what on earth was happening.

I unpacked my clothes again as instructed by an attendant who went through my things to make sure I wasn't carrying any contraband. At the appointed time, Carol came by our room to escort both me and Phyllis to the cafeteria. Phyllis grabbed her cigarettes. We went a few minutes early so I could meet Jim, the current Milk Maid, who would be graduating from Gateway in two days. He showed me the ropes at the beverage station with a charming kind of enthusiasm and said I was a natural. I laughed glibly. Meanwhile, Phyllis' job was to make sure that everyone working in the kitchen had hairnets, so Carol tutored her in her task. The first head to be covered was her own, which was a task unto itself. Her dry, brittle hair broke off as she and Carol worked to stuff it into the net. I was only six hours into rehab, and I could see already that Carol was someone special, possessing almost inexhaustible patience.

After dinner, we had about 45 minutes to catch a smoke, freshen up, and (for those with permission) make phone calls. Because I was new, I was not permitted to make phone calls for the first three days. That was fine by me. Who was I going to call anyway? Jerry? *Maybe* Jack, I thought, but he'd already given me so much that I wanted to leave him some breathing room.

I used my time to finish unpacking, then went out to the nurse's station where a small group of folks had congregated. Carol was there and introduced me to a few more people. Some of them were in my therapy group, and it was obvious they had a little more clean-time under their belts than I did. Two days and some change off of the booze and drugs, I was starting to feel my skin crawl as I shivered in a drenching sweat.

A guy named Milo approached me.

"That's God shaking the poison out of you. You'll be all right, come around tomorrow."

"God, huh?" I said.

Like many times in my childhood, I wished I was invisible. *If I could only hole up in my bed and wait this out*, I thought. I realized this wasn't an option. Instead, I laughed nervously and accepted a bleached-out, well-loved hanky that Milo passed to me. I wiped my forehead clear of the obvious sweat and wished I could at least call Jack.

"C'mon, we better get downstairs if we wanna grab a smoke before Dr. T.'s talk," Milo said. I was all about that.

"And we're gonna wanna get seats up front," he added.

I shuddered at the thought, realizing that a front-row seat would only put me further on display.

The cafeteria was set up theater-style for the evening's lecture by Dr. Twerski. I had no idea who he was and I was surprised, baffled really, when I spied through the motley crowd of patients and staff a man dressed in a refined black jacket and pants with a white shirt. He had a long white mustache and beard that flowed from his sideburns to the middle of his chest. He was surrounded by people who I later learned were the senior administrators of Gateway: Ken Ramsey, Sharon Eakes, and some of the therapists. He was animated and lighthearted, and I noticed that he wore some kind of cap that slid forward on his head as he spoke and laughed with those around him. He rhythmically smoothed his mustache and periodically punched himself in the nose to adjust his glasses, which slid down as he moved about. *He doesn't look like any doctor I've ever seen*, I thought.

I couldn't take my eyes off of Dr. Twerski as Milo, Carol, and I made our way to the front of the room and took our seats. Phyllis was nearby, manically bouncing her knee as she sat in her chosen chair. Carol tugged on my arm.

"Honestly, Terry. You're gonna love this guy," she said.

She is a cheerleader, this one, I thought.

Sharon shushed folks and called everyone "to order."

"We're delighted to have Dr. Twerski, Gateway's founder, here with us this evening to offer you some words of wisdom. Please take your seats and welcome Dr. Twerski."

Everyone quieted down as Dr. Twerski moved to the front of the room, thanking Ms. Eakes.

"Who is new to Gateway this week?" he asked.

No one budged.

"Come on. Don't be shy," he said. "Let's see the newcomers."

I looked around and meekly raised my hand in the air with other new patients.

"Wonderful, wonderful. Welcome to you all! I am so delighted to see you. It gives me great joy to be here with all of you, especially our new community members. You make me happy. Let me tell you why. Knowingly or unknowingly, you enrich my spirit. You give me purpose, and that is a wonderful gift to give to another person," Dr. Twerski said.

I watched this peculiar man as he walked back and forth in the front of the room, hands moving fluidly at emphatic moments of his speech. He was peculiar to me only because I had never seen an Orthodox Jewish rabbi before. I watched and listened as intently as a freshly sober person can. I think I was in awe of him. He would periodically adjust his little black yarmulke (the cap I'd noticed) or smooth his mustache when he paused or deliberated.

Dr. Twerski spoke with conviction and love in his voice. He claimed that happiness is self-fulfilling—that if people neglect to fulfill their inherent capacity or purpose they will experience deep unhappiness. Suppose, for example, that a person is gifted, artistically and musically, but neglects that part of herself and allows it to atrophy. In such a situation, the person is suppressing a potential source of happiness. But if we realize our inherent strengths and abilities and develop our gifts to the fullest extent, then we will be happy in equal measure.

Abraham J. Twerski, MD, founder of Gateway Rehabilitation Center, 1972

As I listened to this man, I recalled that Ms. Eakes had said he was the founder of Gateway. I noted how sincerely engaged he was with his audience, many of whom were, at best, intermittently attentive. And yet he spoke as though addressing a devoted audience, understanding that even if only some of it registered, it might catalyze a change. I realized that I was sitting before someone who was really great.

In his little, nasal voice, he continued.

"The reason I am so delighted to see all of you, and especially our newcomers, is because you are my gift. You are making my dream for this place, this center for recovery, a reality. You are helping me realize my own inherent strengths and abilities, and this gives me great happiness and joy. So, thank you for being here and for offering me the gift of your presence and participation."

Some of us began to applaud, thinking it was the end.

"So," he continued, "let me ask you. How does a lobster grow?"

A few in the audience chuckled. Dr. Twerski was unfazed.

"Lobsters are mushy animals that live in a rigid shell. That rigid shell does not expand. How, then, does the lobster grow? As the lobster grows, its shell becomes very confining. The lobster feels itself under pressure and is uncomfortable. It goes under a rock formation to protect itself from predatory fish. It casts off the shell and produces a new one. Eventually, *that* shell becomes uncomfortable as it grows. So back under the rocks it goes. The lobster repeats this process numerous times. Now this is the crucial point: The stimulus for the lobster to grow is that it feels uncomfortable! Right? Now, if lobsters had doctors, they would never grow!"

Dr. Twerski let out a whiny laugh.

"Because if the lobster felt uncomfortable and visited a doctor, he would get a little Valium. He would get a little Percocet. And he might feel, at best, fine. That awful word. Fine. But in all his 'fineness,' he never casts off the shell. What I think we have to realize is that times of stress are also signals of potential growth. If we use stress and adversity properly, we can grow *through* adversity and *because of* adversity. We can be grateful for adversity and the sign it gives us."

I sat motionless in my seat as I took in Dr. Twerski's words.

"So, in summation, you are lobsters," Dr. Twerski said, laughing.

I laughed too.

"And you have hit a time of adversity in your lives relating to your use of drugs and alcohol, right? And now you are here, using your moment of adversity to cast off your shell."

Dr. Twerski stopped to stretch out his arms and hands, palm up.

"Let us take a moment to truly take this in. By being in this room, you are realizing your inherent capacity to respond to adversity and fulfill your potential. To reach your happiness. You are in a safe harbor 'under the rocks' here, and you have the opportunity to cast off your old shell, the one that no longer works for you. The one that no longer fits you. The secret is out. We have a problem. You would not be here if you didn't have to be here. Let yourself use this safe harbor in a meaningful way. Allow yourself to grow into the full stature of your potential here. That's what you actually deserve," he said.

Dr. Twerski stood just a few feet away from me as he spoke. Sweat dripped from my brow as I shook in my seat, still withdrawing. Embarrassed as I was, I couldn't take my gaze off of him. I searched his deep-set, soulful eyes and found a wisdom, vibrancy, and playfulness there that riveted me to my seat.

The talk ended, and Milo again passed me his hanky.

"Keep it," he said.

Some people exited the room for smokes, while others went to the front to talk with staff and get a word in with Dr. T. I made my way out of the cafeteria. I hit the john, where I vomited up my supper and wiped the sour taste from my face with Milo's gift to me.

Splashing water on my face, I looked in the mirror for just a flash, catching the hollowness of my eyes. Shaking my head, I thought, *If eyes are the window to the soul, I'm in serious trouble.*

I left the bathroom and entered the social area outside the cafeteria. I walked over to a large picture window that showcased a handmade poster reading, "REHAB IS FOR QUITTERS!!!"

I decided to go outside for a cigarette. Phyllis was already out there. When I turned, Dr. Abraham Twerski was standing in front of me.

He reached for my hand and asked, "What is your name?"

"Terry," I replied, startled and embarrassed.

"And how are you doing, Terry?" he asked.

I took a deep and anxious breath.

"Pretty shitty, actually."

"Ah, honesty. I like that. But do you know that you have had a change of heart?" he asked.

"I guess. Maybe?" I stuttered.

"Well, you have, because you would not be here if you hadn't. Something or someone has helped you get to this place. And now, even if you don't believe it, everything is possible for you," he said.

I was on board with cautious optimism, but the idea that everything was possible for me hadn't quite registered. I focused on something more concrete.

"My friend Jack helped me to get here. He's taken me to some meetings too."

"Well, you are blessed to have a friend like him. Now you just have to let yourself be a lobster," he said, laughing. "Like I said up there, you deserve to have a safe harbor to make the kinds of changes you want for yourself. Your change of heart, the one that I was just talking about, will lead to changes in your thinking and behavior. Have you tried to quit before?" he asked.

"Only every day or so," I said, half-smiling.

"What is different this time?" he asked, stroking his beard.

"I asked for help. Outside of myself. I called my friend Jack after I blacked out. I was very weak and incoherent really, but he answered my call. We talked. He helped. And I'm here."

"So now you realize you don't have to fix everything yourself. You must be ready this time."

I bowed my head and offered a sweaty smile.

"You shouldn't bow your head, Terry. You took a step that is tremendously difficult for most people, sometimes too difficult. And now you're here as a consequence of that bravery and you deserve to be relieved of this affliction. To be fulfilled by greater things. Please take advantage of this place."

Lifting my chin with his hand, Dr. Twerski looked me dead in the eye. I felt his observation deep in my heart, where I thought my secrets were safe—my self-loathing, my despair, my loneliness, my shame, my desire to die—all validated by a pantheon of poets. But this sweet old man stood with me and embraced me in all my frailty.

"You are not alone, Terry. And you do not deserve to be alone. Strength shows not only in our ability to persist, but even more in our ability and willingness to start over."

I started to cry.

"You've done that a few times already, haven't you? Starting over?"

I thought of moving from the projects to Grandview Street, of welcoming and raising my brother Donnie, of sifting through syrup-caked bottles and cans to ensure we could get through life one week at a time, of training for my first real job at Koppers.

"Yes," I said. "It feels that way sometimes."

Dr. Twerski put his hand on my shoulder and said, "This place can be a real sanctuary for you. This is your chance to find the fulfillment you deserve. I will be wishing that for you. Please know that."

That conversation set the tone for the rest of my time at Gateway. Day by day, I was coaxed by staff, but especially by myself, to "be a lobster" and to accept, even for a little while, a sanctuary I had never experienced or even realized could exist. I had individual sessions with Suzanne Anderson and I came slowly to believe in her belief in me. In both individual and group sessions, I learned about addiction: a chronic, relapsing brain disease that is progressive and, if untreated, fatal. As Suzanne explained to me, "Addiction is characterized by an obsession of the mind and a compulsion of the body to seek and use drugs despite harmful consequences to one's emotional, mental, physical, and spiritual states, often culminating in self-destructive behaviors." That all sounded like me. And because of that, I had no problem readily admitting that I was an alcoholic or addict. I knew for years that there was absolutely nothing "social" about how I used. Being identified as an alcoholic relieved me. The secret was out and I was doing something about it.

After the first 72 hours, I was permitted to make some phone calls. Suzanne suggested that I call Jack to let him know how I was doing. She also suggested I contact Jerry to invite him to a family session scheduled for the upcoming weekend. She asked that I come back and see her after the calls.

Jack was over the moon to hear my voice. He said he had asked Dr. Twerski to keep an eye out for me, and I told him about our conversation.

"Like he said, you're right where you belong, Terry. Don't let anything sway you from your conviction to be there. Not Jerry, not the needs of your mother. Nothing. This is entirely your time. Things will get tight in therapy, or they usually do, anyway. Old stuff from the past breaks through to the surface and it feels like the last thing in the world you want to deal with, but you're in good hands with Suzanne. Just stay with it, and if you need support, I'm only a call away now."

I promised Jack that I would call if I felt my "addiction talking to me" and thanked him for his support.

I hung up the phone, took some breaths, and dialed our home number. I told Jerry how I was doing and asked if he would come to the family session on Saturday. He immediately challenged everything I said to him—questioning the qualifications of the people working at Gateway, chiding me that I was gullible and stupid to believe what people were telling me, scoffing at my inability to disprove his allegations. By the end of our call, he was noncommittal about attending the family session.

"We'll see," he said, mockingly.

In early recovery, a person's emotional states are incredibly fragile, sometimes even infantile. A person can feel motivated and "on the straight and narrow," only to be thrown off course into a regressive thought or behavior by virtue of contact with a person like Jerry. Recognizing this, I dragged myself to Suzanne's office, plopped in a chair and started weeping.

"I assume it did not go well with Jerry," she said.

"It didn't," I said. "He's merciless."

"Is he coming on Saturday?"

"He wouldn't say."

"What did he say?"

"He said none of you know what you're talking about. That I'm being brainwashed. That I'm stupid for thinking I'm an alcoholic."

"And what about Jack? What did he have to say?" she asked.

"He said I was doing great. Not to give up. That he was proud of me. And that if I needed support, I could call him."

Suzanne sighed.

"You know, Terry, the first step to getting somewhere is deciding that you're not going to stay where you are. You have already determined that you want to get somewhere. And that's been damn hard, but you're doing it anyway. You're already on your way. To somewhere that only you determine. We're all here to be your bumper pads as you make your way over this rocky road. And honestly, it's not going to be easy, but I can promise you it will be worth it. And I know you are worth it. In time, you will need to start thinking about who you want waiting for you at the end of that road."

"What do I do?" I asked.

"Well, for tonight, you rest. I say just attend the community reading session this evening and call it a night. You are doing what you need to do, Terry. It might not feel that way right now, but trust me, you are on a good path."

With each passing day at Gateway, I felt myself growing in strength but I knew a confrontation with Jerry was forthcoming.

9.

AND BRIDGES TO BURN

To my surprise, Jerry showed up for the family session in Suzanne's office on Saturday. He showed up with a few beers under his belt and with his cross hairs fixed on Suzanne. His first shot was to attack her and her credentials. He then fired scatter-shot at the whole Gateway program, saying everyone there was a charlatan peddling lies and making people question their lives.

"You should all be ashamed of yourselves," he said.

Suzanne was unperturbed.

In a calm and deliberate voice, she confronted Jerry's drinking, questioning why he decided to drink before coming to a family session. He sputtered some lame excuse. She asked why he found it so difficult to support me in my decision to get help.

"Why does her sobriety threaten you?" she asked. "And do you feel, going forward, that you could support her?"

He laughed off Suzanne's questions and replied, "If you think any of this intimidates me, you're wrong. There is nothing wrong with my drinking or her drinking! You're all just a bunch of hacks, making a buck on the backs of weak people. You know what? This is a fucking joke."

He laughed, stood, and pointed down at me.

"Get your stuff. We're leaving."

Bewildered, I looked at Jerry and then Suzanne. I didn't know what to do.

Suzanne didn't acknowledge Jerry's presence (or histrionics) at all.

"Terry, you're doing amazing work here. I think you know that. What would you actually like to do?"

In the moment, I felt Jerry's eyes burning into me, melting my resolve. I turned away from both of them and looked into the hall, where I noticed a poster reading, "A major life decision is never a choice, but a realization that the decision has already been made." I absorbed that statement: the notion that some changes are simply inevitable, undeniable, and evident whether we want them to be or not. In just a period of days, I had developed a radically different outlook regarding my future, my possibilities, and (just as importantly) the degree to which my past, including my relationship with Jerry, was warped and wrecked.

"I'm staying," I said.

Jerry reached for a cigarette and fired it up.

"There's no smoking in here, Jerry."

"Oh yeah?" he said.

He took a long drag and defiantly stomped it out on the office floor.

"Do you think you can support Terry by attending future family sessions sober?" she asked.

"That's my decision, right? You can't tell *me* what to do now, can you?"

"If you cannot make a commitment today to come to family sessions sober, then you are no longer invited to attend," she said.

"I guess I won't be here, then," he said.

I closed my eyes and let out a soft cry.

"Fair enough, Jerry. I can show you out. Terry, I'll be right back."

And, that was it. Jerry did not come back. I spent the rest of my time at Gateway focusing on my sobriety. And as the days passed, I felt stronger. Soon enough, I was the person welcoming the newcomers and showing them around. I was in an unlikely state of contentment attending therapy sessions, serving as the cafeteria Milk Maid, talking to Phyllis while she chain-smoked, encouraging Carol's enthusiasm, and steering clear of anyone who might thwart my progress with their cynicism.

On a Sunday afternoon during family visitation, I saw Jack on the grounds walking with Dr. Twerski, who was on site to give another talk. Jack had come to hear him and to visit with me as well. We talked about recovery and work, and he assured me that though there were some changes at Koppers, my job would be there when I returned.

Approaching my "graduation" from Gateway, Suzanne and I had a session to discuss where I was going to go after graduation.

"I talk to you straight, Terry. You know that. If you go back home to Jerry, I'm concerned you'll be setting yourself up for relapse. Everything you have worked so hard on to heal from your addiction—the first steps of recovery, your self-esteem issues, opening up painful childhood memories, addressing family ties, the friendships you are building with people in recovery— all of that goes out the window if you go back there. Jerry is not a bad man. He's a sick man, but not a bad man. But right now, he is categorically unable to keep your best interests at heart, and your chances of relapse are as high as possible if you go back into that environment and live with him."

"I'm scheduled to be out of here in three days, Suzanne. If I don't go home, where do I go, exactly? I don't have any place or anyone else I can live with."

"Are you willing to try to find another place to live? Other than going back with Jerry, I mean."

"If you think it is best for me to find another place to live, I will do it. I trust your judgment," I said.

"Good. This is about taking care of yourself first instead of others. This is living sober," she said. "First, I'm going to make some calls and see if we can find an apartment for you. I've already looked at your health insurance, and they will grant you a treatment extension of three days, so we now have six days to find you something. It does mean you will have to go out and look at apartments if we locate something."

My life as I knew it was upending. The only thing that remained constant was having Jack in my corner, and he would be there when I got out, no matter where I landed. I knew I could count on him.

After some fits and starts, I finally did locate an efficiency apartment in the East End of Pittsburgh. I selected it by reviewing my recovery meeting list and a map to identify parts of town with a good number of meetings that I could walk to. I didn't have a car at the time, so the efficiency of being at the corner of Shady and Maryland did the trick; it was nestled in a veritable constellation of meeting spots. I could walk to the Saturday morning Amberson meeting, Sunday night Sacred Heart meeting, Tuesday afternoon Calvary meeting, and Thursday night Fifth and Negley meeting. I memorized these days, times, and cross streets as if they were sequential codes to a bank vault; metaphorically speaking, it was true.

When I started off (being new to the neighborhood and the recovery process), I often walked in the wrong direction, encountering other members going the other way en route to the meeting. We would sometimes recognize each other and cheerfully yell greetings. Eventually, sensing that I was lost, I would realize that they were going to the meeting, too, and I had probably missed a turn. When that happened, I would make my best inconspicuous, mid-gait U-turn and try to catch up with whomever I had seen, figuring that they were on the right path. I'm sure at least one of them must have noticed my lemming tactic at some point, but no one was ungracious enough to say anything about it. Still, I made a mental note to build extra time into my travel schedule until I mastered my routes.

Jack was as committed to my sobriety as I was. I didn't ask for it but when I found the apartment, he graciously offered to help me with the security deposit and the first month's rent. I was incredibly grateful for his generosity.

On the first day I returned to work, Jack suggested I arrive early. Mr. Wilson was there to greet me.

"It's great to see you, Terry. Let's get a coffee and come on back to my office," he said.

I followed Mr. Wilson into his corner suite, and he invited me to join him in the "living room" section of the suite, not around his large oak desk in the back of the office. He took up his station at the end of the softly worn leather couch, and I sat in an adjacent wingback guest chair.

"How are you feeling?" Mr. Wilson asked.

"Shaky, but good. I separated from my husband, so I had to find a new place to live. Thank God for Jack. He even helped with that. I'm going to every meeting I can make but I'm glad to be back here."

"We're really proud of you, Terry. This is a fresh start and you deserve that."

To my bewilderment, Mr. Wilson started to laugh, poking my arm and saying, "Hey, do you remember that day when we were doing the press release for the Briar acquisition? You and Margie were taking turns running in and out of the conference room where the board members and I were meeting. You remember that day?" he asked, chuckling.

"I do, actually. It was really crazy. We kept revising the press release. Ad nauseum, in fact. Breakfast went into lunch, lunch went into dinner. It was a wild day. I remember it well. Some antitrust issue came up last minute and threw a wrench into everything, right?"

"Yep. You and Marge were hitting those revisions, ordering food, buying cigarettes and cigars for all of us. Running non-stop."

I didn't know what he was getting at.

Mr. Wilson reached over to his corner table and opened the letter drawer. I watched his hand.

"I'm hoping you can help me with something," he said, reaching into the drawer to fish around for something.

Finally, I spied them. Four "bennies." My heart began to race as fast as it did when I was on them.

"So, on the day of the acquisition," he said. "I found these. Terry, do these look familiar to you?"

Clenching my chest and stammering, I choked out a reply.

"Yeah, I remember those."

Mr. Wilson reached out for my hand.

"Listen, I don't mean to throw you off here. I'll get rid of these. But"— he chuckled a little—"I could swear that on that day when you walked into the conference room, I saw these pills falling out of your pockets. Maybe was there a hole in your pocket? I didn't want to say anything then. I just picked them up as they trailed behind you."

I froze.

"Was I seeing things?" he asked as he collected all of the amphetamines and put them in his own pocket.

"They were mine. Actually, they were falling out of the hem of my skirt. I was pretty far along in my addiction at that point, so I was eating those things like candy. If they were in my pocket and easy to access, they were in my mouth in seconds. If you can believe it, I used to cut an opening in the hem of my skirts and load the pills in there, thinking that would help to control my use by making them harder to get to. Fucking crazy, right? Well, that's addicts. I honestly thought that measure was going to stop me or slow me down. For what it's worth, I'm sorry you had to see that."

"No apology necessary. I'm just glad you're okay."

I thanked him.

"But listen, Terry. I need to talk with you about something, especially in the midst of all the other changes you're experiencing. I want you to hear from me personally that there are some big changes coming to Koppers, too, and there will be a lot of employees transitioning. Because of your work with Jean in human resources, we're going to need your assistance with everything, but you need to know that in about ten to twelve months, your position will be terminated too. I talked with Jack about this and we both agreed that it would be best for you to hear about this now so you can plan accordingly. We didn't want you to be hit by any surprises and we both will be here to help you make a transition when the time comes."

I was stunned by the news, but also grateful to both of them for telling me in advance.

"Jack is planning on having lunch with you and your recovery sponsor today so you all can discuss this. I know it's just your first day back and this is a lot to lay on you, but we felt it was important for you to know now so you can begin to plan for it. What's most important is that you stay close to Jack, your sponsor, and your meetings. You're already doing a great job. I just want you to know we're rooting for you."

Jack walked into the office.

"Can you do lunch today?" he asked.

"Sure, Jack, and thanks, Mr. Wilson. I appreciate your honesty. Oh, and you can flush those pills if you wouldn't mind," I said.

"Will do," he said. "Farewell to all that."

"Amen," I said.

At noon, Jack and I made our way to the Duquesne Club where we met Linda, whom Jack introduced me to several weeks earlier. We had lunch in Koppers' private dining suite, where our scallops were drizzled in the club's renowned Hoelzel dressing and garnished with fresh wedged tomatoes and kalamata olives (hardly the meals I enjoyed in my efficiency apartment). We talked about how I felt I was doing with my recovery and the other major changes in my life. I was situated in my new place and going to recovery meetings every day. I had little contact with Jerry, which I felt very conflicted about. Regardless, with each passing day of new-found clarity, I knew we had to part ways if I wanted to stay clean and sober. It was difficult holding onto myself in this way. Wildly unfamiliar, in fact.

Jack told me that he had heard from Suzanne, whom I was continuing to see on an outpatient basis. She told him I was doing a great job and was even volunteering at Gateway and that they might be hiring a part-time intake specialist.

"You are obviously making a good impression, Terry. Linda and I think you should go for it and apply."

A waiter appeared to refill our waters.

"I'm just a few months sober," I said, almost whispering as he walked away. "Do you think they would even consider me?"

"Well, Suzanne thinks so. You should discuss it with her at your next appointment," he suggested.

"You're going to meetings every day," Linda said. "This part-time job wouldn't interfere with your meetings. It might even become something more permanent when your job at Koppers ends."

I was both grateful and confused by my sponsor Linda's support. I was attending several meetings a week with her, but she could be a little—well, let's call it endearingly cantankerous. Jack still suggested she remain my sponsor, and I followed his advice, which ultimately turned out to be sage; Linda was exactly who I needed at that time.

I was following her "good orderly direction," as they say in recovery. Usually, she was saying things like "First step is to get in the car. Second step is to sit up front at the meeting. Third step is to take the cotton out of your ears and put it in your mouth and listen! And when it's your turn to speak in the meeting, you stand up, tell them your name is Terry and that you're an alcoholic, then you sit your butt down 'cause you done told them all you know!" Though these things were said in the usual recovery-style, tough-love fashion, Linda's words usually had a little extra bite. Her endorsement to apply for this part-time position at Gateway surprised and delighted me. It reflected an approval of me I hadn't thought I'd earned from her yet. I interpreted it as a sign of my progress.

In the months that followed, I attended the Saturday morning Amberson meeting—regularly hitting both the beginners' and speakers' meetings. I would arrive early and set ashtrays and doughnuts out on the tables, help Pat B. make coffee in the kitchen, and clear up or clean anything that required it. The Amberson meetings were huge, with over two hundred people attending most of the time.

Anna Mae G., an old, stalwart member who got sober in the early days when recovery groups were just forming, always arrived early. She would show up dressed to the nines and sparkling with diamonds on her ears, fingers, and neck. In recovery circles, she was a revered "grand dame." I don't know how old Anna Mae was (and she wasn't telling), but her wrinkled, tanned skin told me she had some miles on her; no doubt each of those wrinkles held a story. Anna Mae, for all her glamour, had emphysema and toted an oxygen tank with her, a pack of cigarettes at the ready. When she arrived at the meeting, I'd fetch coffee for her and sit with her for a while, hoping she'd share some wisdom with me.

"The recovery literature says over and over again that faith without works is dead. You're coming here early and helping to set up the meeting. That's you being of service, and if you do that with a grateful heart, you're going to be okay, Terry," she said, patting my hand and firing up a Virginia Slim.

I loved being at the meeting. Anna Mae was charming and generous with her time, as was Pat, who happened to give the best hugs in the recovery rooms. There was also one-armed, mustachioed, and cigarette-smoking Johnny, another old-timer consistently willing to share his stories about addiction and sobriety.

About three months into my recovery, I turned up at the Amberson meeting early to help in the kitchen and Pat was there, politely listening as I dumped a big batch of "poor me's" onto him.

"I don't know what I'm going to do about my marriage," I said. "Jerry is pushing me to come back home, but I don't think I should. My mother is in the hospital again, and I don't know how I'm going to keep up with work, meetings, and hospital visits with her. My sponsor said I should be working steps one, two, and three, but I don't understand this 'turning my will over to God' part," I said.

Hearing enough of my whining, Pat took me by the hand and directed me out of the kitchen into the large meeting room, where people were starting to gather for the meeting.

"How much time do you have now, Terry?" he asked.

"Ninety days today," I said, proudly.

"Excellent! You see that woman over there?" Pat asked.

He turned me by the shoulders toward a bewildered-looking woman who appeared close to my age.

"Yes," I said.

"Well, she has about *90 minutes* of sobriety, and I think you have something to offer her," he said. "If you're willing."

All of a sudden, my 90 days (and all their attendant woes) felt puny in the face of helping a newcomer who reminded me of my own sweaty, disoriented self in my first few days at Gateway.

"Yeah, but I'm a newcomer myself," I said. "I don't have anything to offer yet."

"Okay. A few things about that statement," Pat said, coaching me along a little. "First of all, you know better than to start or end any statement with a 'yeah-but,' right? Next, you do have something to offer. You've been sober for months now."

"That's only because I have nothing else in my life right now," I whined.

"Not buying it," Pat said. "You told me that your work at Gateway is a part-time job, so you're already being of service to others. How is this different? You do have something to offer, Terry. Do you have the little program preamble card I gave you?"

"Yeah," I said, as Pat nodded for me to pull it out of my wallet.

"Read the responsibility statement to me."

I read from the card.

"I am responsible when anyone, anywhere, reaches out for help. I want the hand of recovery always to be there."

"That young woman is here because she wants help, Terry. You know people don't just wake up in the morning and say, 'Hey! I think this is a great day to get sober!' If she is here, she is reaching out her hand. And you are responsible for reaching back."

"I don't know what to say to her," I said.

"Introduce yourself. Tell her how courageous it is that she is here today. Then tell her how you came to sobriety. The rest will take care of itself," Pat said, and with a smile he gently shoved me in Laney's direction.

I never looked back.

Pat opened my heart to service that day, and this one lesson transformed my life, my whole disposition toward others. I learned that, as Laurence Lerner once remarked, "The difference between an outstretched open palm and a helping hand is a simple twist of the wrist." I was reminded that at any time in my life, I can be on either side of the giving or receiving. I was reminded where I came from and what it felt like to be on the palms-up side of this equation when no one was reaching back. I remembered being a child, wanting to help Mama feel good about herself when her drinking got out of hand or when she was sick and laid out for days or when welfare workers threatened to split us up. There was not much I could do about it as a child but now, as a sober adult, I could be of service—to help people feel good about themselves and their future. Some of this work would be within organizations like Gateway and in recovery meetings, but some of it would be more personal and spontaneous. Obvious or not, I realized that it was almost always more gratifying and enlightening to give rather than receive.

As a friend from the recovery meetings told me, "A grateful heart does not have to drink." Pat, in his wisdom, knew that I could not simultaneously bitch about my own life and help a new person with hers. That day, as I nervously blubbered slogans at Laney, circled meetings on a list, threw recovery literature in her face, and pressed my telephone number into her outstretched hand, I learned that being of service to others also meant being in service to myself—that paradoxically, I was helped by helping others.

In those early months, I would meet many kind people who would be of service to me. They would help me through a relapse when I was ending my marriage with Jerry. They would support me when my job ended at Koppers. Eventually, the part-time work I was offered at Gateway led to a chance to take on a full-time position, where I learned a great deal about recovery from a professional perspective. I was encouraged to attend certified addiction trainings that could lead to becoming credentialed to hold other positions in the addictions and recovery field.

Ten months into the job, Suzanne and Jim, a Gateway senior administrator, called me into the Gateway staff lounge for a meeting.

"Terry, there's a job for a DUI therapist at the Turtle Creek Valley drug and alcohol agency located on the South Side. It's a full-time position. We've been talking and we think you would be a great fit there," Jim said.

"Yeah," Suzanne said with a laugh, "Be forewarned that it's a heck of a population to cut your teeth on, but if you can work with drunk drivers, you can work with anyone! It's smooth sailing after that."

"I'm listening," I said, playfully.

"Terry, you're logging all these addiction counseling education hours, supervised employment hours, and even some direct client hours and supervision. That's all great, but if you're serious about this work, about getting certified in Pennsylvania, you'll need to ramp up those direct client and supervision hours. This position will help you to do that."

"This is a lot to take in," I said.

"The discomfort and uncertainty you're feeling," Suzanne said. "That's why it's time to take this leap. Remember Dr. Twerski's lobster lecture?"

I nodded.

"Listen," Jim said, "the director of the DUI program is an old friend of mine, Mike Yates. He's a great guy, and you will love him. And the rest of the staff is awesome. Alas, maybe not as much fun as us," he joked, "but if you're open to this opportunity, we can call Mike today and get you in for an interview as early as tomorrow."

"I would have to update my resume," I said.

"What's stopping you?" Suzanne asked.

"This is really fast," I said. "Maybe too fast."

"We get it, but do you remember when you came to treatment? Jack had you at a recovery meeting within 24 hours, and you were here within three days. Now you're way more constituted to do the kind of work that's ahead of you. You're ready and, if you're serious about wanting to work in recovery, this is the best next step for you. You will have wonderful people there to support you," Jim said.

"Like Dot T.," Suzanne said.

This got my attention.

"You mean the woman I heard speak at Founder's Day in June?"

Suzanne laughed, "Sister, there's only one Dot T.! You know it!"

"She's amazing," I said. "I bought the cassette tape of her talk and listen to it all the time. It's practically warped by now."

"Well, she's been working in Turtle Creek's DUI program for at least a few years now, and if anybody can teach you the ropes, it's Dot."

I could hear in my head something Dot said on one of the tapes: "When we were using, no power in the world could stop the bad things from happening, but now that we're sober, no power in the world can stop the good things from happening."

"I'll do it," I said.

Within 24 hours, I was sitting in Mike Yates's office on 22nd Street on the South Side, being interviewed for the position, which I was offered immediately after our conversation. Jim's vote of confidence had helped. The next day, I started my new job.

At the Turtle Creek Valley agency orientation, I met the other members of the team and learned about their areas of expertise. Mr. Yates had me shadow some of the other therapists, and I attended trainings on treatment, intervention, and aftercare models. The primary goal of the program was to reduce recidivism among DUI offenders. I learned that traditional sanctions, such as paying fines, license suspensions, and even the threat of incarceration, often fail to deter offenders from drinking and driving again. A more useful approach is to determine the root causes of the behavior.

I was trained in brief intervention, cognitive behavioral therapy, and motivational interviewing. I was assigned to run individual counseling sessions, armed with the awareness that Dot T. would run outpatient therapy groups for DUI clients in the same building. Thinking about the state of my life just months earlier, I could barely fathom that Dot and I would be working side by side. Nor could I anticipate the role she would play in my life in the years to come.

10.

DOT T.: BENEFACTOR OF HOPE

If you've ever been to a recovery group meeting, you know what it's like to see people in all stages of recovery. People with one day of sobriety sit next to long-timers with 30 or 40 years under their belts. Meetings are lively and friendly. People laugh—deep belly laughs—and tell stories that are often unbelievable or shocking. You see pairs in corners where sponsors are speaking with their sponsees, guiding them through difficult times. You also encounter the pre-meeting "tractor beam": the coffee and doughnut table. People gather there for their caffeine and sugar fix. There's a lot of sugar in booze, so folks freshly coming off the stuff need those cookies and doughnuts to get through early sobriety. Some people sit quietly, taking in the scene. Others wish they were invisible, but almost all still need three doughnuts and a full cup of coffee to make it through the meeting. They try to reach their seat discreetly without spilling anything. The whole scene is reminiscent of a skating rink at Christmas time: seasoned gliders sharing the space with bumbling novices, but anyone could fall at any time.

Even when the speaker is talking, people are jumping up and down to refill their coffee, send text messages, or head outside for a smoke or phone call. It's a very vivacious atmosphere—sometimes unruly—and if you didn't know any better, you would think you were at a church social with a more motley and unguarded crowd.

But then something amazing happens. When the speaker gets to the "what happened" part of his or her story, the room falls into a weighted silence.

Dot Talley, staff member, Turtle Creek Valley Treatment Programs

145

Coffee runners stop in their tracks. Blurry-eyed, crumb-covered newcomers look up from their doughnuts. People stop fidgeting in their chairs. Late arrivals quietly stand in the doorway out of respect, and, except for the soft gurgling of the coffee pots, you can hear a pin drop in the room.

Why?

Because everyone wants to know "what happened." What got this poor, hopeless son of a bitch—this slob of a drunk—into recovery? How did it all come to be? Did they lose a job? Did their partner throw them out of the house? Were they through their tenth rehab, and their body just couldn't take it anymore? Were their children taken from them? Were they busted for drinking and driving for the third time? Did they have alcohol poisoning? Were they pronounced dead after a serious binge only to survive for the fourth time? Were they homeless and living in a dumpster? Did God tap them on the shoulder to ask, "Hey, asshole, this is your last stop?" And lastly, why did they get it this time and not the hundred times before when they promised themselves and those around them that they would stop?

Wanting to know what happened is a normal human impulse, magnified even more by the unassuming, dank, and lugubrious settings of most recovery meetings: church basements, spare rooms of community centers, etc. The good news is that no one goes to meetings to be wowed by the aesthetics. Meetings are, figuratively speaking, a very Protestant affair: "churches" that come alive solely by virtue of four walls, a more or less sturdy roof, and a group of people gathering with the same fundamental intentions. There's no pretense (and no space for it). After a speaker's shame, guilt, and dirt is thrown onto the table, the next and most important question follows: "What happened? What made you choose life over death?" It's the one part of any meeting when you can hear a pin drop in the room because we want to hear the mystery or miracle of what happened in the person's life—the moment that ripped them from a path of self-destruction towards one of self-redemption.

I remember one such talk that rattled me into a new kind of consciousness and brought me a lasting friendship with the most courageous and wise woman I've ever known. I first heard Dot T. speak at a national recovery event in Akron, Ohio. It's not the most scenic of locales, but it's where recovery for millions of people began. Little did I know that on that cloudy day I would be so moved by Dot's words that I would actively seek out a cassette recording of her talk to play in my car and elsewhere for the subsequent year. For many months, her remarks and insights from the event became a practical gospel to me. I fixated on and mantracized her comment that "Now that we're sober, there is no power in the world that can stop the good things from happening."

Having just finished rehab and having just started my new, full-time job, I wanted good things to happen. It struck me as a transcendently simple idea that if I eliminated one glaring impediment to happiness (substance abuse), good things would enter my life much as water flows effortlessly when sediment is removed from its path. For years, I had heard self-help charlatanry that preached the need to add more to my life, my habits, my routines. I'd even entertained the notion that we should strain to smile when we're sad, with the aim of releasing some now-forgettable or unpronounceable brain chemical or to dupe my own mind and heart into feeling otherwise; I'd tried that without success. And maybe if I'd never met Jack, I would have thought Dot's remarks and demeanor were complete bullshit, too—snake-oil peddling of a sort. But having witnessed Jack's transformation, I understood that the approach that Dot advocated was the real deal. From a macroscopic view, it didn't have to be complex. The removal of the problem was in many ways the solution—or the only possible start of it.

Little did I know that not long after hearing that tape, I would be working with Dot in the same drug and alcohol recovery facility, Turtle Creek Valley D&A, where our true journey together began. As time went on, we not only attended meetings together in Pittsburgh, but she became something like my oracle—a sage consultant who always kept my sobriety and best interests in mind. In other words, she became my sponsor.

I remember hearing Dot remark at a meeting in Pittsburgh (on the day when we finally met) that we're all like wild horses, especially when we identify with our unruly minds. Dot's unusual mixture of candor, bluntness, and wisdom drew me to her and made me listen with extra attention.

I approached her at the end of that meeting with a question in mind.

"Why wild horses?" I asked.

Dot laughed.

"Oh, our minds, especially when we're new to recovery, are just all over the place, biting and kicking us with aggressive and negative thoughts. It takes time for our minds to settle down. The group's recovery program and a sponsor can help with that," she said.

Soon enough, I told her about the tape and how we were, improbably or otherwise, about to be working together.

In just a matter of days, I was standing beside the woman whose words I had memorized from a cassette tape, helping her facilitate a group session for others on the path to recovery. I could hardly believe it.

Passing out worksheets to the group, Dot began.

"Looky here. Alcoholism is the only disease that tells you, 'you ain't got a disease!'"

A few clients groaned. A few muttered lifeless "uh-huh's."

"And listen up," she said, "it's an equal opportunity disease. Look around the room. All of you from all walks of life, aren't you? People who wouldn't normally mix, right? Look around and tell me I'm wrong! You're all in the same room, 'cause you all have the same disease. Your drinking or your drug use, or both, got you here. Now, we can spend time knocking heads about whether or not you're an alcoholic. That's an option. But truthfully, I'm not gonna do that with you. I don't have the energy for all that. I'm old, baby," Dot laughed.

I laughed too. Her candor was refreshing for me and for everyone else in the room.

"And besides," she said, "I can see from the lot of you that you're already having a hard time looking in the mirror and trying to accept what you see. Most of you are refusing to accept the painful reality of your lives. Is that right? The DUI, disappointing your spouse or girlfriend, or whatever. You're paying fees and fines with money you don't have. You're losing your jobs. You're getting your license suspended. Some of you are even looking at jail time, having been here more than once. Ain't that right, Bob?"

Bob stared mutely.

"You too. Over there, Henry. I see you," Dot said, pointing.

Henry laughed in concession.

"This denial, though, is trying to tell you everything's okay! Right?" she said with a laugh. "Never mind that it eats up your dignity, your self-esteem, your integrity, and the love and understanding of your family and friends. That's cool with you, right? All good? But that's how denial is. It has you disavowing and distorting reality even though the evidence is right in front of you. And Lord forbid we admit we have a problem. There's that nasty stigma of saying 'I'm an alcoholic.' No, we can't say that! We don't want anyone to know. Better to just fold up and take everyone down with you. Never mind your neighbor saw you sleeping one off in the front yard! Or saw you staggering down the street from the bar! Or saw you showing up at your kid's baseball game drunk and with a six-pack in your hands! Or family members having coming to bail you outta jail. No, we don't want anyone to know we have a problem," Dot laughed.

I saw the group warming to her, some laughing audibly.

"Oh yeah, baby. That's how it goes. So, me and Terry, we're just going to try and do some education about addiction and alcoholism for y'all. We're going to start there today, and who knows, maybe one or two of you might even come to realize that admitting you've got a problem is the answer to your problem and not a problem in itself."

In all my time in recovery, including my stay at Gateway as a patient and during my professional work there, it was drummed into me that denial is the number-one challenge to recovery. Since addiction is a disease, it is the interventionist's job to aggressively confront substance abusers with the negative consequences of their addiction. What I learned from this first session with Dot was that she exposed denial for what it was, but was able to leave the individual intact. By using humor, she did not demean, attack, or shame. Instead, she implicitly acknowledged that bludgeoning people with the consequences of their behavior does not necessarily help them break through denial. She did not let them

Dot (right) with friends, always ready with a smile

off the hook, but she offered her own brand of compassionate, humorous intervention that grabbed my attention and would inform my own work with DUI clients, families, adolescents, and women from that day forward.

11

MOE: GREAT TEACHERS INSPIRE

That year, a dear friend from my recovery meetings, Joan L., kept a close eye on me. She was a social worker for the county, helping people find their way back to work after periods of unemployment due to layoffs, addiction, incarceration, or related issues. She could tell I was struggling based on how I presented myself at meetings.

On a sunny Saturday morning, I sat on a curb outside the Amberson meeting in Shadyside, smoking a cigarette and watching folks mill about—talking, gossiping, smoking, and slurping coffee while waiting for the next meeting to begin. Joan, a tall and striking woman in her early fifties with salt-and-pepper hair, strode up to me, hollering my name. I rose to my feet to give her a hug.

"How are you doing today, Terry?" she asked.

"I'm good," I replied.

Holding my shoulders, she cocked her head to find some shadow from the sun and get a good look into my eyes.

"Now, I don't know about that," she said. "Listen. You know this is a program of suggestions, right?"

"Yeah," I replied, too exhausted to engage.

"Well, I want to make a suggestion to you. I'm not your sponsor, but you should talk with her about this. I see you're doing everything you need to be doing in your program, but I can also see that you have an emotional struggle going on that extends beyond all this. I want to suggest that you see a social worker I know who might be able to give you additional support for your recovery. In fact, I've already spoken to her. Her name is Ms. Yvette, and she is expecting a call from you. Here's her number. She's with the county mental health and drug and alcohol program. Just try talking with her and let me know what you think."

I hadn't realized that Joan was paying any attention to me, but clearly, she was. Since she had many years of what seemed like solid sobriety, I had always listened closely to her words at meetings. She never offered advice. Instead, she made suggestions in a kind and caring manner that made it easy to follow her "good orderly direction."

Within a week, I was sitting in Ms. Yvette's office, just a block away from where I worked. She was a tall, stately, brown-skinned woman with warm eyes and a deep, kind, resonant voice. Though I can't fully understand or explain it, I felt I was in the presence of royalty when I was with her. Her calm, clear manner gently led me into a space where I could shed light on my weariness, pain, shame, and inadequacy.

In due time, I began talking with Ms. Yvette about my addiction, my blooming sobriety, and the things I was struggling with most: my mother's ongoing illnesses and how they left me feeling emotionally depleted and alone. Then there were childhood memories of neglect and abuse that began to bleed through the fogginess of my brain.

Not too long into my sessions with her, Ms. Yvette asked me a question that would profoundly change the trajectory of my life.

At my scheduled hour on a Tuesday afternoon in 1983, I walked the short block from work to Ms. Yvette's office on South 22nd Street in Pittsburgh's South Side. It was a dreary day that matched my mood. I had started my day at Presbyterian-University Hospital, visiting Mama, who had an infection in the large toe of her right foot. At 6 a.m. I had caught her doctor while he was making the rounds and was able to get an update on her condition. He told me that antibiotics had been started. Her fever was beginning to make a turn in the right direction, but her blood sugar was not yet under control, and they were seriously considering amputating her toe. While walking to my appointment with Ms. Yvette, I felt nothing less than profound gratitude for something very simple but very miraculous: the large toe of my own right foot as it pressed and then released against the ground. I simultaneously imagined the agony and distress my mother might feel in losing her own toe and the possible repercussions of that.

I started my session by discussing Mama's condition with Ms. Yvette. As the hour wore on, it was quite evident to both of us that I was struggling to talk about anything other than my empathy for Mama and her physical crises. Out of the blue, Ms. Yvette asked, "Have you ever thought of going to college?"

I remember feeling confused and bewildered by her question but I responded anyway.

"Not really. Poor kids from the projects don't go to college."

"Yes, but have you ever thought about it?" she asked. "You know, for you. For yourself, Terry."

"No," I replied with a baffled look on my face.

"Why not?" she wanted to know.

"No one ever asked," I replied.

"Well, I'm asking. From the short time that you have been coming here, it's clear that you have spent a good deal of your life looking after and taking care of others. Take today, for example. Do you realize we are technically 53 minutes into our conversation together—about to close up shop—and you have not mentioned yourself or your own life even one time? I know you love your mother and I know that your relationship with her is complicated, all the more so because of her illnesses. But now I think it's time for you to do something for yourself. Something that is yours and yours alone."

"I don't know," I said.

I folded my arms across my chest and crossed my legs. I admit that there was a measure of defiance in this gesture. I'm sure I felt that to focus on myself under the circumstances of Mama's impending amputation would qualify as narcissism.

Staring wide-eyed into nothing, I said, "I know I don't have good command of my emotions, but I do know that right now my heart feels like it's going to burst through my chest."

"Why is that, then? What do you think it is?" Ms. Yvette asked in a soft tone.

"Terror," I snapped.

"And why terror?" she prodded.

"Because I can hardly read and keep things in my head, alright? I stopped doing drugs and alcohol almost two years ago but I still can't comprehend things that I know other people find incredibly simple. Bottom line is that I can't remember shit. Even now, I'm struggling at work with my paperwork and I'm afraid I could get fired. That's hard enough. All the while, my sponsor has me reading recovery literature. I'm doing it but I don't understand half of it and can't retain anything. It may as well be written in Danish. I started on drugs and alcohol so young. I used so hard for 18 years that I really think I've messed up my brain, Yvette. I can't even read simple recovery shit."

Ms. Yvette let my statements hang in the air. She didn't say a word, letting me squirm in the echo of my self-doubt. I couldn't bear the silence.

Does she think I'm stupid? Is she going to boot me out of therapy? Is Joan L. going to get pissed at me when she hears that I was honest?

After what seemed like an interminable amount of time, Ms. Yvette straightened herself in her chair and gently asked me to uncross my arms and legs and place my hands on my thighs. She looked directly into my eyes. I struggled to hold her gaze.

"How does that feel?" she asked.

"Terrifying," I replied.

"Okay. Just try to breathe through this," she encouraged. "Listen, you don't have to do this if you don't feel you are ready. I want you to consider it thoroughly and talk with Joan and your sponsor before you make any decision, but please listen to me. You have spent a great deal of your life, Terry, doing things on your own—taking care of your mother, your brother, and yourself. You're accustomed to making big, urgent, and critical decisions by yourself. Now, *you*, at last, have real support. Lifelong friends and supporters. People who will stand with you. I'm one of those people, if you want my support, too. Joan, Jack, and Dot all care about you. I want to remind you that you have already done the most difficult thing you will ever have to do in your life. You've surrendered your battle with drugs and alcohol and asked for help. Right?"

Looking down, I fidgeted with my hands and responded, "Yes."

"And what happened?"

"Jack took my call."

"And what happened for you because of that?" she asked.

"My life is better. Much better than I could have imagined. Even when it's bad, it doesn't compare to before," I said.

"Haven't you said to me before that you believe Jack was an angel to you?"

"Yeah. I do believe he is an angel. In fact, I know he's my angel," I said, feeling a little foolish and self-conscious, though I teared up as I shared my conviction with Ms. Yvette.

"Well, all I'm asking is that you do the same thing you did with Jack. Under new circumstances and with this new opportunity, believe in *my belief* in you. I *know* you can do this. Going to college won't be easy, but staying clean and sober isn't easy either, and you are doing it a day at a time, right?"

"Yes."

"So, consider this. You don't have to make a decision today. Discuss it honestly with the people who know and love you. Then decide. And if you decide to do this, you will do it the same way you do your sobriety. One action at a time. One day at a time. And I swear to you that I will help you in every way I can. That's my promise."

I left Ms. Yvette's office that day with a sense of hope. The negative chatter and preoccupations that had shrieked in my head during the walk earlier had quieted somehow. As I walked back to my car, tears welled in my eyes. I allowed myself to embrace the possibility that Ms. Yvette actually believed in me, though I could barely comprehend it.

Then a notion took me by surprise. *Maybe she sees my brokenness, but maybe that's not all that she sees.*

I recalled Dr. Twerski's words to me when I was in rehab: "Strength shows itself not only in our ability to persist but even more in our ability and willingness to start over."

I presented the possibility of going to college to my sponsor, Dot, and to Jack and Joan. They all wholeheartedly supported the idea, even with all that was unfolding with my mother's health.

"If not now, then when, Terry?" Jack asked.

In the months that followed, I worked with Ms. Yvette to prepare myself for college. I took academic tests to assess my abilities in math, English, and writing. The results showed that I would benefit from remedial classes in all areas, especially math. I took the classes. A career aptitude test showed that I was well-suited for the humanities and social sciences. Afterwards, Ms. Yvette explained that I would have to take additional academic placement tests to further assess my skill levels and that if I did well, I might be eligible for financial aid.

Over the course of the next year, with great support from Ms. Yvette, Dot, Jack, and others, I painstakingly moved through my remedial classes, placement tests, career aptitude tests, and eventually submitted actual applications to universities, including appeals for school grants, scholarships, and loans.

If not for Ms. Yvette, a compassionate social worker who saw something in me when I saw little in myself, I'm certain I would not have stayed motivated enough to complete the entire process. Finally, on a snowy day in late November 1983, following a session with Ms. Yvette, I walked to the mailbox on Carson Street to drop my applications in the mail. Heavy snowflakes pelted my face and melted on contact as my whole body radiated with the warring feelings of excitement and fear. The weather immediately reminded me of my talk with Jack at Point State Park only a couple years earlier when we had practically frozen in the falling, obscuring snow, just before I had made the decision to go to rehab. I thought of the snow as my ally then, a force that serendipitously materialized when I needed a final push.

In the late spring of 1984, I received an acceptance letter from the University of Pittsburgh. It sent me over the moon and also into a mind-numbing anxiety attack. In that moment of divergent feelings, I wept. I never could have dreamed of such a thing for myself. I knew that this success was actually a team effort with Ms. Yvette and Joan, who had challenged me to be more than what I saw in myself. Their push had allowed me to glimpse my potential and embrace my drive to be of service to others.

I decided that I would become a social worker like my therapist and the men and women I worked with. Although I was already becoming a certified addictions counselor by logging clinically supervised work hours and attending addiction trainings, I now had the opportunity to put academic credentials behind my name.

Although it's fashionable in the United States for students to remain "undeclared" while they explore their academic options and bask in the intellectual grazing that a liberal arts education affords them, I didn't have that luxury. I was already late to the game. At 28, I had to declare my major and get to it. My academic advisor, only a few years my senior, recognized the clarity of my convictions and set me on an academic path that led directly to the University of Pittsburgh's School of Social Work.

The first two years of meeting general education requirements were rocky, as evidenced by the inconsistencies in my academic transcript. With each passing semester, though, my brain became clearer and sharper. My academic standing improved in turn.

By the fall of 1987, I was walking into the University of Pittsburgh Graduate School of Public Health looking for my community organizing class. As a nontraditional student and still somewhat new to university life, I was worried that I had the wrong building. It didn't make sense to me that a social work course on community organizing would be held in the public health sciences building. Students moved fluidly through the hallways, confident in where they were going. Bewildered, I stopped and all but threw my hands up in the air. My mouth was dry and my palms were sweating. *I have no clue what I'm doing here*, I thought. The "negative committee" in my head that Dot always spoke about was convened and in full session. Frankly, I was ready to walk out of the building to face the challenge on a different day or abandon the endeavor entirely. In moments of hardship, the appeal to flee becomes strong—a kind of self-destructive, anti-hero impulse that masks a lack of courage and replaces it with a who-cares conviction suggesting "I didn't want it anyway" when, in fact, I absolutely did.

Then, over my shoulder, I heard someone half-shouting at me. I turned to see a slim, suited, attractive gentleman with graying hair walking in my direction. He carried books and manila folders. He also looked a little harried, and that comforted me in some odd way.

"Hey, babe. Are you looking for Community Organizing? I am too," he said. Fumbling with folders and papers, he mumbled, "Er, ah, the room number is here. Somewhere, anyway."

In his own flustered state, his papers fell to the ground, and I helped him to collect them.

"Oh, oh. Thank you, babe," he said, without making eye contact with me. Before I could even say whether I was looking for the community organizing class, he said, "Oh. Okay, babe. Down here, it looks like. End of the hall."

And he strode off in front of me, dog-eared papers trailing behind.

Taken off guard by my first interaction with Professor Morton Coleman, I followed him down the hall, thinking, *Shit, if he's the instructor, I'm either in really good hands or this is going to be a nightmare.* I picked up the papers that trailed in his wake. They scattered as predictably as footprints.

In class, he shed his jacket, loosened his tie, and rolled up his crisp white shirt sleeves. His first instruction was as follows: "Moe. Call me, Moe."

I took my seat while he distributed course materials and charged into reviewing the syllabus, course outline, weighted assignments, tests, and reading requirements.

"Class participation counts for 30 percent of your grade. Community organizing is about engaging with real social-welfare issues. Over the course of this class, you will meet community leaders, elected officials, nonprofit leaders, and grassroots organizers who are dealing with real social, economic, and policy issues that we face right here in Allegheny County. Think of this as a civic engagement class," he said.

This summary alone intimidated the hell out of me, but as an older, working woman, I felt I had insights that typical college-age students didn't have. By then, my work life was already flourishing. I was employed as a fully certified addictions counselor, working not only with DUI clients but also with families, women, and adolescents.

"So, the reading list," Moe said.

I scribbled away as Moe prattled on about Saul Alinsky, known for his confrontational approach to organizing, and Robert Fisher, who, unlike Alinsky, activated and mobilized communities through collaboration and consensus building.

"The Fisher model is one that I lean toward myself. As a matter of fact, Alinsky probably would have called me and Fisher sellouts, not organizers!" he snickered. "Different strategies for different aims. That's how I see it. My view is don't pick a fight if you don't have to. Yes, people and neighborhoods that are struggling to get basic needs met can be angry. But you can empower them by helping them to identify the resources they do have, building consensus around identified problems and giving communities a public voice."

A few students asked questions about the differences between Alinsky and Fisher. Moe happily spoke at length about both before continuing.

"As community organizers, our job is to work ourselves out of a job. To render our own job void. In effective community organizing, people should feel good about what *they* can do to improve their situation. A good organizer is simply a catalyst to help them see this. We provide tactical support by helping to identify power structures and networks, recruit and mobilize coalitions, build consensus, and then it's our job to get out of the way and leave them to it. To hand it over when it's the responsible time to do so."

The class ended and I was exhilarated. Moe's enthusiasm for social activism lit a flame in me. His comment that "people should feel good about what they can do to improve their situation" spoke to that place in me that desired to be of service in a way that emboldened and empowered others.

Professor "Moe" Coleman

I lingered and approached him after class.

"Professor Coleman," I started.

"Ah, ah, Moe. It's Moe," he said.

He was flustered again, organizing his books and shoving dog-eared and upside-down papers into his folders.

"Oh, okay. Well, I just want to thank you for pointing me in the right direction this morning. Literally and figuratively. And for today's class. I work in the drug and alcohol field already and am studying direct practice but I wanted to try this organizing class. I already find it fascinating."

Mumbling something about phone calls that he needed to return, he said, "Oh, okay, babe. Well, hey, walk with me."

In the short three-block walk back to his office in the Cathedral of Learning, the University of Pittsburgh's prestigious and towering neo-Gothic landmark building, I shared with Moe a very palatable and truncated summary of my life, including how I came to be a "nontraditional student."

"Have a seat," he said, directing me to a chair at a conference table in his office. Moe talked over his shoulder as he moved about, hanging up his suit jacket and rifling through papers on his desk.

"You are lucky to have a good social worker in your corner, to get you pointed in a good direction," he said. "And to clarify about earlier," he said, laughing a little, "you're probably better with directions than I am. That was more luck than anything else."

He gestured toward the surface of his desk, which was in a state of extreme disorganization.

"Maybe," I said, smiling.

He picked up his phone to collect his phone messages.

"Mr. Coleman, social work is where I want to be, but this field of community organizing puts all the one-on-one work into a larger context. I have an idea for a project I'm considering, but it's very rudimentary right now," I said. "I'd love to hear what you think."

Moe was only half-listening as he moved to the conference table and flipped through telephone messages on pink papers, mumbling something about the mayor. On a tablet I saw a to-do list of people he needed to call. The list included university Chancellor Wesley Posvar, a U.S. congressman, Pennsylvania's governor, foundation executives, and prominent city leaders. Other notes on the page included references to an Institute of Politics governance structure, including a catalog of board, staff, and fundraising issues accompanied by his trademark line doodles in the margins.

Embarrassed now by seeing how busy he was with important tasks, I stood up and moved away from the table as he reached for the phone.

"I'm gonna go," I said.

"Okay, babe. See you next class," Moe said.

As I walked down the short corridor and into the hustle and bustle of students changing classes, I heard Moe say, "Hi, Ann. It's Moe for Congressman Coyne."

Who is this guy? I wondered.

(Left to right) Moe; Fred Thieman, then president, The Buhl Foundation; State Representative Dan Frankel; Marc Cherna, director, Allegheny County Department of Human Services

161

Now fully engaged in my junior year at Pitt, I still found it difficult to juggle recovery meetings, studies, work, finances, and caring for my mother, whose health had taken yet another turn for the worse. I was doing an objectively decent job at work and in my classes, but I didn't feel that way at all. I thought I was a fraud, an impostor, and I was certain that one day soon my professors or my boss would find me out and the whole "ruse" would unravel.

Even so, studying at a university was changing my life. My cognitive capacity broadened and I was drawing connections between my work in the addictions field and my studies, linking the social, economic, and political conditions of women in general to investigate the implications for women living with addiction in inhospitable contexts. I knew that I wanted to help make women's lives better and I was hopeful that my new academic training would dovetail with my professional experiences to help me do this.

My community organizing classes with Moe fused together all of these worlds and aspirations. Throughout my junior year, Moe taught us how organizing engages and empowers people, especially those who are marginalized, underserved, and underrepresented. The goal, he said, was to improve the quality of their lives by increasing their influence and decision-making power. He explained the roles of the organizer. We discussed strategies and tactics to engage citizens, including how to build and mobilize coalitions, how to identify formal and informal power structures within communities, and the best models for creating the desired changes.

Beyond the textbook, beyond abstractions and theories, Moe brought in real, live, accomplished organizers who were engaged in efforts to bring about change in our local communities. These were ground-level stories from community civic leaders from organizations like ACTION-Housing, which worked to construct affordable housing in some of Pittsburgh's poorest neighborhoods. We heard from the executive director of a community development corporation that mobilized a citizens' resistance movement to halt the University of Pittsburgh's plans for expansion near a residential neighborhood. Most importantly, I benefited from Moe's personal stories of community organizing, going back to his first job as an organizer at the Anna Heldman Settlement House in Pittsburgh's historic Hill District. He told anecdotes from his experiences during the civil rights movement, along with stories from his tenure as a top aide in the Pittsburgh mayor's office. He even shared insights from his time working as a consultant to Henry Ford II in developing a "model city" in Detroit.

Every speaker and story I heard sparked creative ideas in my mind. An original vision for a project of my own began to emerge. I knew my efforts towards conceptualizing my own project would be imprecise at first, but I recognized that my initial awkwardness might turn into a real facility for organizing, if I could only remain patient. Keeping my recovery work in mind, I knew it was just a matter of taking small, incremental steps towards my vision.

Up to the midpoint of Moe's course, we spent much of our time discussing the "locality development model" of community organizing as laid out by Jack Rothman, a sociologist and social worker whose conceptualization of community interventions was a keystone in academic settings across the United States. Nevertheless, his "place-based" model of organizing was confounding my ability to clarify and crystallize my thinking on how to improve the recovery experience of women dealing with traumas beyond addiction itself. This was becoming my mission and my quandary.

At my job, I had recently learned about the work of Dr. Stephanie Covington, a clinician in California and a pioneer in the field of women's issues and their relationship to addiction, trauma, and recovery. Almost no one at this time was looking at gender-specific responses and trauma-informed approaches to addressing addiction. Gateway Rehabilitation Center had only recently begun a women's group at its inpatient facility in Aliquippa, 15 miles north-west of Pittsburgh, and Turtle Creek Valley had just received a small grant to develop a women's outpatient program. I knew we were onto something. In the mid-1980s, in the Pittsburgh region, these two slowly developing programs were the only two gender-specific options for women in recovery. I was grateful to work at one of those agencies and participate in some of the women's groups but I recognized a glaring need for this treatment to be offered on a broader scale. What we were doing—a trial version, if you will— was good work, but it wasn't nearly enough.

One of our assignments in Moe's class was to apply one of the organizing models we had studied to a specific issue. I was both ecstatic and terrified by the project. Because I was an academic novice, the overlapping qualities of the various models confused me. In some measure, I was able to distinguish them, but when I tried to apply them to a potential project, things were less than tidy.

As I sat in class, Moe's voice became muffled from my perspective, and I stared out the nearby window at an image of myself kneeling on the torn linoleum floor of my family's cold, bare apartment. Mama, in this image, was drunk and unresponsive. I leaned down to make sure she was breathing. I reached for the cigarette that still burned between her immobile, nicotine-stained fingers, trying not to drop the ashes. They fell onto the floor anyway—lifeless and tireless. I puffed on the cigarette before I crushed it out in the nearby ashtray. A half-consumed bottle of cheap red wine stained the formica coffee table nearby. I set the bottle upright and gulped what was left in her glass. Donnie cried in his crib, demanding my attention. I sighed, a sound no one in that moment heard or cared about.

Other students began laughing at something Moe said, which brought me back into the classroom. In that same moment, I thought about what it means to be truly abandoned.

"Okay, we're done today," Moe said, chuckling. "On your way out, put your proposed project topics on the desk. Next time, our speaker will be the executive secretary to Mayor Caliguiri. He will be discussing the second Renaissance of the City of Pittsburgh. Be here on time," he barked.

Students chattered as they collected their belongings and shuffled out toward their next classes.

Feeling deflated, I scribbled down on the assignment sheet: *Women and recovery from addictions. Treatment options? Social planning? Social action? Organizing for women's treatment programs?*

I gathered my things and walked to the front of the room, dropping my assignment on the desk. It was a vague, imperfect germ of an idea, but it was something.

Moe was unrolling his shirt sleeves and collecting his materials.

"Which way are you going, babe?" he asked.

"The Cathedral," I replied.

"Good. Walk with me then."

Moe swung his jacket over his shoulder and gathered up his disheveled folders and books. We walked out into the bright sunlight.

"So, what's going on?" he asked. "I thought that I could count on you to keep the dialogue going in class, but you've clammed up on me lately. What's up?"

"Oh, I don't know, Moe. I'm feeling confused about this organizing project. I don't get the models. They blend together to me. And this 'place-based' organizing is throwing me off. I don't have a geographic community or neighborhood where I want to work," I said.

"And what else?" he asked.

I felt caught off guard by his questions, convinced that he was fishing for something deeper. I didn't realize that my emotional retreat in class had been so obvious. There was something disarming about Moe's casual and friendly manner.

As we walked down Fifth Avenue toward the Cathedral of Learning, our conversation was regularly interrupted by friends, colleagues, and students (old and new) who greeted Moe on the street or asked him quick questions. He struck me in that moment—while we ambled down the sidewalk with eager disciples running parallel to us—as something close to Socrates: a walking reservoir of wisdom but also modest, a little gruff, and devoid of pretense. I noticed how he treated everyone equally, gave each person his undivided attention, and offered advice or a time to meet to discuss things further. *Who is this guy?* I continued to wonder.

When we finally made it to the Cathedral, we hadn't finished our conversation.

"Let's grab lunch. You have time?" he asked.

"Ah, yeah," I stammered. Panic raced through me because I didn't even have enough money for lunch. Just some spare change, which I was saving to buy a box of Kraft macaroni and cheese for dinner. Moe, even then, knew precious little about my background, including the anxiety that often surrounded when my next meal would be.

We went into an Arby's on the ground floor of the Cathedral, and Moe ordered sandwiches for both of us.

"Moe, I'm not hungry. Really," I said.

"Nah. You gotta eat, babe. Come on, let me get this."

He plopped his things on the counter and rummaged through his pockets for money. The folders slid and papers went everywhere. Moe's dishevelment, I'm now convinced, was part and parcel of his brilliance and "process." I couldn't fault him. I accepted Moe in all his imperfection, maybe because a more composed version of him would have lacked the compassion, patience, and insight that defined him.

Moe continued to fumble to retrieve his money while I picked up his folders and class assignments from the floor.

"Ahhh, thanks, babe," he said.

Out in the hallway, with everything in hand, we pushed through the noisy mob of students waiting for elevators to get to their classes.

"Twenty-three," Moe yelled. I pushed the button for the floor and waited for us to ascend. Anyone who worked or had classes in Pitt's Cathedral of Learning knew that you had to build "elevator waiting time" into your schedule if you wanted to get anywhere on time. As we waited in that cramped, slow-moving box, students, staff, and faculty greeted Moe with a shout, a slap on the back, a personal joke, or concerns about a pressing issue. It was starting to dawn on me that Moe was someone very special. He saw people and attended to them exactly where they were. Because of his community organizing background, I sometimes forgot that he was also a seasoned social worker.

We finally arrived at his office.

"Have a seat, babe. Feel free to eat while I check my telephone messages."

He opened a desk drawer and pulled out a warm diet Coke and a handful of rumpled napkins.

"To go with the sandwich," he said, pushing them my way. "Ah, ah, I gotta make this call to Dave," he said, confident that I would know who Dave was.

"Should I go?" I asked nervously.

"No, no, no. Sit. Eat. I'll just be a minute," he said. He had the phone pinched between his ear and shoulder as he dialed the telephone.

I took my lunch and backpack and sat at the conference table adjacent to his desk. As I nibbled away at my sandwich, I snapped open the warm soda and looked around the room. The office itself was nothing to write home about, but the furniture was beautiful.

Wiping my hands on a napkin so as not to stain anything, I ran my hand along the smooth, reddish-brown grain of the mahogany conference table that featured elegant, carved legs and long stretchers that ran from end to end. The chairs didn't match the French style of the table; they were wooden and colonial-looking. Surrounding us were antique, mahogany, barrister-style stacking bookcases with leaded glass and brass knobs. A smaller mahogany lateral-file writing desk sat in the corner of the room with a traditional emerald green and brass banker's lamp.

Simply put, I was out of my element. I thought about my Radio Flyer wagon and its screeching wheel. I thought about splitting part of a calcified government-issued cheese block with Eddie while we sat with our legs dangled over the Inky Wall, making each other laugh with jokes and stories from the neighborhood.

I watched as Moe picked at his sandwich and spoke enthusiastically with "Dave"—who turned out to be the executive secretary to then Pittsburgh Mayor Caliguiri. They talked about a new public-private initiative that community leaders were considering to create a cultural arts district in Pittsburgh. The call was taking some time, and I wondered if I should just go. From the way he anxiously flipped through the stack of pink phone messages on his desk, I could see they demanded his attention.

Sensing my impatience, Moe turned to me and said, "Eat, babe. I'll be with you in just a minute."

I nodded.

I finished my sandwich, a meal for which I was very grateful, and stood to put my things in the trash. I moved past the window and stopped to take in the view. Moe's office was on the 23rd floor of the Cathedral, on the Forbes Avenue side of the building. The view outside flowed along Forbes, catching the entrance of the Carnegie Museum of Natural History, the oak tree-lined parklet that led to the main branch of the Carnegie Library. From another window, I could see the perfectly manicured lawns of Phipps Conservatory and Botanical Gardens, including the rolling glass domes that house ever-changing seasonal floral displays and a renowned collection of orchids, ferns, palms, and cacti. I was struck in that moment by the physical beauty surrounding the campus and wondered, *How on earth did I manage to get here?*

I returned to the conference table and opened my backpack, pulling out my notes from class. Moe finished his call, bit into his now-soggy and cold sandwich, and spat it at me as he asked, "Okay, babe. Let's talk. What's going on with you?"

"I'm confused with these models of organizing and how to situate my project because I don't have a specific neighborhood I want to work in," I muttered.

"Okay, babe. We'll get to that. First, tell me what's going on with you. Not with the class," he said.

"I don't know what to say to that," I said, embarrassed.

"Look, you bring a lot to class, and I can tell it's hard for you being an older student. I can see that. But you chime in. You ask good questions. That's good. It helps the other students a lot more than you realize. But something's different. Something's up."

"So, I do this work in addictions, right? Well, I'm doing more work now with women addicts and I want to do more than just treat their addiction."

I looked at Moe. I sensed that he knew I was deflecting his question and was waiting for me to get to the point.

"I'm in recovery, Moe. I know these women need more, because I needed more. In a lot of ways, I was lucky. I met a friend through the job I was working at, a friend who got so drunk at work that they sent him to rehab. He got sober and stayed sober. Months later, I called him one night and he *happened* to pick up the phone. He *happened* to care. I don't want other women to rely on luck to get them through what could be the most excruciating and life-altering change they ever have to make."

I sat there across from Moe, blushing for having shared what I did. I wished that I could reel all the words back into my mouth, but I couldn't.

Moe jumped in.

"Hey, babe. Listen. First of all, it takes a lot of courage to get on a straight path, so good for you. That's great! And now you want to help others, which is even better. The best organizing work comes when you have direct experience. Always. So, let's figure this out together. This is a good thing. As for this project, I know you have some questions written down, so let's start there."

"I don't know if this will make any sense," I said.

"Fun fact: When you are organizing, things rarely make any sense in the beginning. Sometimes halfway through, too," he laughed. "That's why you organize to make order out of things. To identify problems, to clarify questions, to sort through resources or the lack thereof. To challenge the status quo. That's the whole point of this work. You don't have to know all the answers now. Just sort through the questions."

Reassured, I told Moe about Dr. Stephanie Covington's groundbreaking work on gender-specific, trauma-informed treatment for women and how only two treatment providers locally were exploring this kind of programming for recovering women. I told him about a friend of mine named Billy, a gay man who had left Pittsburgh for California to become an AIDS activist. Billy had explained to me that gay men's issues were manifold: living with a new disease, under the threat of death, and with all the stigma that came with being gay and "diseased." Billy explained that society considered those afflicted with AIDS as "good as dead" or "socially dead." I shared with Moe that I was learning how AIDS activism was forming in a social and political environment that forced gay men with AIDS to organize as *people* with AIDS to push for improved social services and medical research. I told Moe that this same approach might be applicable to women who were dealing with addiction and trauma, seeking recovery and improved social services.

The common thread was the need to create solidarity among a community not defined by neighborhood boundaries.

Moe chomped away at his sandwich and dipped greasy, limp fries into a vat of ketchup as he listened to me. From time to time, he scribbled down notes as I talked.

"Good thinking so far. Go on," he said.

"I want to better help women in recovery," I said. "I am one of these women, Moe. Sure, I'm in recovery, and I'm doing good work with a therapist, but it's been a long slog for me, dealing with some serious demons from my past. From my professional experience, I can see that men and women with addiction deal with different types of issues and cope or 'manage' in different ways, too. If that's the case, maybe they require different treatment models. I know I'm not the only recovering woman who is now dealing with multiple issues— sexual abuse, neglect, domestic violence, family separation. These are not things that women can comfortably deal with in a co-ed setting. Nor should any woman have to. Safe places with women-centered treatment models, like what Dr. Covington talks about, need to be created so that women can get to the core issues beyond their addictions. I'm convinced that if these things are not dealt with in a safe and professional setting, they will undermine a woman's recovery."

"I think you're absolutely right on that," Moe said, no longer eating or taking notes, but simply giving me his full attention.

I felt a rush of urgency. Rarely had I seen him entirely focused on the task at hand, but that didn't mean he wasn't paying attention all along.

"I don't know why I'm telling you all this, Moe. All I really know is that I'm not supposed to be here. I have been through more than I thought I could handle. I actually lived with a death wish for so many years, trying to shove down the memories of my own traumas with every drink and drug I took. And that worked. At least, it worked until it stopped working. At some point, it *always* stops working. That's why addicts always need more. One day I got sober by the grace of something a lot larger than me, and every repressed memory that I kept at bay with my addictions suddenly demanded my undivided attention. Over the years, with the help of a small group of friends and the kindness of some good professionals, I've been able to sustain my work. But now I want to create something for others. Something that is systematic, holistic, inclusive, and compassionate for women like me. I want to create a space where women can heal their traumas while firmly establishing their sobriety. Something we needed yesterday!"

Moe nodded, looking off to his left while he thought of something.

"I'm sorry," I said, lowering and shaking my head.

"Listen, babe. You don't ever apologize for overcoming hardships. I'm humbled by your story. Even more humbled that you felt comfortable enough to share it with me."

"I honestly didn't mean to go into all of that," I said. "I had no intention of sharing all this with you today, but after everything we've discussed in class and everything I've witnessed at my job, I know that I must do something for women. We must do better by women. It might sound like gallows humor, but long-timers in recovery say all the time that *recovery is about living or dying.* I believe that. For me, this is honestly about saving lives."

"Sometimes it is exactly about that," Moe said. "So, tell me what you want to do. Tell me about your ideas and let's see if we can clarify some of your community organizing questions."

For the next hour, Moe and I discussed the idea of creating a long-term, trauma-informed treatment program for women. With that as the aim, we talked through Rothman's three organizing models—community development, social action, and social planning. Moe clarified each one for me, and I took notes as he spoke.

"It sounds like what I'm talking about doing might be a little bit of each?" I asked.

"Yep, babe. That's right. For your project, we'll have to create a model that incorporates all three of them."

"How do I begin?" I asked.

"Good question. You're going to have to do an environmental scan and needs assessment to determine if there is, in fact, a gap in services and therefore a need for such a program. Based on what you're telling me from your experiences alone, that's the case. If your research bears that out, you'll want to do a SWOT analysis to determine the strengths, weaknesses, opportunities, and threats of what you are proposing."

"Needs assessment?" I asked.

"Sure. The question is really this. Who are your authenticators? Who are the people who can verify that your ideas are worth pursuing?" he asked.

"I suppose I would go first to the drug and alcohol agency where I work and ask for a letter of support, then go to treatment agencies and even family and child services agencies, including county programs. I can request letters of support from them too."

"Yes! But before you do that, complete your scan and let's discuss that, because it will inform your letter requesting support. For our next meeting, have your scan completed and bring along a list of the agencies you plan to contact. We'll then work on a letter and begin to flesh out how to build organizational scaffolding to operationalize everything."

"I will have all that for you at our next meeting, Moe."

"This is all great, babe. Great! Do you feel clearer about things now?" Moe asked.

"Yes," I said, smiling. "And no."

"That's okay. Things should be as clear as mud right now. It'll sort out. The important thing is that you are clear about your heart's desire. I have a lot of students, and sometimes their ideas are much more abstract. More removed from personal experience. You have a good idea and personal, direct experience with what you're talking about. That's where the best work comes from. Continue to lean into these ideas, and this project will take off. I know it will."

"Thank you so much, Moe," I said.

I stood and began to push my chair in.

"Terry," he said. "Maybe no one has told you this before, but you're brave. It takes a lot of courage to put yourself out there like this. Not only to share what you did with me, but to pursue this idea and try to make it real."

Moe's phone rang, and he flew out of his seat to grab the call, yelling over his shoulder, "Okay, okay, see you in class!"

I collected my things and left his office, welcoming the wait at the elevator. On the way down, the ride was completely different. The campus had emptied out considerably, so I was alone in what amounted to a meditative chamber. A quiet and warm sensation rose up inside me. I realized that I had shared these things with Moe because he did for me exactly what I wanted to do for women living with addictions and trauma. He showed me enough of himself for me to see that he was a good man; through his gestures of welcome and trust, I felt comfortable enough to walk into his office, share some of my story, and accept his guidance. He saw me and created a safe space for me to speak my truth. He mirrored for me exactly what I hoped to create for a community of women in recovery.

In the elevator, I recalled a story I had heard about a homeless woman who went to a free clinic once a month to see the doctor. The doctor, upon seeing her condition, didn't judge her disheveled appearance or the scraps of life that she carried with her in bags and bundles. Instead, he saw and treated her conditions with kindness, care, and presence. After her first few appointments, the woman would show up at the clinic on days when the doctor wasn't there. The staff observed that she would go to the open door of the doctor's exam room, step one foot into the room, and then step back out again. She would repeat this several times; when she was satisfied, she would leave the building. Obviously, the doctor's care for her was such a striking contrast to what she experienced in everyday life that she felt the need to remind herself of the compassionate treatment he offered—to confirm that it had actually happened, that it was a good, intact, and undisturbed thing. His care had become a reality and memory that no one could tarnish, and his office was a sanctuary she could revisit (and count on) in the future.

It dawned on me that the places where we are truly seen and heard are holy places for us. Floundering in a snowstorm in Point State Park with Jack. At Gateway Rehab with Dr. Twerski, where I and the rest of the "lobsters" began to heal. Alone after work with my cassette, listening to Dot as she dropped her wisdom in my ear. I thought about how Moe had created another holy place for me, allowing me to reach into my own truth and access my deepest self. I could not have known that Moe would hold this safe space for me for many years to come. In his company, I found a holy place that I would be blessed to visit time and again.

12

LATIKA: TEACHER

Back in my office at Turtle Creek Valley, I sat in a small and dank office space across from my new client, Latika. As soon as she entered the room, I recognized she would be, in euphemistic terms, "unreceptive to feedback."

I offered her a seat.

"Look," she said, beginning to sit down, "I'll tell you whatever you want to hear so we can get this shit done with and I can get the fuck outta here. I drank three Colt 45s but I wasn't drunk. Them cops, they just have it in for us black folks. DUI? That's bullshit. A bullshit story. Fuck him and fuck you too."

I took a deep breath.

"Well, Latika, I'm sorry you feel that way, because you are court-ordered to be here. That means that we have to spend some time together discussing what brought you here. So how would you like this to go? You can keep that big fat chip on your shoulder and give me a hard time. Believe me, you won't be the first to do that," I said with a chuckle.

"But I'll only tolerate that for a short while. After that, I'll be required to write you up and terminate you for noncompliance, and you'll go back before the judge. Another option"—I paused briefly for effect— "is figuring out how we're going to move forward together."

Latika slumped in the wobbly desk chair at the side of my desk. Baggy pants hung down below her hips, and she wore an oversized Bob Marley T-shirt that covered her slight frame. Her eyes darted back and forth as she repeatedly snapped an elastic bracelet against her wrist. She meant to indicate annoyance or, maybe, deliberation. Her head was twitching as she rocked herself from side to side. It looked like crack cocaine withdrawal to me (I had seen it many times), but she certainly wasn't telling.

"So, what's it going to be, Latika? *I* know you don't want to be here. *You* know you don't want to be here. But we have a problem, because you *need* to be here. First, I have some paperwork I need to go through with you. I'm going to ask you some questions about your drinking, drug use, family life, childhood, education, and work life. And then we're going to figure out the best treatment plan for you. I'd like to do this with you. You don't have to believe in it, understand it, or even like it, but we do have to get through this so you can meet your court requirements and maybe, just maybe, you'll even get something out of this."

"I ain't no alcoholic and I ain't going to no meetings," she snapped.

"Well, here's the deal. Let's get through this form first before you make any statements about what you're going to do. Who knows? Maybe by doing this you'll learn something about yourself that you didn't know."

"Right," Latika said, snorting.

"Here's what I know, Latika. If you're drinking to the point where your blood alcohol is two times the legal limit and you've been busted with a DUI not once but twice, that tells me there's something going on with you. We're not going to know what that is if you just show up here week after week to butt heads with me. I want to help you. I don't know what's going on in your life that got you to drinking, but maybe together we can start to sort this out."

Latika tapped her right foot against the chair, and her rocking escalated as beads of sweat gathered above her brow. Tears welled in her eyes.

"You don't have to do this by yourself," I said.

As though someone or something had laced her up in a straitjacket, Latika wrapped her arms around herself and sat up tall and rigid in her seat. In a quick flash, her eyes ricocheted like pinballs before they locked on some spot on the wall. She gazed with what war veterans call a "thousand-yard stare." She was gone, and all I could do was be there. I sat looking at her as tears cascaded from some place behind her cold, deadened gaze.

"I'd like to give you a box of tissues, Latika. Would that be all right?" I asked.

No response.

"Latika, can you look at me, please?"

No response.

I lifted a tissue from the box and reached to put it in her hand, and with a blink of her eyes, she bowed her head and wept.

"I don't know what just happened for you, Latika, but I want you to know that you are safe here, and whatever you need to talk about, you can do that here with me."

Latika suppressed her sobbing.

"I still ain't no alcoholic. I'll do what I gotta do to beat this thing, but don't think you're gonna get an easy ride from me," she said.

I knew we hadn't made the agency-mandated progress we were supposed to make—namely, getting the psycho-social evaluation completed—but progress was made in earning her trust, which was a big step for both of us.

"It sounds like we have a plan, Latika. You show up for your sessions, and we'll figure this out as we go along. One session at a time. How does that sound?"

"Yeah, same time next week," she said, and got up to leave.

I sat there in my basement office, gazing at the slant of the sun's evening rays, which struggled to penetrate my grimy window that sat just below the sidewalk grate outside. Like Latika, in that moment, I slipped away into a soothing abyss of nothingness. I rested there for a while until the images of all the women I had worked with brought me back to reality. Countless women, who, through the process of drug and alcohol treatment, had brushed up against the ghosts in their closets long enough to know they were in there, but not long enough to confront or release them.

After my first meeting with Latika, I was haunted by the conviction that we could and needed to do better for these women. We were missing something with them. At Turtle Creek Valley, where I worked, the protocols were excellent in diagnosing whether a client had a substance abuse disorder, but our treatment model didn't go far enough. I knew this because I was one of these women myself. I was working with Dot and my therapist at the time and I was still making progress. I knew there was a way back to and through the trauma that many women experience, but in the early 1980s, drug and alcohol treatment programs were still primarily designed to treat male clients. The stigma associated with alcoholism and addiction served to keep women in the shadows, but women were showing up for treatment in greater numbers, and programs were ill-equipped to deal with them. Treatment models were undeniably "androcentric," designed with a male bias, consciously or otherwise. The goal of this male-centered model was to push through and break down one's denial of alcoholism, a very real and cunning aspect of addiction. Tactics at that time involved shaming strategies to push male clients to connect with their emotions around their addictive behaviors. It was an outside-in approach.

What I had discovered in my own personal work and with women in early recovery was that in general, women were already in touch with the feelings related to their addictions. In my own case, I was already consumed with remorse, guilt, shame, and fear because of where my addiction had taken me. I didn't need the then-standard browbeating to get in touch with my fear or shame related to regular "blackout" drinking. I didn't need to be shamed into feeling guilt and remorse for driving drunk with my nieces and nephews in the back of a pickup truck, where I could have killed them. I already felt disgust with myself for having had drunken sex with men on the prowl and for all other self-destructive attempts to resolve my childhood abuse issues. In sum, I was already in full and acute contact with my feelings and I certainly didn't need to be emotionally and psychologically battered into grasping that I was powerless over my drinking.

Like me, Latika and other women didn't need to be shamed into knowing that their current situation was connected to the traumas of their past. The addiction field's androcentric model of treatment created an unintended form of prejudice toward women clients by trying to make them fit into its definition of the disease of addiction. Its views, roles, and models were predicated upon a culture of masculine standards.

In my own agency, funds had recently been raised to establish an outpatient women's group that was quickly gaining in popularity. Additionally, in conversations with agency leadership, we received the go-ahead to develop new intake protocols that included taking histories on sexual abuse, eating disorders, physical and emotional abuse, and domestic violence—all issues that could be linked to addictive behavior and which women are more likely to experience than men.

The following week, Latika walked into my office for our second required counseling session, just as jittery as before.

"What we gonna do today?" she asked, giving me a piercing stare.

"Well, we're going to finish filling out the paperwork we started last time. All you have to do today is sit back and answer some questions. Would you like a coffee or something before we get started?"

"Coffee. Cream. Four packets of sugar," she said.

"You got it," I said.

Noticing Latika's fidgety state, and having learned the importance of giving only half a cup of coffee to people with the jitters, I fixed her drink and offered her more if she wanted it.

"Okay, let's get going," I said. "Now, I want you to know that I will be asking some personal questions here. If you have difficulty with anything, we can take it slow."

"Right," she said.

"So, I'm going to dive right in. Last time we finished up with some of your basic intake information. This next section is going to be about your sexual history."

She grunted disapprovingly.

"At what age did you first have sexual activity?"

With a quick and far-off look in her eyes, Latika said, "Eleven."

"All right. And who was that with?" I asked.

Staring out the window, she said, "My brother."

"Okay. And how long did that go on?" I asked.

Latika stared off and numbly stirred her coffee. Her eyes settled on the cross-stitched Serenity Prayer that hung on my wood-paneled wall.

"Till my daddy found out," she said. "Round about thirteen."

179

"What happened then?" I asked.

"Daddy whooped the shit out of him," she said, dazed.

"And then what happened, Latika?"

Taking a deep breath that brought her back into the room, she looked me straight in the eye and said, "He picked up right where my brother left off."

I plucked a tissue from the box on my desk and offered it to her.

"Latika, I am so sorry," I said.

With this simple gesture, she released a river of tears that had been stored in her for a lifetime. I sat quietly and bore witness to her pain.

After a while, she asked for a glass of water, which I brought to her.

"Latika, first of all I want to say how brave you are for giving voice to those experiences. I'm honored that you feel safe enough to talk with me about it even though we are still getting to know each other. May I ask you another question?" I asked.

"Yeah," she said, lowering her head.

"Have you ever told anyone about this?"

"Nah," she said.

"May I ask why?"

"No one ever asked," she said, without missing a beat.

In that moment, I realized that through our women's program and new intake processes we were providing a desperately needed service to women in recovery not just from addiction, but from underlying trauma as well.

Latika and I continued to work together and I referred her to the new women's outpatient group, where I hoped she would find additional support. She stayed actively involved in both programs, and, in a few months' time, it was evident that she was making major progress. Something clicked for her that was born out of several crucial factors: her access to a support group with a shared aim of sobriety, a scheduled time and place for meetings, and her recognition that she had an advocate in me—someone who truly cared about her.

When our one-on-one therapy sessions were ending, we met for a final time in my office, and I asked Latika if she had any final thoughts or feelings that she wanted us to discuss together.

"Miss Terry," she said. "When you started asking me questions about my past, I felt I was heading in a dark way. But now, praise God, I'm feeling hope all around me. I come here every week and look at that prayer on your wall and I say that prayer at the meetings. I know I have a walk to do and I do wish I had some place to stay because you know them memories are talking at me all the time. But I know I have God at my back and I'm gonna make it through this."

"You are an example of what it means to step out in faith, Latika. I know we're wrapping up here, but please stay involved in the women's group and keep close to your sponsor."

"I will, Miss Terry. Thank you for the kindness you've shown me."

"The pleasure was mine, Latika. You've taught me a great deal, too."

About six months later, I received a call from Latika, who had completed the women's group three months earlier. She called because she wanted me to know that she had relapsed and was entering an inpatient treatment facility. When I asked what lead to her relapse, she sighed.

"After group, I felt I was done working on those things from my daddy and brother but I'm coming to see that you can't just ignore someone who gave you so much to remember. Those memories are pushing and shoving me in all directions. They break my heart, to tell you the truth. To know they cared about me so little, and to feel so small, so powerless, and little myself. I used again, but I know it was the wrong choice. Gateway is gonna have a bed for me in two days. I just wanted you to know."

"I'm glad you called me, Latika. Just keep doing the next right thing for you. The relapse may feel like a setback, but if it gets you to inpatient treatment, then that's a good thing. You are not alone. Just know that," I said.

"May I reach out to you, Miss Terry, when I get out of treatment?" she asked.

"Of course, you can. Please do. I'll be here," I said.

That was the last time I heard from Latika. Later, I learned through the grapevine that she had left treatment in her third week at Gateway. For whatever reason, she was not able to complete the program. I suspect her suffering couldn't be quelled.

The agency's outpatient group for women continued to be successful and taught us new things about women's treatment needs. I also continued my direct counseling with women and used gender-specific intake methods that helped me confirm that in the addiction recovery field, there remained a need for long-term services for women like Latika.

Latika's story lit a spark in me to take action on creating a long-term, continuum-of-care program specifically for women. One that would invite them to share their stories and would provide the holistic emotional, mental, physical, and spiritual support they would need to make the journey back to themselves—to embrace their struggle and their strength. I wanted to found a program worthy of Latika and women like her—a sanctuary where women could heal.

13.

GIDEON: IN ALL OF MY HOUSE

Not long after Latika's disappearance, Dot and I were well into our time of working together at Turtle Creek Valley. The full weight of my own past was continuing to surface in the form of fragmented and disorienting memories of physical and sexual abuse I had suffered as a child and young adult. It wasn't just my mind that was fragmented. Physically, I was experiencing a tightness around my chest and had difficulty breathing. My feet and hands would tingle and go numb. When I tried to discuss these things with a therapist, my throat closed off and I would lose my voice. My sleeping was horrible. I had developed night terrors. During these episodes, scents and bits of past memories pushed through—disturbing my mind and body, leaving me thrashing about, sweating, and struggling to wake up. When I did awaken, I was frightened and hypervigilant, unable to fall asleep again.

In the midst of my struggles to address my past, I continued to attend to Mama's compounding medical conditions. I also tried, sometimes fruitlessly, to be a conscientious student. The idea I had shared and discussed with Moe, Dot, and others—of establishing an agency for women in recovery—felt unachievable until Mama's health stabilized and until I could get my own head and heart restored.

Around this time, Mama was hospitalized yet again for an infection in the ball of her foot. Complications with her sugar kept her in the hospital for most of a month while the infection worsened and developed into gangrene. The doctors determined that her foot would have to go.

Mama stayed in the hospital for almost three months following the surgery. The doctors didn't think she would make it through. Despite my responsibilities at work and school, I started every morning with a visit to see her. At the hospital I would catch up with the medical team, probing them for updates about her health. After work or school, I visited her again. In between my classes, meetings, homework, therapy appointments, and meetings, I ran to her apartment to water plants, sort mail, clean the floors, and pay her bills.

When Mama was finally released from the hospital, I sat by her side as she tried to establish a new relationship with the painful phantom that was once her foot. The pain was excruciating for her. As usual, I bore the weight of her heaviness (literally and figuratively) and commanded my own pain and sorrow to retreat underground. For weeks and months, I pressed on as her caretaker and cheerleader, supporting her through the simple things she had taken for granted: making a meal, taking a shower, dressing, grocery shopping, doing housework. Together we trudged as one conjoined entity, and though I offered her a smile on my face and a lilt in my voice, my own weakness was becoming undeniable. She was not the only one dealing with phantom pain.

One day I sat on the floor of her apartment. I was situated at the foot of the recliner where she sat while I carefully unwrapped the bandage at the bottom of her leg.

"Well, it looks like you had a workout today, Mama. Moving about the apartment like we did, it's no wonder. How does it feel?" I asked.

She remained silent while I wrung out the soft and soapy washcloth to clean her obviously tender wound.

Mama winced in pain as I touched the bottom of her leg. She had reluctantly worn a prosthetic foot at the beginning, but it was never a good fit. It rubbed on the wound in an irritating way. The wound itself was healing ever so slowly because of her diabetes.

"How does it feel?" she repeated, mockingly. "It hurts."

"Well, I can see that, Mama. I think we should call the doctor and get you in to see him."

With that, Mama gazed out the window of the apartment toward the trees across the street. I was glad that she was "going away" in that moment, because I didn't have the emotional energy to talk about it, to argue, or to be the object of her frustration. I continued to quietly and gently clean the wound at the bottom of her leg, which was on the verge of infection. I washed her stump, placed a clean piece of gauze around it, and loosely wrapped it in an Ace bandage. Finally, I gently shimmied the two-ply prosthetic soft socks up her leg.

"There you go, Mama. That ought to hold you until morning."

She looked at me without speaking.

"Come on," I said, "let's get you into bed."

In just a few months, Mama was hospitalized again, this time with pneumonia. Her doctor determined that with the infection in her leg, she would need another amputation. This would be Mama's third chop, but it would have to wait because while she was in the hospital, she suffered a heart attack. Shocked and traumatized, I did what was natural for me and I went onto auto-pilot, attending to Mama and dragging myself to work, to school, to meetings.

Again, Mama was tapping at death's door, relying on me as her primary caretaker. Both Eddie and Donnie now were married and tending to families of their own. We hadn't heard from Eddie in years. Donnie surfaced from time to time, providing much needed intermittent support. I was weary of the situation and weary of Mama. I loved and loathed her simultaneously— wishing her dead and well at the same time. As I worked to take care of her, I worked privately and with my therapist to address the sexual abuse I had suffered at my mother's hands. I didn't feel a sense of hatred per se. Only profound sadness. She was a damaged person, and I had known this fact forever, intuiting it at a remarkably young age. I also knew that there was still some irreconcilable schism between her and her own mother and family that no one would ever confront. It was something big and ugly in their relationship that kept all of the family away from us, even when my mother was in the hospital for months on end, being cut on, cut off, and carted away.

Mama's heart surgery began just hours later and it was riddled with complications. She remained in the cardiac intensive care unit for six weeks before she could transition to "step down" care. In the first two weeks of her stay, only a few family members visited to see how she was. With visitations limited to only two 15-minute periods a day, the support for her (and me) declined rapidly, reduced to a few periodic cards from aunts and distant relatives, which I would read to her in her room. Most of the cards conveyed half-hearted, boilerplate sentiments. Some only signed their names, without any inclusion of "love." I did my best to make sure everyone in the family stayed updated on her status, but this disparity in effort only made me more aware of their indifference.

I went to see Mama at the hospital one night, but she was down for tests, so I left her a note telling her that I'd be back in the morning. I decided to swing by and catch the beginners' recovery meeting at Fifth and Negley.

The topic was powerlessness, and as the meeting went around the room, I half-listened to folks while they shared their stories. I was more drawn into the deep sadness and powerlessness I felt in myself than to any words exchanged in the room. I had lost a lot of weight. I felt both depressed and anxious, and my breathing felt constricted. I also struggled to stay present for anything beyond dealing with Mama's illnesses. I could only really focus when I was at her bedside, where I knew I must be fully present and available for her. Beyond that, I floated in a dreamlike world.

At the end of the meeting, a few attendees looked unburdened—lightened by whatever they had released or learned in the company of others who also were struggling. As for me, on the way home from that meeting, I wept.

When I entered my apartment, I fed my cats and collapsed in bed. In the middle of the night, I rose up to sit on the edge of my bed, shuffling through the events of my evening. I saw Mama's empty hospital bed and the card sent to her by neighbors in her building. I saw the note I had written to her on the back of the envelope, with a heart and smiley face.

I thought back to the meeting on powerlessness a few hours earlier. While I was there, I saw Mark, a homeless man I knew, sitting at a collapsible table, making a cup of coffee and eating doughnuts with a deep sense of tranquility and gratitude. I saw Pat B.'s kindness toward him, offering questions and encouragement. I heard Tom C. say, "I'm happy every day because I wake up and make a decision to be happy." And I wondered why I couldn't be, if not "happy," more like them. If I didn't become more like them, I wondered how could I hope to help anyone in the way I intended.

I checked my answering machine and heard an old, soon-to-expire message. Mama's faint voice said, "I may miss you tonight. They're taking me down for another X-ray. If I do, I'll see you in the morning. I love you." Every time she called me at night (on the rare occasion I missed seeing her at the hospital), I didn't know if I would see her in the morning, if she'd even stay alive. She was always dangling over the precipice, and I felt that way too.

Dot finally noticed what I was failing to hide. She strolled into my office one day, plopping herself down in a chair before squaring off with me.

"Look here now," she said. "Let me get a good look into them eyes of yours."

I reluctantly lifted my head from some paperwork to look at her.

"Tell me how you're doing. And don't you say 'fine,' because both you and I know that ain't the truth."

Dot was, along with Jack, the only other person in my inner circle who "got me" and loved me unconditionally. It was useless to try to get something past her, because she always called me out. She loved me enough to be straight with me about everything.

"I'm bottoming out," I said. "That's the truth. I don't have anything left. I'm trying to be there for Mama and for everything else I have to do but I'm worn down. For weeks, I've been feeling like I can't breathe and my head's all fuzzy. I can't eat. I can't sleep. I don't even know how I'm functioning."

"You keeping up with your therapy?" she asked.

"Yes."

"You keeping up with meetings?"

"Yes."

"You right with God?" she asked.

"I don't know how to answer that, Dot. I'm tired and alone and so sad about all that's happening to Mama. No one deserves what she's dealing with."

"Maybe no one deserves what you're dealing with either. Listen up. You know I'm gonna tell you that feeling alone is not a bad thing. It's actually a good thing."

I shook my head in disagreement.

"That's okay. Shake your head. Look at me like you're baffled. But it's true. Being lonely is a natural part of what makes us human. We need to have that place crying out to be filled. You know why?" she asked.

"No, I have nothing," I said.

Dot just smiled at me.

"Child, that's because it's the place in us that only God can fill. It's that place in us that belongs only to our God and it forces us to reach out to our Higher Power to make us whole. Now, I know you got a lot on your plate. You're weary, and I get that. If you weren't weary, I'd be worried about you! But please rest. Rest in the fact that God has your back."

I wasn't hearing it.

"All my life I have taken care of Mama," I said. "My whole damn life. She never told me to take care of things, of course. She never explicitly said, 'You are the caretaker,' but it was understood and necessary. That's the way it's always been. I sometimes feel like I existed to relieve her pain. There has never been a place for me in my family. Never a place for any of my needs. And the needs I do have, I have to push underground because Mama's problems are so overwhelming and always have been. So catastrophic and life-threatening. She eclipses me, okay? Sometimes I feel like I shouldn't even exist."

Gazing out the window, a soft snow fell in my mind and I saw a parade of images float by. Images of me collecting pop bottles to buy food for the family. Images of Mama lying on the floor, half-dead and covered in vomit. Images of Bobby Morano snatching me from the street and shoving his penis down my throat. Images of Donnie in a soiled diaper, wailing in the crib while Mama and Bill sipped Seven and Sevens in the kitchen, oblivious and unreachable. Images of Mama in the hospital bed, me at her side, and a doctor whispering in my ear, "If you have something you need to say to her, you may want to do it now. She may not make it." What would I say to her? I saw myself in Stan's Café, dancing with "Jumbo Jim" and Mama swaying with a drink by the jukebox, winking with approval because enduring all this meant that a burger was on the way and that was somehow good. A worthwhile bargain.

In a trance-like state, I looked up at Dot.

"It is an odd thing," I said, "to feel like you are simultaneously the most important and the least important person in your family. The zenith and the nadir. Is that even possible? To be two extreme opposites at the same time?

And if it's possible, wouldn't a person stretched across the poles of that continuum simply vanish into thin air?"

"Walk with me," Dot said.

Dot led me to the group room. It was around dusk then, just after our shift had ended, and I could see the blood-orange hues of the sun coming through the window. We sat in the folding chairs of an otherwise empty circle.

"Listen up, baby girl," Dot began. "Let me tell you a story." I turned toward her.

"So, there was this dude named Gideon," she said. "And one day he was coming out of where they pressed the wine. Who knows, maybe he was one of us," she said, chuckling, gesturing towards the recovery space around us.

"Anyway, he was walking down the road when the angel of the Lord called out to him and said 'Hail, Gideon, man of valor and might, the Lord is with you.'"

Dot smiled.

"Gideon looked over his shoulder and didn't see anyone. Thought maybe he shouldn't have had that last pull on the wine bag."

We laughed.

"Anyway, he continued on his way. Then the angel of the Lord called out again, 'Hail, Gideon, man of valor and might, the Lord is with you.' He was still confused, so he turned and looked to the sky and said, 'You talking to me?' And the angel of the Lord said again, 'Gideon, man of valor and might, the Lord is with you.' So, Gideon stopped in his tracks and turned to the sky and said, 'Let me ask you something, then. Every year the Midianites come through our village and turn up our crops, burn our fields, and steal our children into slavery. I want to know, if the Lord is with me, what would it be like if the Lord *wasn't* with me?'"

Dot pulled her hand up to her face—her fingernails painted ruby red— to suppress a chuckle.

"Oh, that Gideon," she said. "Now, the angel of the Lord just calmly replied, 'Hail, Gideon. If there is something in your life that is not right, go in your power and make it right.' And Gideon looked to the sky and said, 'But you don't understand. In all my land, my village is the least, and in all my village, my house is the least, and in all my house, I am the least.' You see, Terry, that Gideon suffered from a case of the 'yeah, buts.' Just like us. You need to stop drinking—'yeah, but.' You need to get some more help—'yeah, but.' You need to start this recovery program you never stop talking about— 'yeah, but.' But the voice said again, 'Gideon, man of valor and might. With me at your side, go in your power and make what is wrong right.'"

Recognizing my tears, Dot passed me a tissue and said, "Blow."

I did. It reminded me of Eddie and of the way he tried to protect or console me in my moments of unraveling.

"Go in your power and make what is wrong right. Now do you understand the story?" Dot asked.

"Yes and no. I'm tripped up on the idea of being the least," I said.

"The moral of the story is to go in your power. To acknowledge the power you already have, 'cause God made you and gave it to you. All you have to do is claim it as yours. And share it in a way that brings relief in this world. It's there waiting for you. You just have to walk in that power and make what's wrong right."

Easier said than done, I thought.

I reflected on the story, but I was distracted by how the soft hues of the late-afternoon sun caught the champagne color in Dot's skin. She appeared to be shimmering in the light.

"You with me?" Dot asked.

"Yeah, I think so."

"You remember that day you came into my office, and I was on the phone with that attorney?" she asked.

"I do."

"You remember what that mess was about?"

"Well, yeah," I said with a deep exhale. "That was some deep shit, Dot."

190

"Yeah, well, you were the one bringing the wisdom that day," she said with a reflective distance. "That's how this works. Give and take."

I thought back to that day. I had never seen Dot "undone" like that. At the time, I perceived her in an idealized way, as an international recovery group speaker who sponsored people all over the world. She was the one people sought for help, not the one who needed it.

I remembered her in her office that day, standing at her desk, talking on the phone. She was sporting an iconic Tina Turner wig, shaggy and spiky with a deep honey base and dark roots. It flopped and danced about as Dot spoke in urgent and hushed tones into the phone. Seeing she was in the middle of something, I mouthed, "I'll catch you later," but she waved me into her office anyway and motioned for me to close the door.

I entered the office. Dot scratched down some notes, finished her call, and then sat and turned toward me.

Beads of sweat were visible on her face. She exhaled deeply as she adjusted her wig and reached for my hands.

"Hey, Dot. What's up?" I asked, concerned.

"Oh, child. The Lord is pressing in on me," she said.

"What's going on, Dot?"

"I'll just be straight with you. No point in dancing around or giving you some smoke and mirrors about who I am and who I'm not. I've been on the lam all this time with an outstanding arrest warrant in California. For something I did back when I was still shootin' dope," she said.

"Holy shit," I said, involuntarily. "For real?"

"Yeah, well, I was just now talking to an attorney. We're sorting through how I might turn myself in."

Physically shaking, Dot wrung the palms of her hands as the spiked ends of her wig shimmered. She shuddered in fear.

"Fuck, Dot. You're really gonna do that?"

"I'm thinking on it. Praying on it. I don't know what will happen. They could lock me up. My attorney is looking at statutes of limitation and such. Maybe they'll drop the charge because it's been so long. Maybe not. But I'm thinking about my family—my grandbabies. It's the thought that I am letting them down by not telling the truth and the thought that I'm being a fool if I send myself away from them."

She teared up, lifting a hand to the sky.

"Oh, Lord, what am I gonna do?" she cried.

"Hey. Come on," I said, reaching for her hands. "Listen, you obviously are working this through with your support group. And, if you're having talks with an attorney, you're ready to make amends and restitution."

Dot dropped her head, and the tips of her wig tickled my nose. She cried.

"Listen, I know you're scared. If you weren't afraid, I'd be worried about you," I said, trying to get a laugh out of her by using one of her "lines" myself.

It worked. Dot lifted her head, snot dripping from her nose. I handed her a tissue.

"God has you. I have you. Miss Esther, your mentor, has you. And a whole heap of people from around the world have you, Dot. And I know that somewhere Reverend Toomey's Baptist church has a 24/7 prayer circle praying for you!"

She smiled.

"You know I'm only gonna say the same thing you say to me when I'm being foolish or scared about something that I *think* is unmanageable."

"I know," she said.

"What's the worst that can happen, and can you survive it? You were the one who showed me how change, even change that seems outright awful, actually pushes a person in a new direction. Usually a better one, especially if it's a push towards the *truth,* right?"

"Oh, baby girl, you're bringing the wisdom today," Dot said with a sniffle.

"Well, I have a good teacher."

Reflecting back on that time in Dot's life, on that moment of candor when she shared something so raw and unflattering, I saw then the lesson she was trying to impart with her story of Gideon. Although she had spent years in private terror ("on the lam"), she went in her power that day and made the call to the Sheriff's Office in California to turn herself in to the authorities. She made what was wrong right. And in the end, it all worked out. Dot didn't do jail time. It's as though the universe, in a moment of genuine karmic justice, evaluated what Dot had done since then and allowed that good to eclipse whatever infraction or crime she had committed before.

While Dot showed courage in "going in her power," I was struck even more by her sheer vulnerability, her fear, and how she had allowed me to witness all of it. Just witnessing it changed me—changed us, really. Seeing her not as someone better than me or more than me, but as someone the same as me, deepened our relationship. After that, our interaction was more authentic, more honest, and truly mutual. As with Jack, "lifting the veil" to see the rounded and imperfect version of Dot made me think more rather than less of her.

Now, back in the group therapy room long after that incident, Dot was taking the lead and reminding me of my power and of God's love for me.

"Look, you may not feel worthy of God's love, but guess what? You got it anyway. It's there. Now use it. You know God loved you when you were a low-down thieving and cheating alcoholic drug addict. He loved you then! Now how much more you think He's gonna love you since you cleaned up and know where you took off your underwear last night? Huh? Now that you're educating yourself and building a life for yourself and the people you care about? Now that you're chasing something beautiful? Healing yourself so you can help people other than yourself?"

Taking my hand, Dot continued, "Listen, God is not to be impressed, understand? He loved you then and He loves you now. All you have to do is walk with faith, walk in your power, and in that space of love you're going to make your situation right."

At that stage in my recovery, I had no clear idea where I was with the divine or with ideas of faith and love. I was working hard to get the talons of the

Catholic Church out of my head and heart and I knew my deep sense of unworthiness was tied in some measure to that early indoctrination. I didn't have a strong belief in God; but I did believe in Dot and thought I could make myself believe in her belief.

"I'm here, and you have a good support system around you," she said, "so you're on the right path. But something is demanding your attention, and I don't think it's your Mama anymore. Maybe you're being called to do something higher now. Something outside and beyond yourself. Just like Gideon."

Dot sighed and looked up at the ceiling. I looked, too, and we enjoyed that silence together for a few moments.

"C'mon, now," she said. "Let's pray. Dear Heavenly Father, we come to You today asking for Your blessing and direction for Miss Terry as she seeks, dear Father, Your guidance and wisdom in finding support for this next part of her journey to embrace life and Your love for her. Help her, Father, to walk in her power and accept Your love so that she may walk with strength and dignity into those places in her past that, with Your blessing, will free her to be the woman she is meant to be. Grant her the strength to realize her vision, to lessen the pain of those who are suffering. We ask these things in the name of Your Son, Our Dear Lord and Savior, Jesus Christ. Amen."

"Amen," I said.

14

IF YOU BUILD IT, THEY WILL COME

In 1989, the movie "Field of Dreams" came out. It's about an Iowa farmer, played by Kevin Costner, who hears a voice in his cornfield tell him, "If you build it, he will come." The farmer interprets this message as encouragement to build a baseball diamond on his farm. He believes that if he does, Shoeless Joe Jackson will appear alongside seven other Chicago White Sox players accused of taking bribes to intentionally lose the 1919 World Series. Their reappearance would signify redemption, resolution, and the chance to resume the activity they loved most.

I saw the movie in a local theater, and though I found it somewhat sappy, I was taken by its fundamental message. I had already been contemplating and beginning to develop with Moe the idea of creating a treatment program for women. I found the main character's willingness to listen to his inner voice and follow his dream a message for me as well. The tagline, "If you build it, [they] will come," swirled in my head amidst a hail of reasons why my dream could not become a reality.

As was often the case when I felt torn about a decision, I sought out Dot's wisdom. After my last client left for the day, I poked my head into her office.

"Hey, Dot. Can I get your ear on something?"

"Sure, I've got some time for you. I need a break from these treatment plans, anyway."

"Yeah, so you know about what's happening with this women's program, and I told you about that client of mine, Latika, who needed support beyond 28-day inpatient treatment. I don't know what has happened to her since then, but I can't get her out of my head. I know we should be providing better services for women."

I sighed, catching my breath.

"Anyway, the other night I was coming out of my recovery meeting and I ran into another woman who seemed to be struggling and she really pushed at me. She actually went out of her way to say 'You're Terry Miller. I know you're already doing work with women addicts, but we need more help and you can do something about it. There's no place for women like me to go! And Tom Murphy would help!'" (Tom Murphy was a state representative with an interest in recovery programs at that time).

I continued to tell Dot my thoughts and concerns: the lack of research demonstrating the benefits of trauma-informed, gender-specific treatment; the lack of evidence that long-term programs were of any benefit; the presence of only one long-term co-ed treatment facility in the region; the ridiculously long waiting lists for treatment; the talk at the federal level about increasing drug and alcohol recovery funding and how Pennsylvania could potentially receive millions of dollars for this purpose; and finally, that maybe some of this funding could be used for women's treatment programs like my "moon shot" idea.

"Looky here," Dot said, noticeably impatient. "You've been sitting with this for some time now and not talking about it. And what have I told you about being in your head by yourself? You know that is a dangerous place to be. You have to treat your mind like a bad neighborhood. Never go there alone," she said, laughing.

She continued.

"You know that negative committee is sittin' in that head of yours, at a big long shiny conference table just waitin' to take you down. It would love to see this whole idea of yours drop off the cliff. You know that, right? That low self-esteem is shouting at you, and self-doubt's yippin' in your ear, too. I'm sure all the fears about this new idea and about your Mama's health are sitting at the head of the table, gavel in hand, trying to get a hold of this whole mess. 'All those in favor of sabotaging Terry's dream, say I.'"

I laughed a little.

"Right, girl. Come on now. You know I'm speaking truth. Now, if God gave you one small, positive voice to sit up there with that hostile negative committee, where would she be and what would she be saying? C'mon, now, tell me about her," Dot chided me with a laugh.

196

"This is silly," I said.

"Humor me."

I pushed back in my chair and looked into Dot's eyes.

"Well, she'd probably be sitting somewhere in the middle of the table," I said.

"And who is she?" Dot asked.

"My dreamer. My confidence, I guess. That part of me that feels that anything is possible."

"Go on," Dot said.

"And because she's so small," I said, "she'd probably be sitting on a booster chair."

This time we both laughed loudly.

"Ah, go on, girl," Dot retorted. "Tell me about Miss Booster Chair."

"Knowing her voice isn't very strong, she would probably be holding a megaphone to be heard by the committee," I said.

"What would this child, your dreamer with the megaphone sitting on the booster chair say?" Dot asked.

"She would lift that megaphone to her mouth and say, 'I have everything I need today to move forward and make what is wrong right.' And she would say, 'If we build it, they will come.'"

"Now, there you go," Dot said. "I see you're still keeping that Gideon story in your back pocket. You need to remember that it's not natural for our minds to be on our side. Hard truth, but there it is. The mind will always look to take you down a dark road, so you need to be vigilant and remember what this child in the booster chair is saying. All of her wisdom is yours, and it's always available. And one day very, very soon, she's gonna be gaveling that meeting, taking the place of fear. You hear me?"

"I do, Dot. Thanks. You rock," I said.

"Well, for now, just go about figuring out how to get this program started for these women. I know you have your own struggles going on, but keep on working that through in therapy and through your recovery program. This work to create a new program for women, you being of service in this very special way, will help you move through your past. I promise you."

"If you say so, Dot."

"That professor you're always telling me about? Moe? Didn't he give you a task to get started on some so-and-so analysis?"

"Yeah, a SWOT analysis," I replied.

"Well, get to it. Circle the wagons, baby. I'm on for the ride too. I already talked to our director here, and Turtle Creek Valley is going to write a letter of support for your idea. You build it and they will come. And you know you already got God and me interested, so you're pretty well on your way," she said, laughing.

I took Dot's words to heart and reached out to Moe to discuss the idea with him further and see if I could use my project plan as a field placement opportunity, with him as my advisor. He agreed to support me, and over the course of the next two years, with Moe at my side, I went to work. I was assisted by a team of committed drug and alcohol professionals, women's treatment experts, persons in recovery, attorneys, community leaders, accountants, and respected elected officials. Under my leadership, we launched an effort to conceptualize and establish POWER—the Pennsylvania Organization for Women in Early Recovery, a women-centered, trauma-informed halfway-house program.

Mary, the woman who had approached me that night in November 1989, recommended that we speak with State Representative Murphy as soon as possible. He became a big supporter of our efforts. He provided office space for some of our meetings and offered the support of his office manager, who helped to identify possible sites for the program.

We began the process to incorporate as a 501(c)(3) charitable nonprofit, with the assembled team agreeing to serve as the inaugural board of directors. In short order, we all were working to develop a draft program proposal that would be submitted to the Pennsylvania Office of Drug and Alcohol Programs.

I met twice a week with Moe, and he provided invaluable guidance and direction to our fledgling and very fluid startup operations. In just a few months, some possible sites for the program had been identified and it was time to move the organizational operation into the field.

❇

Tom Murphy's office manager took us to tour possible program sites in Pittsburgh, but none of them—mainly empty warehouses—felt like a good home for POWER.

Then, unexpectedly, we learned from the Catholic Diocese of Pittsburgh that a convent would be up for lease in Swissvale, a small community east of Pittsburgh. We went to visit the convent at St. Anselm's Church, not knowing what to expect. Our appointment was with Sister Joyce, one of the parish nuns and the assistant to Father Cheetham, St. Anselm's pastor.

As soon as I set foot on the church campus, I felt this was going to be our home.

The grounds were beautifully maintained, with a field of ivy growing among a cathedral of trees in the center of the campus. To the right was a small stone patio where I assumed the nuns congregated. The convent featured a porch dressed in red and purple fuchsias and a walkway dotted with white begonias leading up to the arched entryway. Straight ahead was the church, and to the left was the grade school. It was the grade school that gave me the willies. Not because of past ghosts, but because I knew any proposal to locate a drug and alcohol agency on a church campus adjacent to where children went to school would be a hard sell to the community. My archived notes reflect this concern: *What is our message? If we don't define it, the community will define it for us. This must be clearly and thoughtfully considered and, above all, honest.*

The board president and I met Sister Joyce in the rectory behind the church. Unlike any nun I had ever studied with, she was dressed in fashionable clothing and had a head full of beautiful curls that matched her bubbly personality. I remember breathing in and thinking to myself, *This is a good sign.*

Sister Joyce welcomed us, and we chatted for a while about the church's history, the campus, the Sisters of Charity, and how the convent came to be available for lease.

"The convent is a wonderful building, and we would love to hold on to it," she said. "Leasing will allow us to do that for the time being, but we now only have about five of our sisters living in the abbey, and it was built to house 25 of us."

"Where will the sisters go?" I asked.

"We have a smaller house at the end of Church Street that will accommodate them nicely, so we will be moving them there in the coming month," she said.

She inhaled excitedly, collecting herself. Clasping her hands together, she said, "So please tell me about POWER."

We launched into our vision for POWER, explaining our hope to create a safe space where women in recovery from addiction to harmful substances could have time to address their addictions while also healing those things that may have drawn them to those substances and behaviors in the first place. We explained to Sister Joyce how, at that time, there were only six co-ed, long-term treatment beds for women in Southwestern Pennsylvania and only a few dozen in the entire state. We explained our desire to create a women-centered, trauma-informed program that could be a model for other jurisdictions.

"People who suffer with addiction have a medical problem," I said. "When they pick up a drink or some other mind-altering substance, they deviate from a state of health and present with a set of symptoms that are progressive, chronic, and, if not treated, fatal."

Sister Joyce nodded.

"These are not bad people trying to get good, but sick people who are trying to get well. I know, because I am one of them," I continued.

"Go on," she said.

"I made my way to recovery in 1982. I experienced divine intervention of a sort. A power greater than me put my dear friend, Jack, in my path. He showed me, by power of example, that it is possible to go from a deep emotional, mental, and spiritual low to a life of sobriety. I witnessed his sobriety in action, when he was tested in the worst possible way. Just a short while into his recovery, his wife of many years died suddenly. Jack had no time to brace for it and I expected him to crumble. But then I watched him remain sober throughout this ordeal, handling it with grace and dignity."

Sister Joyce smiled.

"Inspired by Jack, I went to Gateway Rehab. I needed every one of those 28 days to get the drugs and alcohol out of my system. In fact, I ended up staying for 31 days. There are many women who need more than 28 days. In my case, I had been using, without interruption, for almost 20 years. Since then, I have been attending support group meetings and counseling to help me through my walk in sobriety."

Sister Joyce listened respectfully.

"Recovery is about cultivating belief. About seeing good things happen to people who are like you—just as compromised, just as strained. But it's also about having access to a place where it's possible for women to witness recovery with others and, with professional support, apply it to their own lives. This communal experience does several things. It gives hope to those who were hopeless, and it lifts people out of isolation, helping them to see they are not alone."

Sister Joyce scribbled down some notes.

"So, you're part of this whole story, then," she said, looking up from her notepad.

"I am. I'm one of these women, Sister Joyce. I dealt with neglect, abuse, hunger, mental illness, and alcoholism throughout my childhood. Those wounds are not mended by short-term fixes, so I needed focused, safe, and inclusive long-term treatment, but it was not available to me. I have been fortunate to continue to make it through, but even today I am dealing with significant abuse issues. Women need their own protected place to heal. The kind of place we hope to establish in a holy place like this."

I gazed out the window and then back at her.

"I just want to say that I have been very blessed to have some very wonderful people around me over the years. People who loved me and believed in me until I was able to love and believe in myself. And I have also had some not-so-kind people in my life," I said. "I want to put something in place that will provide women with what they need to stabilize themselves in recovery by creating a program and support community that will address their emotional, mental, physical, *and* spiritual needs."

"Belief and the space to cultivate it. I understand," Sister Joyce said. "And I appreciate you sharing some of your story, too. Now how about we go and tour the convent? We can visit with Father Cheetham when we're done, and then see where things stand from there."

We crossed the church campus and entered the convent, where we were greeted by several of the Sisters of Charity. They cheerfully welcomed us into their home and joined us for the tour. We started in the community kitchen and dining hall and then we made our way to the third floor to view the bathrooms and individual living rooms. All the rooms on the third floor were empty, but all were modestly furnished, with ample space for a single bed and small dresser. Some had their own sinks. The second floor also had space for offices and a large communal gathering space. Everything looked perfectly suited to match the logistical demands of our proposed program.

We returned to the first floor, where there was a bathroom, more offices, and a chapel. Upon entering the chapel, I went into a pew and knelt down. I felt the power and sacredness of the space, and in my heart, I knew this was the place for our program. While the nuns congregated outside, talking quietly, I prayed that the meeting would go well and that POWER would find a home here.

I returned to the rest of the group standing outside the chapel.

"It's so peaceful here," I said.

"Yes, it is," said Sister Joyce. "We treasure this place. Shall we see if Father Cheetham is ready to meet?"

Sister Joyce took us to the conference room, where Father William Cheetham joined us. I was struck by his gentle manner and kind eyes. Sister Joyce launched the conversation, enthusiastically relaying who we were and what we hoped to do with the convent should he and the church council, diocese, and community agree to host us as tenants. I had the feeling that she was already on our side, but this was purely intuitive; she hadn't tipped her hand yet, which made me respect her all the more. When she had finished summarizing our mission, I chimed in to explain our proposed program design: a gynocentric treatment model for women as opposed to the more traditional, androcentric model used by treatment facilities at that time. Father Cheetham listened attentively, asking questions along the way.

While we talked, I looked at both Father Cheetham and Sister Joyce, trying to read their body language. Despite Sister Joyce's initial enthusiasm over what I had shared during our first conversation, I sensed that I was being a little stilted and overly formal in this next phase of our conversation. In my head I heard a plea: *Just be honest. If you speak with your heart, they will receive it with their hearts.*

I breathed in and exhaled deeply, trying to calm down. I looked across the table at Father Cheetham and went for it.

"Father Cheetham, you have a wonderful campus here, and the convent is an inspiring building. It was an honor to meet some of the sisters who have lived in this space. It's obvious, even to an outsider like me, how much they love it. Talking with them, and I won't speak for Sister Joyce, they seem excited about our proposed idea for a future use of the convent. At the risk of sounding too metaphysical, when we went into the chapel, I felt the collective energy of decades of women living together in this community. These women have lived here with a common purpose to be of service to one another and to the larger community through spiritual devotion and growth. I admire and respect that."

I continued.

"This building is an undeniably holy place. I suppose that all we are asking of you is that you allow us to continue to use it as that—as a sacred place where a woman, any woman with a true and honest desire to live a sober and spiritual life, can come to share their experience, strength, and hope with others who are seeking the same thing. In this way, the legacy and blessings of this place will live on in the women of POWER."

Father Cheetham said nothing.

"To cultivate belief. That's what you said earlier," Sister Joyce said.

"Exactly," I said. "And hope. Realistic hope."

Father Cheetham looked at me, not skeptically, but discerningly.

"Well," he said, adjusting in his seat, "this does seem to be a noble and appropriate use of the sisters' house."

"Thank you," we said. "That's our intention."

"I will take your idea into counsel with Sister Joyce and our church council, and we will be in touch. We are, of course, meeting with others who are proposing alternative uses for the building. I just want you to know that this is not the only option we are considering," he said.

"Understood."

We stood up to leave, and I shook Father Cheetham's hand.

"I want you to know," I said, "that I began this project as a field study to earn my bachelor's degree in social work. My advisor gave me the task of identifying a list of words to help me define my vision for the project. One of the words I listed was 'inspirational,' and when I looked up the root word for inspire, it said…"

"To breathe life into," Father Cheetham said, smiling.

"That is exactly what we hope to do here, Father. To breathe life into the women who will come through our doors, and to honor this space that has inspired spiritual growth in all the women who have already resided here. Even if nothing comes of this request, we want to say thank you for welcoming us here, for giving us the chance to meet all of you."

In the days that followed, Father Cheetham met with his church council and told them about our proposal. Our leadership team was then invited to meet with them and share our vision for POWER. Within a few weeks, after some healthy debate and conversation, the church council agreed to further discussion of the reuse of the convent as a recovery program, this time including community involvement.

At this stage I quickly learned how critical both Sister Joyce and Father Cheetham had been to our efforts; they were officially on board with our proposed project and its aims. Still, I knew it was not going to be an easy request of the Swissvale community. There were a number of hurdles to overcome before we could officially claim the space for POWER.

Early in my community organizing classes, Moe had taught us about NIMBY (not in my backyard) syndrome: the tendency for communities and individuals to endorse humanitarian causes abstractly, but to resist the placement of facilities serving those causes in their own neighborhood. That's why Moe insisted that I work to clarify our message to the community, showing how the presence of our program would actually enhance the community's image and value.

After many discussions with the POWER team, we determined that our message should encompass both addiction and recovery. We would explain that addiction is an *illness*, not a "bad" or "immoral" behavior. We would point out that addiction is an equal-opportunity disease that impacts everyone, directly and indirectly. Virtually everyone can think of at least one person in their web of family and friends who is afflicted and they know that these loved ones are not "bad" people, but individuals who need help. And if our loved ones need help and a chance at recovery, then, I intended to ask, can't we, as the community of Swissvale, agree to offer recovery services to meet the needs of those suffering from addiction? I believed this was a story that any person or community should want to be a part of, and I was hoping the residents of Swissvale would feel the same. Still, even with a well-honed message, I knew I could count on at least a moderate degree of opposition.

In between meetings, our leadership team spent time on the phone with Father Cheetham and corresponded with him and Sister Joyce so they had all the information they needed to discuss our proposal with other community stakeholders. In the course of our conversations, they helped us refine our vision and mission, both of them becoming active advocates for our cause. Like Moe, they pressed us to think about any issues that might put local residents at odds with the idea of welcoming our program into the community. We discussed the particular stigma attached to women with addiction, along with public safety, community input, and parking issues. Father Cheetham was gracious with his time in helping us sort through these matters. I've always considered it the mark of a caring collaborator when he or she can handle the meticulous, unsexy nuances of a project and the more alluring, big-picture concerns with equal tenacity. Father Cheetham was a generous person and proved himself to be an important ally of POWER.

In a wonderful turn of events, after receiving approval from the church council to move forward with exploration of our proposal, Father Cheetham spoke from the pulpit on a Sunday, telling his parishioners about the inspirational meetings he was having with a proposed program called POWER and the opportunity it presented for Swissvale. We couldn't have asked for a better spokesperson than Father Cheetham to welcome us into the community for dialogue.

In the weeks that followed, POWER came together as an organization. Our 501(c)(3) approval came through, and we had our first official board of directors' meeting in keeping with our bylaws and articles of incorporation. Representative Murphy served as an important liaison in Harrisburg. Simultaneously, the board broke into working groups to develop our proposal for funding. Everyone involved with POWER participated in this effort to develop a program overview, evidence of expertise and capabilities, contracts and services to be offered, proposed fee structures, quality assurance and evaluation processes, coordination of services, staffing and governance, management requirements, and finance and budget projections.

To accompany the proposal, we gathered letters of support from a host of highly regarded agencies alongside the local women's center and homeless shelter. Then in summer 1990, we were officially invited to submit a proposal to operate to the State Office of Drug and Alcohol Programs (ODAP). Representative Murphy offered a personal recommendation to the appropriate cabinet member in state government. As we sent the proposal to Harrisburg, I continued to believe that *if we build it, they will come.*

In the meantime, the Swissvale town hall meeting was looming. Our challenge was to educate the community about our proposed program and respond persuasively to any concerns. Our efforts were moving forward in a very positive way, but the outcome of our public meeting with the residents of Swissvale would likely determine our fate.

Moe and I, along with board and committee members, met regularly to flesh out the community outreach strategy. In one of our personal meetings, I advised Moe that the town hall meeting was scheduled, that Father Cheetham would announce the event from his pulpit on Sunday and encourage everyone to attend, and that we expected a good turnout.

"That's good, babe. How does that feel?" Moe asked.

"I'm scared to death," I said. "This is it, you know. I mean, if we don't nail this meeting, it's all over."

"Let's talk strategy, then," Moe said.

"So, our message is about addiction *and* recovery with a heavy focus on recovery," I said.

"Good," he said.

"I have some ideas about that. We also want to put squarely on the table what the community's fears are. We should begin to address them and invite the residents to say what they are, but I think it's important to launch that proactively, rather than getting painted into a corner where we have to be reactive."

"Good idea. Responsive, not reactive," he said.

"In terms of the meeting structure, here is what we have in mind. Father Cheetham opens the meeting with a prayer. Then we have Swissvale Mayor Martoni say a few words about why he believes it is so important to support this effort, so the attendees can hear from their own leader. I'll thank everyone for coming. The board has been invited, of course, and we will have good representation, including the mayor, a few borough council members, and Representatives Ron Cowell and Tom Murphy. Then, we thought it would be great to have Representative Murphy speak about alcohol addiction. He speaks often about how we all know somebody who is living with the illness of addiction. I think his remarks could be powerful," I said.

"Yeah, Murphy's passionate, all right. He'll do a great job," Moe said.

"Then we'll talk about treatment and recovery and explain how there are precious few treatment beds in the state for women. I will discuss how the feds are opening up funding streams to support states in addressing addiction and how Pennsylvania is very open to the idea of gender-specific treatment programs for women. We'll talk about our experience of touring St. Anselm's convent and why we feel it is beautifully suited to house and help women who are seeking to restore their lives. I want to emphasize how our program is in many ways a continuation of the convent's existing mission."

Moe nodded, endorsing the strategy so far. I continued.

"I also reached out to an old friend, Linda S., who went through a co-ed halfway house in Butler County [north of Pittsburgh]. She's been clean for six years now, and I asked if she would come and tell her story and talk about why a long-term facility was so crucial to her recovery. I'm hoping she'll explain what it means to be in recovery—emphasizing the emotional, physical, and spiritual elements of that reclamation. Hearing her personal experience, putting a face on the issue, will drive things home in a concrete way. Then the team thought it would be good to say more about the kind of women that would come to POWER, describing how they would be voluntary admissions—women who are ready and have a desire to reclaim their lives."

"What about larger community issues?" Moe asked.

"Right. We assume parking will be an issue, so we have begun to negotiate parking slots with the owner of the lot in the strip mall across the street. There will be no parking on McClure or Church Streets. The residents will not have vehicles."

"What about safety issues?"

"Yes, that's definitely going to come up. The women will be all voluntary admissions and family visits will be on Sundays with staff supervision. All visitors have to be sober and clean."

"What about convicted clients?" Moe asked.

"Well, this did come up in an earlier meeting. We'll have to see how that goes, but perhaps we can initially offer that none of the clients will be convicted offenders? Maybe that's a place to start. Maybe this can change over time, but it might be viewed as a gesture of good faith to the community."

"Since you are so close to the school and church," he said, "it's the best approach. But you can expect plenty of pushback even with this concession."

"What do you think of the idea of offering a way to get buy-in from the community?" Moe asked. "I'm not certain how that might play out, but on-the-spot participation would go a long way in actually getting your program doors open. And it empowers them too."

Because Moe had one of the best organizing minds ever, our strategy sessions together were invaluable to me. I could not have asked for a better advisor, mentor, and instructor to help me stay grounded and focused on our strategic plan, goals, objectives, and the tasks at hand, especially in the midst of my own personal struggles.

My mother was back in the hospital by this time, facing another surgery. In addition to tending to her, I also was dealing with acute body memories related to past traumatic episodes. Headaches, lightheadedness, and shortness of breath all plagued me. With Dot's support, I pushed through as I prepared for Mama's surgery and the POWER town hall meeting.

About 70 Swissvale residents turned out for the meeting. It was obvious from the start that having Father Cheetham, Mayor Martoni, and Swissvale state representatives present was key to our success. People filed into the school auditorium, chatting with the local officials and one another. I stood next to Father Cheetham, and he introduced me to the locals. There were residents, school board members, church council members, and borough council and zoning board members, all eager to learn about POWER.

The meeting proceeded as designed. Father Cheetham opened the meeting, the mayor spoke, and Representative Murphy gave an impassioned talk on the wide-ranging impact of addiction and how we all are touched by it. I talked about POWER and recovery, and Linda S. told her story. After Linda's remarks, we opened up the meeting for discussion to address any questions and concerns the community might have.

There were several questions about parking and other logistical concerns. One parishioner wanted to know if there were other planned uses for the building. Father Cheetham explained that the only other entity expressing interest in the convent was an insurance company. No one seemed particularly animated about the notion of an insurance company inhabiting the convent, despite its relative innocuousness.

I decided to chime in at that point, recalling the first conversation I'd had with Sister Joyce.

"Although the decision for the use of St. Anselm's convent ultimately rests with the church and the residents of Swissvale, our hope is that you will seriously consider our request to continue to use the building for its intended purpose—to house women who, like the Sisters of Charity, are on a spiritual journey."

The energy in the room seemed overwhelmingly positive and welcoming. Then, almost on cue, a resident asked about convicted felons being admitted to POWER and how we would keep the community safe. "There are children nearby," she said.

"We really appreciate your question," I said, "because it is something that we have reflected on a good deal. Let's be honest. Although we are well-intentioned and want to create something transformative here in your community—in your backyard—you don't know us. But you do know Father Cheetham and you do know Mayor Martoni and Representative Cowell. We would not be here this evening with all of you if *they* didn't believe this is an important and worthy cause that will not be a risk to the community. Understanding that this particular issue would be a concern of the community, we can place a moratorium on admitting women who are convicted of drug-related crimes. We also could create a community advisory board as a way to keep communication open between our program and the community. If any of you here tonight would like to serve on the board, you are welcome to sign up tonight before you leave."

I scribbled headings on a sheet of paper and placed it next to a pen at the table in the front of the room.

A few zoning questions followed regarding an existing moratorium on the creation of new human service programs in Swissvale. Members of the zoning board answered the questions honestly, noting that this was an ongoing dialogue and that residents were invited to participate in any upcoming zoning board meetings.

Glancing around the room, I asked if there were any more questions. People spoke to one another in low voices, but nobody raised a hand. Just as I was getting ready to thank the group and adjourn the meeting, a woman named Louanne, who I later learned was a member of the local school board, stood up and said in an authoritative and booming voice, "I have something I want to say."

I acknowledged her with a welcoming smile, but I had a sinking feeling in my stomach, something bordering on dread—a momentary belief that maybe, in an instant, this whole thing would unravel.

Louanne rose and looked at those of us in the front of the room.

"We should thank Terry and the others for coming here to tell us about POWER," she started. Looking around at her neighbors, she continued, "I've listened to all of the speakers and to the good questions that I knew we would ask."

People shook their heads affirmatively.

"What I want to say is that I think that Swissvale has a unique opportunity here. Every week we come to church and we listen to messages of fellowship and service and what it means to be a good, faith-abiding person—a good mother, father, daughter, or son. We hear about how God loves us, sins and all, just the way we are, and that we should love one another.

"I think we, as citizens of Swissvale, are being given a chance to demonstrate that we don't just talk about loving our neighbors here. We can actually *show that love* by supporting a program like this. Maybe if we do this, we can be an example for other communities to follow suit. We all know someone who has a problem. We have an opportunity to do the right thing here. I for one am going to sign up to be on the community advisory board," she concluded, "because I want to be a part of this process."

Some people nodded affirmatively, so I decided to respond.

"Thank you, Louanne, for your powerful words and for your willingness to serve both POWER and the community on the committee. There is a great deal of work to do, and for this project to thrive, we need ongoing input from the community."

I handed Louanne the community advisory board sign up sheet and then continued, "None of us here tonight can say how all of this will turn out. I can only tell you that we will be respectful, responsible, and good neighbors, and that we will move forward with you, showing respect and reverence for what this facility has symbolized in the past and for what it promises to become while we are here. Thank you all for your time and your questions. I could not think of a better place for POWER to call home."

We wrapped up the meeting by inviting attendees to sign up for the community committee, and by announcing the date of the first zoning board meeting to discuss POWER.

"We hope to see some of you there," I said.

Recovery literature refers to times in our lives when we "stand at a turning point." When I reflect on these early months of POWER's startup, I see them as turning points for me and for the project itself. Personally, and through my work establishing POWER, I was changing for the better—noticeably healing. In those early months, with Moe's support, I was stepping up as a leader for the first time in my life, inhabiting the role with a fledgling confidence I had never experienced before. Moe was one of the few people who had believed in me until I was able to believe in myself. Even when my role felt foreign to me, I managed to embrace it in the moments that counted.

In the months that followed, events surrounding the establishment of POWER moved forward, though haltingly, in a positive manner. The success of the town hall meeting and the establishment of the community committee went a long way to create goodwill in the community. St. Anselm's church council and the Catholic Diocese approved the use of their convent to house POWER. Residents signed up to be on the community committee. Many showed up at zoning board meetings, and the zoning board lifted the moratorium on new social service agencies in Swissvale. The residents made that happen through their enthusiasm and belief in our mission, allowing us to repurpose the convent. The POWER board continued to refine treatment protocols, address funding issues, and discuss staffing needs, all while we awaited news about the status of our proposal to establish the facility.

In the meantime, I sought out Dot for advice.

"Don't forget," she said. "There's a difference between 'fake it till you make it' and 'acting as if.' If you fake it, you may not make it. 'Acting as if' means stepping out on faith and trusting that if you do the footwork, it will all come into being. That's something different. That's the real deal."

"We have to start making renovations on the building if we want to get the doors open before the end of the year," I said. "And we don't have a hint yet from ODAP whether our program is going to get approval. So now what?"

"You know what to do," Dot said. "Go and talk to Moe and see what he has up his sleeve. He's got your back on this."

"Yeah, I have a meeting with him later today."

"Then keep breathing, baby. You got this. God did not bring you this far, out of all that pain and nonsense, just to drop out on you now. Keep that in your pocket, with Gideon."

As expected, Moe did have a plan. We had to do the legwork, of course, but we were able to negotiate a line of credit with the county, to be repaid when the state contract came through. I wasn't sure whether this was a wise assumption or an exercise in blind faith. Either way, the county line of credit would help us pay workers to upgrade and renovate the convent. We also accessed a county program called Allegheny Works, where tradesmen served as mentors to ex-offenders or the unemployed and gave them hands-on experience in the trades they were learning. We were able to use the Allegheny County line of credit to support these workers and trainees. It was inspiring to see that even the renovation and early stages of POWER incorporated and embraced the overall mission of the organization.

Moe's steadfast guidance and support as POWER came to fruition cannot be overstated. Far more than just an advisor, Moe was becoming a close friend. He understood my passion for the project, including its relationship to my own personal struggles, and he never doubted that I could attain my goals. Even so, I could only tell him so much.

15.

INSIDIOUS

I continued to heed Dot's advice to step out on faith as we neared the opening of POWER. We now had a loan that needed to be repaid. We were purchasing furniture to fill the house. Staff were being interviewed and hired. Meetings were underway with the community committee. And as of early July 1991, we still had no financial commitment from the state Office of Drug and Alcohol Programs.

Dot was proud, because I was certainly "acting as if" by this point.

Through late 1990 and early 1991, I was emotionally and physically decompensating. The POWER startup was in full swing, Mama was hospitalized several more times, and I was still working part-time for the children's program at Turtle Creek Valley, while also working towards my graduate degree. Though all these demands created enough stress to cause my fatigue, I was also holding an unspeakable secret that caused me great fear, dread, and shame.

Asking for help didn't come naturally to me, but I had been sober long enough to know that I was backsliding because of this secret, and I needed to speak honestly, specifically to Dot.

Knocking on her office door, I asked, "Hey, Dot, can we grab some lunch today?"

"Sure, baby girl. Let me sign off on these treatment plans, and we can go."

I nodded and stood there sheepishly as she wrapped up her paperwork and gathered her bag and keys. Locking the door behind her, we headed out and down Carson Street to Cupka's, a local spot with spicy wings that Dot loved.

We found a place to sit and I looked on as Dot pulled her bottle of triple-hot hot sauce from her purse.

"My Mama's," she said.

She soaked the chicken wing in the sauce, delicately loosened the meat from the bone, and then went to town eating. I wished I could do the same.

"You gonna tell me what's eating at you, child?" she asked, pouring more hot sauce onto one of her chicken wings.

"I'm a mess, Dot."

"You've been a mess for a while, girl. A lot on your plate for sure with your Mama and POWER, plus school 'n all. But we've been talking about all this, so I'm guessing there's something else on your heart that you're not talking about."

"Yeah," I said, sucking in a deep breath.

Rubbing my hands together, I tried to muster the strength to tell her what was on my mind.

Dot dipped some fries into a vat of Heinz 57.

"Come on, girl. Invite your Higher Power into this conversation and just spill it. I got you, and so does He."

I visibly began to shake and stammered, "I'm so embarrassed, Dot. And scared. I feel like I'm going crazy. You know I had been seeing that therapist for a while?"

"Yes, I do, but you quit that therapy a while back now, right? I seem to recall you were doing some good work around your childhood issues. So, why'd you quit?"

"My therapist got inappropriate with me!" I blurted out in a stifled breath.

This got Dot's attention. Looking up from her food, she dropped her wings into the basket, licked her teeth, and wiped her red-stained fingers on a napkin.

"What?" she exclaimed, shaking her head.

"I didn't really *quit* therapy. My therapy was stopped," I said, trembling.

"All right now. Just keep talking."

"I was in the middle of working on some memory around my father.

I couldn't get my breath, my body hurt, and my mind was fuzzy. Like how I feel right now," I said, feeling that I was about to pass out.

"You're doing a good job, Terry. Keep going."

"She called me one day and said she had a 9 p.m. cancellation and that I needed to come in to see her. I was so out of it, Dot. I went."

"Right," Dot said, drawing out the word, adopting a steely look.

"She kept insisting that I looked like I needed a hug. That she could see I was in pain. She insisted again that I needed a hug, but that I needed to ask for it. She said she wanted to take care of me, but that I needed to ask for it. I just sat there, frozen, weeping on her couch. The next thing I remember, she was sitting beside me, stroking my hair, saying I had asked for it and that was a good thing. I was dizzy and felt like I was about to faint. My stomach heaved, and I had difficulty breathing. I just wanted to flee, to get out of there. But I was frozen and couldn't think straight, let alone drive. She insisted on taking me home. I got in her car, and she took me to her house instead."

My head hung low, and a dizzying swirl of snow blew through it.

"I'm so confused and embarrassed, Dot. I wanted to believe her. I was too weak to refuse her advances. After all I shared with her, she acted just like every other predator in my past, but it was even more insidious. She terminated my treatment, but insisted that if anyone asked, I should say I quit. I have been saying that. I don't know why. I feel so stupid."

"Oh, baby," Dot said caringly. "First of all, lift up your head. You didn't do anything wrong. Second, I'm gonna ask you a question and I want you to be honest with me, you hear?"

"I feel really sick, Dot. I think I'm gonna throw up."

"I see that. Your color's all drained from you. But that's just because you're getting rid of that secret now. It's all out now. But I want you to lift your head and look at me."

I lifted my head, but I could not look into Dot's eyes.

"Now, be straight with me. Did this woman put her hands on you?"

I felt a tight band cinch around my chest. Breathlessly and faintly, I winced while saying, "Yes, but I let it happen."

"Oh, baby girl. May I hold your hands?" she asked.

Somehow, I managed to relay to Dot what the last year of my life had been like, coming to feel that what was happening with my former therapist was inappropriate and wrong and trying desperately to push her out of my life. I had felt confused by her professions of love toward me and confounded by my going along with it, even while her advances made me physically sick, disembodied, and disconnected from my thoughts, feelings, and memories. She was a constant, malignant fixture in my life that I couldn't seem to shake.

Though I couldn't articulate it, my former therapist seemed to sense my pulling away. Redoubling her efforts to maintain my silence about what had happened between us, she forced her way, uninvited, into every area of my life. Though I was going through the motions and maintaining appearances, I no longer had a real sense of who I was. I had lost my essence. I had lost myself—much as I had felt throughout my childhood and addiction.

Dot held my hands, her thumbs rubbing the tops of them.

"Oh, child, I'm so, so sorry," she said.

It soothed me to see her strong hands holding mine, bringing me fully into the present moment.

"Okay, a couple of things," she began. "I know that she is still embedded in your life in many ways, and I'm not sure that we can do anything about that right now. What you *can* do is focus on getting yourself some help. Let me say something again, Terry, in case it isn't clicking yet. You did not do anything wrong. That woman is a predatory therapist, which is one of the worst betrayals a person can endure. Taking advantage of you when you were in a vulnerable state like that. It makes me sick to my stomach," she confessed. "If it's all right with you, I'd like to make a call down to the rape crisis center to see if they can get you into treatment there. You will need to talk with someone. Today. Do you think you can do that?" she asked.

I nodded.

"I knew you were carrying a heavy burden, but I had no idea it was this, of course. Just like our clients, you know that the healing begins when we first name it, then follow up with action. Right?"

"I do know that," I said, wiping my nose on my sleeve. "And it's been so hard to reconcile that while I'm helping others with their own struggles, I'm dealing with this insanity in my own life. I hate it. I feel so ashamed and it makes me feel like a fraud."

"Oh, Terry. It took a lot of courage to open up about this. You've done the most difficult piece now. No matter what your relationship turned into with that woman, *you need to remember that you did not ask for it and you did not do anything wrong!*" she stressed. "You needed to do the very thing that we counsel our clients about all the time—ask for help. The hard part's done. So, let's get back to the office and we'll make that call to get the ball rolling. You can stay with me while I do that, and they may even have someone you can see right away."

"Thanks, Dot. God, I'm a mess," I said, crying and searching for a tissue.

Dot put a napkin in my hand and said, "Blow. You'll be okay, baby."

She reassured me as she put her hand in mine to make the walk back to the office.

"We got this," she said.

As we entered the office, Dot instructed our secretary, "Reschedule my next appointment."

We closed her office door and she put the call on speaker. She requested to speak with a rape crisis specialist named Robin. After hearing my situation, Robin recommended a trauma specialist who had some specific expertise in working with trauma survivors, but also with cult survivors. Considering how the therapist had seemed to groom and exploit my vulnerabilities, Robin felt this would be the best way for me to proceed, and she offered to make a call to Dr. Marijke van Linden to see if she could get me in as soon as possible.

It was incredibly difficult to ask for help, especially at that time, while everything was progressing so positively with POWER. Dot was quick to remind me that regardless of the good news in one quadrant of my life, I was subjecting myself to prolonged emotional and physical abuse and getting worse with each passing day.

"The difference now, Terry," she assured me, "is that because this secret is in the light of day, you will get better."

Dot moved mountains to get me the help I needed while simultaneously guiding me in completing what was, for me, a landmark and life-defining project—the establishment of POWER. With Dot and my recovery support group at my side, I began the very long and slow process of healing in my work with Dr. van Linden.

For more than six months, I met with Dr. van Linden several times a week. Through it all, I somehow managed to stay on top of everything else in my life.

In truth, it was difficult. Not only because I was working to recapture and process the experiences of traumas, but because the present-day trauma was undeniably linked to the abuses in my past. They had left me feeling exploited, ashamed, isolated, empty, angry, depressed, and cognitively impaired. There were times when I felt I was truly losing my mind.

In time, I came to believe that Dr. van Linden was genuinely invested in my well-being, and, of course, Dot was a constant and anchoring presence in my life.

At the time, I wasn't able to tell those working on POWER what was going on in my life, and unfortunately that included Moe. I compartmentalized my life out of necessity and I feigned composure to make sure the project advanced. Although there were many days when I wanted to confide in Moe and others, I couldn't. This matter was too far out in left field, and I had to accept that some struggles had to remain within a tight and trusted support network.

Finally, in fall 1991, after months of hand-wringing, some relief arrived. We learned that the State Office of Drug and Alcohol Programs was going to fund POWER. It was no longer a leap of faith or an "acting as if" scenario. It was, as Dot liked to say, "the real deal."

It was such a bittersweet moment for me. On one hand, I was over the moon that all our conceptualizing, proposing, conversing, deliberating, petitioning, and organizing (not to mention the physical work of renovating the convent itself) had paid off. At the same time, in the eight months leading up to this moment, I continued to receive outpatient treatment for the abuse and trauma I had endured, and I also continued to care for Mama, whose physical and mental health was increasingly deteriorating. The bitter irony was not lost on me—that no one more desperately needed the holistic, wraparound, recovery services that POWER offered than I did.

My work with Dr. van Linden continued, and though I struggled with dissociative episodes, body memories, depression, and toxic shame that dragged me down into moments of immense self-loathing, I somehow pushed forward by leaning on my support network and every Zen-, Buddhist-, Taoist-, recovery-, and Dot-derived maxim I could collect: *Act as if, go beyond the beyond, emptiness is the path upon which the enlightened person travels, one day at a time (sometimes one hour at a time), breathe, to thine own self be true,* and on and on. At the time, they were not cheap platitudes or tea-bag mantras, but essential touchstones keeping me afloat.

On November 7, 1991, the doors of POWER finally opened, and, the next day, a woman named Harriett arrived as POWER's first client. I recall the staff's excitement as everyone fussed all around her. After completing her intake form, she was fed a meal (the first one ever served there) and given a tour of the facility. And because she was our first client, we allowed her to select her own room.

The opening of POWER, 1991

On that first day as POWER's first executive director, I sat in my office and looked out at the scene. Harriett, a heroin addict, was a wisp of a thing, weighing in at 102 pounds. Our staff members carried her bag to her room, reviewed house policies with her, and offered her some fresh-baked blueberry muffins. At one point, Harriett, surveying the facility in her scruffy jeans and bleached blonde hair, turned and looked into my office. She sensed that I had something to do with the place and she mouthed the words "thank you." I will never forget that moment. In my mind I was looking at Phyllis from Gateway, at Latika, and—in light of everything I was dealing with at that time—at myself.

Me giving remarks at the opening of POWER

Tom Murphy, then state representative and former mayor, City of Pittsburgh, making remarks at POWER opening, 1991

Still, although I had realized my vision and reached the apparent finish line, this was not the conclusion of a "happily ever after" story. By the time POWER's doors opened, I was plain exhausted. Through my work with Dr. van Linden—and in consultation with legal counsel—I determined to file a complaint against my former therapist. Upon receiving the news, she immediately ceased all communication and engagement with me. I could finally breathe a sigh of relief.

At the insistence of the board, especially members who said, "This was your dream, your vision, so of course you've got to be the executive director," I reluctantly continued in that role, but only for ten months. During that time, I continued my intrapersonal work, delving deeper into blurred and distorted memories of the therapeutic abuse, experiencing flashbacks with crystalline clarity while other twisted recollections from much further in my past drove through to the forefront.

It was evident to both Dot and Dr. van Linden that I was physically and emotionally withering. I knew it, too, and I also knew that if I did not step down from my position, I would destroy what I had spent the last two years of my life helping to create. With deep regret, in August 1992, I resigned my post as executive director and took a position on POWER's board of directors.

Though I was an active board member for some time, when I go back and look at meeting minutes from those early years, I have almost no real recollection of my time on the board. My reduced role was necessary, as I was mentally and physically compromised. I was completing my master's degree in social work at that time and, even when I look at the papers that I wrote back then, I have only a fuzzy recollection of the classes, instructors, and the work completed. What I remember is that I adopted a "one day at a time" approach to earning my graduate degree, an approach I was daily learning to master. My resilience did ultimately pay off, though; it afforded me a new opportunity.

When I told Moe that I needed to step down as POWER's executive director, he did not press me to stay, because even he could see I wasn't doing well. I figured that at best he would offer me some kind words: standard fare.

"My mother's back in the hospital, Moe. With Lord knows what this time. The doctors are still trying to figure it out. I'm trying to keep up with everything, but I'm so worn out."

I still couldn't bring myself to tell Moe about my work with Dr. van Linden and what had prompted it.

Moe sympathized with me for about 15 seconds.

"Ah, it's going to be okay, babe. You'll be okay."

It was obvious that he was mentally scrambling to offer some deeper consolation or encouragement.

"Hey. Hey! Here's an idea! Why don't you come and work with me at the Institute until we figure out what's next for you?"

The University of Pittsburgh's Institute of Politics was a new entity, one Moe had founded on his own principles of community organizing and "finding common ground."

After sharing his offer, Moe was beaming, excited about this spontaneous idea.

In truth, he couldn't have made a kinder or timelier offer. I needed time to heal from everything imaginable, especially as fragments of my life were resurfacing in bits and pieces, adding more complication to my healing process. But working with Moe, whom I had come to admire and who I believed understood, in some measure, the complexities of what I was dealing with, was an inspiring opportunity, however compromised I felt. Moe was my teacher, my mentor— and he had become my friend, too.

I said yes to his offer and never looked back.

The early years of my time at the University of Pittsburgh Institute of Politics are a fuzzy time for me. My mother's health continued to fail, and on top of that, Dot had been diagnosed with cancer.

A devout Christian woman, Dot opted to forgo traditional medicine, instead heading to Chicago for treatment at a faith-based facility. I stayed in touch with her throughout her time there, but in the end, she wound up coming home to Pittsburgh to wrap up her affairs. Reverend Toomey and the fellowship of the Second Baptist Church in Homestead held a 24/7 vigil over Dot, lifting her up to the Lord.

I visited her for the last time on May 25, 1993. She was resting as comfortably as possible in her bed at South Side Hospital, where a circle of church women stood hand in hand, heads bowed, praying, "Good Lord, relieve Sister Dot from her anguish and lift her up out of this bed of sickness."

I acknowledged the women when I entered Dot's room.

"Do you want to pray with us, sister? To intercede with the Lord on Sister Dot's behalf?" one asked.

"Hallelujah," the others chanted with their heads bowed and hands to the sky.

"I'm just paying my respects," I said.

I pulled up a chair and sat at the side of Dot's bed, holding her hand, gazing into her eyes.

The sisters prayed and chanted while the machines attached to Dot beeped and hissed in the background.

"Hey, Dot," I said, squeezing her hand. "So, you know I still have that negative committee running wild in my head, but that little one, the positive voice, is sitting on the booster chair with the megaphone. She's still there, thanks to you. But I've got to tell you something, Dot. I've got you sitting at that table alongside that little one, too. I'm gonna keep leaning on your wisdom 'til I get my own. Thank you for loving me. For teaching me. For just putting up with me."

I lowered my face into a tissue.

"Thank you for guiding me. For all the gifts you've shared with me. I will find my way in this life because you got me on good spiritual footing, so I know I'll be all right, like Gideon."

"It's time for you to go. I know that. And it's okay for you to rise up. You can't keep God waiting for so long, right? I don't know much, Dot. I only know that I didn't want you to leave here before I had the chance to thank you and say goodbye. You are one of the angels. One of the real ones. The real deal, right?"

As I looked into Dot's calm and peaceful face, the faintest of smiles came upon her lips as I said goodbye. I needed to believe that she heard me. I believe she did.

Dot's sisters in faith continued their vigil, appealing to the Good Lord to raise her up and heal her of this illness. Sighing deeply, I lifted Dot's hand to my mouth and kissed it.

"Goodbye, my dear friend."

I left her room for Mama's, just a floor above.

Dot passed quietly on May 26, 1993.

16.

MAMA'S BIRTHDAY SURPRISE

From her wheelchair, parked at the top of Lane 52 at Mt. Lebanon Bowling Lanes, Mama turned her head in the direction of the obnoxious man in Lane 51 who was belly-aching, loud and clear.

Clapping his hands and spinning around in the air after each ill-fated toss, he declared in his booming voice, "Oh my God, I can't hit a pin to save my life!" Relishing the attention he drew from others in the lanes around him, he laughed into the air.

Mama squinted intently in his direction. Years of laser surgeries, cataract removals, and corneal surgeries had left her legally blind. She tried hard to focus on him but couldn't get a clear read.

He was a big, barrel-chested man with thick dark hair and a large nose. It appeared that his voice sounded familiar to her. She strained to look in his direction each time he bellowed his litany of complaints; maybe she was just outright annoyed with him.

Again, she lowered her head to her hand—half tired, half contemplative. This was a familiar posture for Mama in her wheelchair: head propped up on her fist, lost in deep thought like Rodin's "The Thinker." I often wondered what was going through her head, but I seldom asked. Perhaps I didn't really want to know. By that point in our relationship, I had come to accept that whole dimensions of her life were gated off from me.

Mama returned to her own game.

As I looked on from the back of the bowling alley, I recalled how just a couple years earlier, she had mentioned that she hadn't bowled since she was a teenager. She had vehemently resisted getting into her first wheelchair, but following her third amputation, she conceded. In no time at all, she was out and about again, doing things she never imagined she could. After many surgeries and amputations, she accepted her disabilities as completely as one can, and when she did, her whole life opened up.

Once she fully committed to her wheelchair, she became an advocate for the disabled. She helped to organize protests when Pittsburgh's transit system determined that it was going to cut services for people with disabilities. She established a "Square Wheelers" dance group. She custom-designed and assembled portable pocket hangers to attach to wheelchairs, so that people could have their hands free to get around and still carry their personal belongings with them. Lastly, she took up bowling in a league for folks with disabilities.

"I didn't realize how much I missed the lanes," she told me after joining the league. "It has something to do with the scents."

Mama laughed at herself.

"The smell of Aqua Velva, cigarettes, half-eaten cheeseburgers, stale beer, sweaty polyester, the aroma of hundreds of feet placed in shoes worn by thousands of other people. I don't know," she laughed. "You can't beat it!"

I chuckled as I recalled her words, shifting my eyes to the seating area around Lane 52.

"Come on, Marie, you're up next," her friends called.

Mama wheeled herself over to the lane, put her hand over the gust of compressed air, pulled a ball out of the gate, focused hard on the head pin, then let her ball fly. The ball made its way down the center of the lane, taking out nine of the ten soldiers standing at the end of it.

"Yeah, Marie. Let's go! Get that spare," her teammates screamed.

"Not bad for an old lady, huh?" she quipped, laughing.

Her teammates were jiving in their wheelchairs and high-fiving one another. Their raucousness was infectious, a beautiful spectacle for bystanders. From adjacent lanes, people lifted their heads from seemingly grim business to watch the jubilant old women celebrate a good throw.

"Yeah, you old lady. How old are you today, anyway?" one of her friends asked.

"I've spent my life keeping folks guessing," she said, "and I'm not about to change that for you."

Mama wheeled herself back to the gate and waited for her preferred ball, one with a pink stripe and a glitter pattern embedded within it. The glitter made me think of Dot, my perennially luminous friend and mentor who had helped me out of my own mire. She had helped me retain the strength to take care of Mama and start POWER. Dot wasn't there with us, but she seemed to appear in this subtle feature of the bowling ball; the glitter, to me, was her little celestial nod.

Balancing the ball on her lap, Mama wheeled herself to the top of the lane. She focused hard, licked her lips, squinted again, reeled her arm back, and let the ball go with a thud, willing it down the long and shiny lane. It moved with painstaking sluggishness as it tightroped its way along the edge of the gutter. We all tried to will it to stay in the lane, ascribing great importance to the outcome: a spare in a dank bowling alley, thrown by a woman who had suffered so much and who insisted on living while she still could.

I needed her to get that spare.

Everyone in the lanes around us yelled "Go! Go! Go!" as though the air from their booming voices would move the ball along faster, or keep it balanced.

The obnoxious man in the next lane joined in on the "Go! Go! Go!" too, yelling with excitement.

Mama glanced at him briefly while he cheered, but returned her attention to the ball. Just as it was about to tip into the gutter at the end of the lane, it brushed against the ten pin—ever so slightly—and pushed it over.

"Woohoo! A spare!" her friends cried.

"Yeah, baby, we'll take it. Way to go, Marie!" her friend Becky squealed.

Standing in the back of the bowling alley, I watched as Mama laughed and celebrated with her friends. Their wheelchairs were configured in a half circle, so they did a seated version of "the wave." Folks in the lanes next to them automatically joined in, and before I knew it, all the way down the lanes, people were clapping and doing the wave. Up and down along the bowling alley, people were giggling, saluting Mama with drinks held high in the air—

just having a good time. It was one of those spontaneous moments in which everybody was magically and willingly in tune.

I watched from the back of the bowling alley, smiling and drinking in the scene. Mama still didn't know I was there.

She was laughing so hard that she had to stop and brace her upper chest. I don't think I ever saw her laugh like that—not without some drink in her, but she hadn't had one in a long time. She had stopped drinking, improbably, after the second amputation.

I stayed there in the back, watching her heaving laughter, witnessing a moment that was just for her and her friends, happy that she was happy.

Years of sickness, hospitalization, surgeries, amputations, and rehabilitations can make a person downright bitter. Mama had experienced all this and so much more. She had every right to be a miserable and embittered person, but she worked hard not to show it. If she was bitter, she drove it inside, shelving it deep within herself. Outwardly, it showed itself as depression. Besides the prospect of death, which had hung over us for many years, Mama's depression ran deep through both of us.

I'd spent my whole life at Mama's side, caring for her with no steady support from my family. Whatever happened between Mama and her family must have been so horrible. Horrible enough that when my Grandma knew my mother was at death's door, she did not come to see her. Perhaps my aunt and uncle were shielding her from this hardship. She was quite elderly by this time. But to me, because no one in the family discussed things with me, it felt like more of the loneliness I had experienced as a child. My Aunt Jean would sometimes bring Grandma to see my mother at the hospital, but there didn't seem to be any love in it. I sensed that her appearances were obligatory in nature, and Mama knew it too. The visits only made her feel worse, and I was left trying to help heal her spirit as well as her body in their wake.

Her depression became my depression.

But somehow Mama and I pushed through. In the face of despair and the constant presence of death, I watched Mama reach through her pain, her fear, and her brokenness into what I see now as her own spiritual potential. Bankrupt in every other area of her life, she dove into her spiritual core and rose up with a delicate, growing sense of hope. I don't know how she did it. It was not always this way, certainly not in the early years of our walk with death, but ironically, as the end was upon us, Mama tapped into that spirit and surrendered to it, boldly choosing to lean into life in her own twilight.

After one of her open-heart surgeries, I remember asking her how she kept on.

"I put the hand of my courage in the hand of my fear, and I take a step," she said.

I recall how much *I* needed to hear that, because my own heart and spirit were weary and angry, having spent my life watching someone I loved being cut on, cut up, cut off, and carted away from me.

Her strength eventually became my strength.

On her 65th birthday, I stood in the shadows in the back of Mt. Lebanon Lanes and watched with a sense of delight as Mama's spare caused the whole place to erupt in gaiety. With Donna Summer's "Bad Girls" blaring in the background, everyone was laughing and high-fiving, and the women around Lane 52 were swirling in their wheelchairs. Mama was happy in a pure, unmannered way I had never seen before. I thought her dentures were going to fly out of her mouth; she was laughing that hard. She always worried about that, actually, and she typically covered her mouth when she laughed to avoid the potential embarrassment. But not today.

This was her moment, and she was celebrating herself, laughing boisterously with her dentures in full view.

You go, girl, I thought. *Good for you!*

Still, I was choked up. I felt, with some certainty, that it would be her last birthday. Within a few months I would know that I was right.

Looking on at the scene of Mama and her friends, engrossed in the simple joys of being alive, I was overwhelmed with a sense of grace. There was something childlike, innocent, and beautiful about what I was witnessing in them. The way their lightheartedness affected everyone in that remote little bowling alley bordered on divine. It was a delicious feeling, and I ate it up.

"Not bad for an old blind lady," one of Mama's friends jived.

"I'll show you how blind I am! I'll come over there and hit you with my cane, you old bat," she joked back.

The laughing continued as everyone made way for the next bowler.

Mama returned to her position just to the left of the lane. The man in Lane 51 looked in her direction. Then, with a shrug, he turned to throw another ball down the lane in his own alley.

My younger brother Donnie, his wife Margie, and their son Donnie Jr., as well as a friend, Michelle, were all there with me, lurking around in the back of the bowling alley, lying in wait to surprise her.

"Does she know yet?" they asked.

"No, not yet," I said, "but what a scene it's been around here."

The man in Lane 51 flung another ball down toward the pins. This time it was a winner. A strike.

"Woohoo," he yelled, as he looked back over Mama's head, in my direction.

Laughing, he cried out, "Hey, hey. Look at me. A strike. Am I good or what?"

Mama now appeared very annoyed with him. She may have been legally blind, but she had a cold and confused look on her face. I'm sure that others around the alley were finding the man's celebrations tactless too.

Looking in his direction, Mama tilted her head back, raised her left pointer finger to the corner of her left eye and pulled it back. This helped her to focus better. She gazed at him as he danced about. She looked puzzled and exasperated by his antics.

With a deep sigh, she returned her head to rest on her fist and watched as her teammates played on.

The man in Lane 51 spun another ball out of his large hand—another strike. Jubilant, he laughed and danced around in self-satisfaction.

Looking again in Mama's direction, he yelled over her head, "Did you see that, girl? Two in a row now!"

This time, Mama craned her neck in the direction of the man. Squinting hard, she tried to get a read on him. Slowly, she began to wheel herself in his direction.

"It's time," I said, to Donnie and the others.

Quietly and slowly, we all made our way out of the darkness of the back of the bowling alley and moved toward Mama's bowling league. Kitty, one of the organizers of the Competitors bowling team, turned and looked in my direction. She knew me from my participation with the group at bowling tournaments and annual holiday parties.

Kitty is a great woman. A lifetime Pittsburgher, she has one of the thickest Pittsburgh accents I have ever heard. She spied me as I made my way from the back of the bowling alley, and just as she was ready to give us a big, unabashed "Hey, Ter, how yinz doin'?" I raised my finger to my lips, clenched my teeth, and shook my head *NO!!!*

Inside my head I was screaming, *Kitty, for God's sake, please, no, don't say a word.* Grimacing, I continued to shake my head, quietly shushing her with my finger to my lips, begging her to remain silent.

It seemed like an eternity. She looked shocked and a little pissed off. Scrunching her face and rearing her head back, she looked in Mama's direction. I continued my mime-like plead for silence.

Hand in hand, Donnie, the others, and I walked toward Mama. Finally, when I was within several feet of Mama's back, the loud, burly man in Lane 51 turned in her direction and boasted again, "I say, Sis, did you see that? Two in a row. Am I awesome or what?"

Mama slowly rolled in his direction.

"Who is this?" she asked. "Who is he talking to?"

The man now looked directly at Mama and started to walk slowly in her direction. By that time, I was behind her.

Mama looked toward the man, and then with one quick flick of the wrist, she spun herself around in my direction and sucked in her breath. I was right up on her, and through her cloudy gaze it was hard for Mama to make me out, but she knew my scent.

"Terry? It's you, right?" she asked with a tremor in her voice.

"Yeah, Mama, it's me," I replied.

I leaned into her face and rubbed my nose against hers. I could see tears forming in the clouds of her eyes. By this time, Kitty had taken charge of alerting the crowd that something big was going on and that everyone needed to be quiet. An eerie hush had fallen over the lanes nearest us.

Mama reached out and pulled me into her. I hugged her and whispered in her ear.

"I love you, Mama. I came here today to surprise you on your birthday. What do you think about that?"

"Well, I'm really surprised!" she said with a tear in her eye.

"Donnie, Marge, and DJ are here too," I said.

They came around on cue to give Mama a hug.

"Hey, Mom. Happy birthday," Donnie said.

"Oh, I just don't know what to say. Did you know about this, Kitty?" Mama yelled.

Kitty shook her head no—still a little wounded about her role as a zero-hour accomplice.

"So, Mama," I said, "I thought about this being your birthday and all and I wanted to bring you the best prize I could think of."

"Oh honey, this is the best present I could have. You and Donnie and the others here," she said with a warm embrace.

"Well, I'm glad, Mama, but there's one more part to this surprise today," I said.

"Oh, honey," she started. "What on earth could possibly top this? Unless you have a big birthday cake for me too," she said, jokingly.

Slowly stepping back, I released myself from Mama's embrace. Moving behind her, I clutched the handles of her wheelchair and slowly turned her around in the direction of the loud, obnoxious man in Lane 51.

Bending into her ear, I whispered, "Happy birthday, Ma."

Mama sat stunned for a moment. She looked hard through the blur of tears and years of eye surgeries to examine the man in Lane 51, who by now was kneeling close in front of her.

Mom and Eddie reunion, 1994

Looking at him and drawing in his scent through her running nose, she touched his face and looked back at me.

"Oh, Terry … it's you, Eddie, isn't it?"

"Yeah, Ma. It's me. Terry brought us all together for your birthday," he said.

"I knew it was you," Mama cried. "My heart knew it. I knew. I heard your beautiful voice. That beautiful Grandinetti voice, and my heart knew, but I couldn't imagine it was true, the way you were acting."

"We wanted to surprise you, Ma. We are here to celebrate you," Eddie said.

Mama and Eddie hugged and held on to each other, her head on his shoulder. They laughed and cried nervously. I stood back and snapped a few photos. They would be the last photos I would take of her in a moment of light and hope. I told Kitty about our ruse, and a murmur broke out among the crowd as friends and strangers applauded and cried at witnessing a mother-and-son embrace—one that had taken me 12 years to coordinate.

Mama hadn't seen Eddie in over a decade. Following his two tours in Vietnam in the early 1970s, he came back to the United States, married, and settled in Florida. There, he studied to become

Joyful homecoming for Mama and Eddie

a respiratory therapist, eventually taking a job with the Veterans Administration. He and his wife had two children, a boy and a girl, two years apart like me and Eddie.

From the time they were married, there was an odd tension between Mama and both Eddie and his wife. All I knew was that Marilyn, my father's sister, was still very involved with Eddie's family. This left Mama permanently on the outs, feeling that Marilyn had usurped her role as mother and grandmother. And she had. Mama's sins from the past kept pace with her throughout her life, and this was one way they played out. Eddie had seen Mama touch me inappropriately when I was a child, and I'm sure Marilyn knew about it too. I'm also sure she knew about Mama's drinking and infidelities and how my father's angry retaliation was taken out on me. He had long since died of a heart attack at age 47, so he was not in the picture. Maybe Marilyn's focused embrace of Eddie's family was her way of atoning for my father's abusive behavior and protecting Eddie's children from Mama's wanton ways. Whatever the case, it worked. Eddie and his family were virtually removed from our lives until their marriage ended in divorce in the early 1990s.

A lot was happening in Eddie's life at that time. He had been working on a book of poetry about his experiences in Vietnam, which was published in 1991. Its title says it all: *Vietnam Trilogy: And God Died Too.* After that, his home was hit by Hurricane Andrew in 1992, creating great upheaval for the family and culminating in a difficult divorce. Much to Marilyn's chagrin, this turmoil in Eddie's life led him to reach out to me. We began corresponding and eventually this included an exchange of letters between Eddie and Mama.

Though Eddie had long been out of our lives, he was finally here in one of the last moments when Mama would have felt comfortable and dignified seeing him. We were all together, finally, in a healing moment. All of us, in the same place and at the same time, had come to honor and celebrate this woman who had given us life. On that day, at least, we were her present, and she was ours.

❊

As a child, I saw caseworkers show up unannounced at our apartment in the projects, interrogating Mama about men coming in and out and the lack of food in the refrigerator, demanding rent and utility receipts, and threatening to separate our family. I saw the bewilderment, fear, and shame in my mother as she sat in a puddle of humiliation following these raids. It broke my heart to see Mama like that. How badly I wanted to fix her; how badly I wanted to help her stop drinking and make herself healthy with a few obvious and simple choices, so that she wouldn't feel so bad about herself.

I wondered for years, as an adult, if things were as bad as I remembered. Like Mama, I drank my way through those early years and beyond. Not until I got sober and started working with Ms. Yvette did I begin to question my recollection of things. Then, many years later, my memories were corroborated by Eddie and by Mama herself.

When Mama passed, I inherited her personal belongings. There was not much. I mourned her death terribly, as though my own child had died. And, in truth, she was that to me. My bereavement lasted well over a year. My world turned topsy-turvy. Seismic emotional shifts left me feeling insecure and emotionally, mentally, and physically unstable. Familiar and oddly comforting childhood dread, terror, and depression consumed me in those early months as I dragged the loss around with me.

Included in her personal belongings was a box that I assumed contained family photos and such. It sat in my living room for months, haunting me, begging to be opened. On a night when I was particularly consumed with grief and needed desperately to connect with her, I pulled out of a sealed plastic bag a throw that she made and used for years to cover herself. It held her scent; I breathed deeply into it. Now engaged fully in my grief, I ventured into Mama's box. What I found evoked immediate shame that unnerved me, but also validated my childhood recollections.

First, I saw baby doctor visit books for Eddie and me. Eddie's visits were filled out for two years, mine for several months. Then, rooting through the box, I found evidence to support and fill in the holes of my Swiss-cheese memory. There were citations sent to Mama following welfare caseworkers' visitations, noting the presence of alcohol in the home and empty food cupboards, men's clothing and other signs of a man living in or frequenting the home, possible fraudulent use of government assistance, child endangerment, and threats to remove the children from the home. There was a letter from an attorney expressing a willingness to represent Mama in her efforts to keep us together. Wrapped in brittle rubber bands were copies of every rent receipt, every paid gas and electric bill, and empty food stamp books with date notations in the corner in Mama's handwriting. Receipts for groceries and clothing or fabric purchases were all organized by date. A Dark Horse whiskey shot glass audibly rolled around in the box.

Underneath the papers and reports was a mishmash collection of Mama's family photos. Pictures from her childhood, with her parents and siblings, depicted a life that seemed full and abounding in love, attention, connection—showing a sense of belonging, camaraderie, and affection. First Holy Communion pictures, family reunion photos, photos of her grandparents, holiday photos, one of Mama singing with her sister Jean and older brother Paul. Wholesome, beautiful family photos.

Some of the photos were familiar to me—ones that Mama had shared with me over the years; some I had never seen before.

Mama in Arlington Heights Projects, 1955

I mentally interrogated the holdings of my mother's life contained in this old waxed LaHave Brothers "Louisiana Nuggets" sweet potato box. I was struck by the obvious disconnect between her childhood years and what her life had become. The evidence was right there before me, indicating that things had been reasonably happy and normal for her before they had gone terribly wrong. What? When? Why? It was all a mystery to me, but there was no denying that something horrible had fractured Mama's relationship with her family and caused her great shame.

In the bottom of the box, I found a black-and-white photo of my mother, taken when she lived in the projects. In it, she sits on a linoleum tiled floor and stares blankly into a camera. Her knees are drawn up toward her chest with her hands around them. The room is barren and feels cold. I wondered who took the photo. I looked at my mother leaning against an empty wall and felt that I had been meant to find the photo (and her) at that exact moment.

Her eyes were not blank, as I had first interpreted them. They were pleading, imploring. I stared at her and realized that in the last years of her life she had done penance for things that had happened earlier in her life and ours. She had, to the best of her ability, pursued some fumbling attempt at atonement. Though her efforts were derailed time and again by her health or her pride, she fought back each time, and I witnessed it. I was at her side. I felt her determination and sense of urgency. Most notably, she had stopped drinking after her second amputation, when it would have been the easiest possible time to escalate her drinking or double down on her indifference and self-destructiveness. She chose the opposite path, and I admire her for that.

She and I made "living amends" to each other, reshaping our relationship while we still could. She knew that I forgave her. She knew that she had done wrong in many ways, and she acknowledged it. Amidst all the surgeries and long hospital stays, I bore witness (improbable as it may sound) to her growth. The more she suffered, the more she felt an insatiable thirst to be of service to others—the very calling by which I had come to define and rebuild my life, beginning with my work at Gateway many years earlier. To see her manifest at last as the person she was and wanted to be and to see that we both shared that same fundamental desire bonded us. Her growth and change healed and soothed me, making it possible for the twilight of her life to function not as the end of a tragedy, but as a flash of redemption.

Mama finally succumbed to death's long pull on her on April 24, 1995.

17.

A REUNION

On a beautiful day in the spring of 2006, I put on my sunglasses as I left the University of Pittsburgh's Alumni Hall to walk over to the University Club, where I was meeting Jack and Jean for lunch. Thoughts of Jack went through my mind as I recalled how instrumental he had been in helping me get my life turned around.

My heart swelled with joy and even pride as I considered how our relationship had changed over the years. In those early years of my recovery, Jack was always there for me, a crucial part of my support network, right up there with my recovery mentors. Then, over time, there came a point when Jack reached out to me for help. I felt totally ill-equipped to assist him. After all, he had a few years of recovery on me and his transformation into sobriety and clarity had been extreme, graceful, and (as far as I could see) seamless. As I passed the grassy area across the street from Pitt's Cathedral of Learning, crowded with sunbathing, Frisbee-throwing, hacky-sacking students, I smiled to myself as I recalled the first time Jack had asked me for help.

About a year or so into my recovery, I sat in my office at the Koppers Company, processing visa applications for our construction site managers for a job in Ankara, Turkey. I was finishing a call with the U.S. Consulate General in Washington when Jack unexpectedly blew into my office, impeccably dressed in a Joseph A. Bank blue herringbone suit, and quickly closed the door behind him.

Recently retired and about three years into his recovery from alcoholism, Jack was doing amazingly well. He had been invited to sit on the board of directors of Gateway Rehabilitation Center by Dr. Twerski, the organization's founder, and he was very active in recovery circles. I knew that Jack was coming to Koppers this day to have lunch with some of his former cronies, but I was surprised when he breezed into my office.

"Hey, Jack," I said, greeting him with a smile and hug. "How the hell are you, friend?"

Sitting across from me, anxiously twirling his fedora in his hands, he spoke up.

"Oh, Terry. I think I'm doing something wrong," he said.

I cocked my head to attention.

"What, Jack? Shit, did you drink?" I asked.

"No, no, it's not that," he said, almost panting. "It's something else. You know that my sponsor died this past year."

"I do. John, right? You guys were really close. You were even close with his wife, Jean, if I'm remembering correctly," I said. "And you got a new sponsor, right? I thought it was going well."

"Yes, Martin. He's great, but I don't know if I can talk to him about what's going on."

"Shit, Jack. What is it?"

"Oh, fuck," he said. "Look, it's Jean. John's wife. His widow. My *sponsor's* widow. I've been seeing her, supporting her since John's passing. You know, helping with legal matters and stuff like that. Oh, God."

"What, Jack?"

"I've fallen in love with her, Terry. And I feel so bad. I shouldn't and didn't mean for this to happen, but it has. I don't know what to do or who to talk to about it," he stammered tearfully.

I could see Jack's obvious angst and anxiety, and I felt my own heart racing in my chest as I considered what to say to him. *Holy shit* was the main thought going through my head.

"Okay, okay. So, you haven't spoken to Martin yet," I said.

"No, I'm afraid of what he will say."

"Yeah, that's understandable. Okay, well, I have to ask. First, does Jean have feelings for you too?"

"Yes. And, she is struggling with this too. We didn't mean for this to happen. It's only about a year since John passed, and we both feel so conflicted," he said.

"Okay, well, if I were in this situation, I know you would tell me to talk to my sponsor, but I get that you feel concerned about doing that right now," I said.

I paused, feeling too flummoxed to conjure up any advice. I said what I could, unfiltered.

"Look, you have to talk with someone besides me. I don't know how to counsel you. So let me ask—would you feel comfortable talking with Dr. Twerski about this? The two of you have become good friends and maybe he can provide some direction to you. Or what about your minister over at your church? Maybe both you and Jean can talk with him," I suggested.

"Those are really good ideas, Terry, but I'm not sure."

"Listen, Jack, I'm new at this recovery stuff, as you know. I don't know what to tell you, except that I know when shit comes up, we have to talk about it, because as you have told me, speaking about our problems punches the power out of them, and what stays stuck in between our ears is usually bullshit and can send us back toward a drink. Right?"

He nodded.

"You and Jean haven't done anything wrong," I said. "You have found each other. That's all. There's no shame in that," I said, trying to console him.

"You're right. You're right. And I'll call Dr. Twerski today," he said.

"I think that's a good idea."

I rose from my chair and gave him a hug.

We both breathed in deeply and exhaled loudly. Finally, he flashed one of his trademark million-dollar smiles and said to me in his best Pittsburghese, "Listen to you, now, being all sober 'n 'at!"

We laughed, exchanging Pittsburgh-style "yinzer" remarks raucously enough to attract the attention of Miss Kniss, who came in to ask us to keep it down a little.

All these years later, as I headed up the steps to the University Club to meet Jack and Jean, I was taken by the simple beauty of a cluster of daffodils fully in bloom. I also noticed the lemony scent of budding magnolia trees that lined the stairway. In honor of my selection as director of Pitt's Institute of Politics in 2005, Jack and Jean wanted to take me to lunch at the Duquesne Club downtown to celebrate. But with my new designation, I now had privileges at Pitt's University Club, so I invited Jack and Jean to be *my guests* for lunch.

It wasn't intended as some grand, showy gesture to invite them to lunch, but rather an opportunity to share my thanks with both of them—thanks that they both deserved. Though we had stayed in touch mainly by calls and email over the 20-plus years of our shared sobriety, I wanted to see Jack and Jean to express my gratitude for their unwavering support of me. If Jack had not answered his phone on that snowy winter night in 1981 when I called on him for help in the midst of a blackout, I don't believe I would be alive. If I hadn't witnessed his emotional strength on the day of his wife's memorial and funeral, I would not have seen the power of his sobriety, resilience, and grace. Merely witnessing his transformation in recovery made me think that mine was possible too. I would not have a real life, the version of life I now cherish, without having known him.

I entered the University Club lobby, and seated in the high-back leather chairs were Jack and Jean, both lounging with a cup of coffee and a copy of the *New York Times* and *Pittsburgh Post-Gazette*, respectively. Though they were octogenarians by then, they both were elegant, sophisticated, and thoroughly comfortable with themselves.

Jack spotted me, smiled, and had to work a bit to rise to his feet.

"These old legs," he said, laughing a little.

"Ah, you look great, Jack. And Jean. It's so great to see you both," I said, hugging them.

After exchanging greetings, we bypassed the elegant spiral staircase and took the elevator to the Fraternity Grille on the second floor.

The tables were full and buzzing with lively conversations between university faculty and visiting scholars, Pitt leadership and international dignitaries, and alumni, including foundation executives and elected officials. Moe Coleman was there too, at a table with an executive from The Pittsburgh Foundation, discussing a local government efficiency and effectiveness initiative she was interested in supporting. I smiled and nodded in Moe's direction as Jack, Jean, and I were directed to a reserved window table.

Looking around the room, I could not help but feel a moment of pride in what I had made of my life. I thought about how decades earlier I had wished for nothing more than the peace that would come with death. On this day, sitting across from Jack and Jean, I hoped they could see that their investment in me—their kindness and generosity of heart—and a lot of hard work on my part had brought us to this meeting. I experienced a sense of gratitude and deep humility as I looked around the room of distinguished guests, knowing that I was one of them—not more than or less than the others, but the same. I simply belonged.

(Left to right) Former Pennsylvania Governor Dick Thornburgh, then Pennsylvania Governor Tom Corbett, Terry Miller, Elsie and Henry Hillman, and former Pennsylvania Governor Tom Ridge at the Elsie Hillman Lifetime Achievement Award for Excellence in Community Service Ceremony

An Institute of Politics colleague came by and said hello, asking if I would call him regarding a project on first responders and emergency preparedness. I said I'd be in touch.

Jack snapped his napkin onto his lap and grinned at me as he took a sip of water.

"Well, Terry. Regional leaders, foundation executives, and elected officials. Look at you," he said, smiling genuinely.

"You must be so proud of yourself for what you have accomplished," Jean said. "As you should be. Well, we couldn't be prouder of you."

"Like parents," Jack said, playfully.

"On my way over here," I said, "I was reflecting on that call I made to you in 1981. In a blackout, to boot. Some serious intuition was moving in my life then. I never thought I would be grateful for having a blackout but I am for that night. I remember reading a quotation from Jonas Salk where he said, 'Intuition will tell the thinking mind where to look next.' That night it led me to you and because you responded as you did, we are here today."

Jack smiled sheepishly while fiddling with his napkin.

"Well, all things work together for good, Terry," he said.

I took a deep breath.

"From the sounds of it, you're doing some really important work here at the University," Jack continued.

"I do think it's important, Jack. But the truth is, I couldn't have done any of it without you. Who knows where I would be if you hadn't picked up the phone that night?"

"You would have been fine," Jack said, dismissing my remarks.

"None of that is guaranteed. Not at all. Either way, right now, regardless of the change of scenery, I'm only doing what I learned to do so well from you, and from others in recovery circles. I'm just trying to be of service. When you think of it, what I get to do at the Institute is to bring together people with disparate points of view, from different backgrounds, who have a common problem and help them find a common solution. Does that sound familiar?"

He laughed.

"Yeah," he said, "I seem to recall some other organization that's doing that kind of work."

I pointed Moe out to Jack and Jean and shared with them how influential he had been in helping me and our team establish POWER. I also mentioned that he was the founder of the Institute of Politics and brought me on as his deputy when I needed to step away from my position as POWER's executive director.

"Moe's a master community organizer, a collaborative leader, and a genius, if you ask me," I gushed.

"How so?" Jack asked.

"He's the kind of guy who is not interested in getting credit for the work he does. He's focused on others' interests and less on self-interest. He understands that if you really want to accomplish good work on behalf of struggling communities, the environment, or vulnerable populations, you have to inclusively engage people to help them take ownership of the problem *and* the solution. It sounds easy, but it takes a special kind of person to do this work. Someone who is close enough to people to hear their concerns, but far enough ahead to lead them toward solutions and assist in implementing them," I explained.

"Well, the Chancellor named you as director after Moe stepped down, so they must see those same leadership qualities in you," Jack said, patting my hand.

"That's nice of you to say. I'm humbled by the Chancellor's recognition of me and my work. It's an honor," I replied.

"We're so proud of you, Terry," Jean repeated.

Over a lunch of broccoli cheese soup and lobster roll sandwiches, Jack, Jean, and I walked down memory lane, talking about those early years of recovery.

"I remember an early recovery meeting with you, Jack. The Fifth and Negley meeting in the basement. A small room. Very small, as I recall. It was a beginners' meeting. People were sitting around on old couches and chairs. Some of us were on the floor. That one lone lamp sitting askew on a broken table in the corner. The room was so full of smoke it felt like an opium den.

Literally, hands reaching through a blue haze of smoke with raspy, rattling voices saying, 'Hi, my name's Joe, welcome.' Or Mary. Or Sam. Oddly, they all sounded the same. Must have been the smoke."

We all laughed.

"Yeah, those old smoking meetings. That was some serious anonymity," he joked.

Over our dessert of chocolate mousse cake and coffee, we talked about the good and bad times: the sudden death of Jean's son, Chip; the birth of Jack's grandchildren; the establishment and growth of POWER; Jack's involvement on Gateway's board; my graduation from the university; Dot's life; my mother's life. Through it all, we had supported each other and stayed in touch enough to help each other through life's joys and difficult upheavals.

As I walked Jack and Jean back to their car, a sense of sadness came over me. As both were in their mid-eighties, it dawned on me that this could be the last time I would ever see them. My heart sank as I contemplated this. Though he still had that beautiful sparkle in his eye, I noted the unsteadiness in Jack's legs, the tremor in his hands, and the odd pastiness in his usually sharp, healthy, and ruddy complexion.

"You're okay to drive, right?" I asked.

"Heck, yeah," Jack said with a low chuckle.

"All right, but give me a call when you get home, okay?"

Jack grabbed me by the shoulders and kissed my forehead.

"Sure, honey. Now you get back to that office. I know you have some calls of your own to make," he commanded.

"Right," I said, giving both him and Jean hugs.

"Talk soon. I love you," I said as the car doors closed and I waved them off.

On my walk back to my office, I reflected on our talk and on my work at the Institute. Building on the strong foundation of the agency developed by Moe, I was able to broaden the breadth and scope of our impact. I could hardly believe my good fortune to work with such amazing, thoughtful

Terry presenting at an IOP Leadership Session

community leaders in our efforts to improve policies that translated into actionable steps and improved community outcomes.

Over the next year, as I charged into my role as director of the Institute of Politics, I connected with Jack from time to time by email. He reported to me on doctor appointments and on his visits with his grandchildren.

Terry with Moe and Allegheny County Chief Executive Rich Fitzgerald (at left) discussing policy options for financially distressed municipalities in 2016

Moe: teacher, mentor, friend, family

Then, in mid-2008, the emails all but stopped coming. We missed each other with phone calls, and the momentum of my job kept me moving at a dizzying pace. I told myself that Jack must be well or I would hear otherwise. Then, in December, I picked up a newspaper and read Jack's obituary.

I was able to make it to the memorial service at Westminster Church. The last time I had been in that church was for his wife's funeral, when I was still active in my addiction and couldn't even make it through the service without being stoned. At Jack's memorial, I stood in the standing-room-only church sanctuary, *sober*, as the minister and Jack's family read Scripture and told stories to honor the man who was to them a sober and loving father, stepfather, grandfather, and husband. In the back of the church, I wept for the man who had saved my life and who had been a loving presence for so long that I could hardly remember a time without him.

I drove home from his memorial, knowing that Jack was at peace and that he had lived well. I took a slight detour so I could drive through the Fort Pitt Tunnel and catch the famous view of downtown Pittsburgh and Point State Park, where Jack and I had conversed in a snowstorm—a conversation that not only changed my life, but saved it. There was no snow this time. ✳

Jack, Jean, and Terry, 2007

EPILOGUE

I grew up without books. Sure, from time to time, there were cheesy Harlequin romance novels strewn about our flat, passed along to my mother by neighbors: *Return to Love, When You Have Found Me, Scoundrel's Captive,* and *It's Wise to Forget.* I remember those titles with their steamy covers of chiseled men and scantily clad lovers, but no children's books were around at all. No Dr. Seuss's *The Cat in the Hat,* or E. B. White's *Charlotte's Web,* or Margaret Wise Brown's beloved bedtime classic, *Goodnight Moon.* I wouldn't say that Mama didn't want to read to us. I just assume that because of her emotional and physical troubles—in conjunction with getting the rent paid, the utilities on, the clothes on our backs, and food in our mouths—children's books didn't rank high on the list and thus fell through the cracks.

Nor was there any money to pay the book bill at parochial school. At the time, it was a source of great shame for me, as the good nuns of the Order of St. Francis of Assisi seemed to delight in both publicly embarrassing students who did not pay their book bill and withholding books from them as a form of punishment. For this reason, I had to stay after school to "borrow" books so that I could read my assignments for the next day. Something so simple stymied my reading and learning ability, creating a deficiency that has followed me throughout my life. On the positive side, however, it also forced me to be highly proactive and organized in my work, which has been a lifelong skill that has served me well. On that note—thank you, Sister Anastasia!

Now that I'm retired and in a new stage of life, to be writing and reading as a passion is beyond gratifying. This work, including the development of this book, has allowed me to express what has been inside me all along and has given me the gift of clarity. I understand myself better and I have relinquished the defeatist attitude and the overall bleak emotional sway that past life experiences held over me for many years.

In the years following the establishment of POWER, I obtained my master's degree in social work and then, at Moe Coleman's invitation, joined the staff of the University of Pittsburgh's Institute of Politics. POWER remains a thriving organization, still pursuing its mission to support women (and now men, too) in recovery from substance abuse. Approximately 20,000 people and counting have utilized its programs. I am humbled by that achievement and by the continued good work of POWER's leadership, team, and supporters. I remain on POWER's advisory council, which is to me a great blessing. It is a way for me to sustain my connection with that early vision and dream now that it's a living, thriving reality.

My 25 years at the Institute of Politics were also fulfilling, even formative. Moe brought me on board in 1992. Then, in 2005, the Chancellor named me director, and I was privileged to continue Moe's tradition and my own established pattern of servant leadership by organizing, facilitating, and producing nonpartisan, high-level policy forums and educational publications that guided regional policymaking. I spent every day involved in projects aimed at improving the quality of life of the people of southwestern Pennsylvania. Over the years, many recommendations put forth through the politically neutral, research-based work of our Institute's policy committees and special task forces were implemented, achieving significant and positive policy outcomes.

In more recent years, I was privileged to work with public-sector leaders to address policy issues dear to my heart. In 2016, the U.S. Attorney for the Western District of Pennsylvania asked me to participate on a special task force on the opioid and heroin epidemic. The task force's work culminated in a report that I co-authored, which provided policy, educational, intervention, and community recommendations, many of which have been implemented. The task force's work and its outcomes provided a national model of an effective community-level response to this horrendous epidemic.

In 2016, I also created a donor-advised fund, the Our Daily Bread Fund, at The Pittsburgh Foundation, a community philanthropic foundation. The fund's purpose is to support the Greater Pittsburgh Community Food Bank in its efforts to eliminate hunger. As I've learned from experience, you cannot tell a hungry child today that you gave them a meal yesterday. I hope to drive support into the fund, including revenue generated from the sale of this book, for years to come. Please visit **pittsburghfoundation.org/our-daily-bread-fund** for more information.

To have been associated with the good work of the Institute of Politics and to be one of the many benefactors of Moe Coleman's living legacy for more than 25 years is nothing short of miraculous. I know I am not supposed to be here.

As a child, sitting against the Inky Wall at the top of Fort Hill, stealing cigarettes, and drinking Mama's booze to numb my hopelessness and loneliness or looking down on the fiery mill on the South Side and the twinkling lights of the city, I never could have imagined that one day I would be an upstanding, highly regarded, and respected leader in my community. To have offered meaningful public service to the Pittsburgh region, the Commonwealth of Pennsylvania—and even our nation—has been a high honor.

Sadly, in 2018, physical health issues pushed me into early retirement. I am well aware of the vast research conducted on the poor physical, behavioral, and emotional outcomes of the children who live through poverty and on their exposure to food insecurity, neglect, abuse, and all the rest. I am living proof of those research findings. Some of my health issues are genetic, but others are directly related to the physical, emotional, and nutritional deficiencies of my youth. It's painful and challenging to accept that at times, but I counter and eventually mute that feeling by simply treating myself well now. Now that I'm in retirement, I write, meditate, do yoga, swim, and study. And with the support of my partner, Mary Ellen, I love, I play, and I travel.

Yes, I found love!

Mary Ellen and I met in 2014, after orbiting each other for years in Pittsburgh social and professional circles; in December 2016, we married. Moe walked me down the aisle, and Mary Ellen's children made the march with her; her grandchildren—our grandchildren—Elliot and Evan served as our ring bearer and flower girl, respectively.

Mary Ellen is kind, smart, funny and strong-willed, and she loves fiercely. We are good together. Perhaps it's because we are older and have had our fair share of wildly unhealthy relationships or maybe it's because the years ahead of us are fewer than those behind us, but whatever the reason, we are committed to being of service to ourselves and to each other. We are respectful and honest and we "stay current" with each other. That means that when there is turmoil brewing between us somewhere under the surface, we unpack it in the moment and address it before it mushrooms into something that can pollute and sabotage our relationship. It's not easy, because it involves regularly taking risks and being vulnerable. But we do it—sometimes with grace, usually without— because the rewards of risking and sharing our weaknesses, our wounds, and our hearts, especially when we are deep in fear, far outweigh any supposed benefits of living in the fantasy world of denial. It's hard work, but we are both worthy of it.

I also am learning how to be in a family. It feels odd at age 65, but here I am doing it anyway. I am blessed to have amazing longtime friends in my life who support and love me. I would not be in my new family without them. Today, I am learning how to be a good and responsible partner, sister, stepmother, and grandmother. I have a good relationship with my sisters-in-law, Phyllis, Cheryl, and Carol, and am developing strong relations with Mary Ellen's children, my stepchildren: her son Matthew and his partner Kris; her daughter, Kate; and Stephen, her youngest. Like Mary Ellen herself, her children are beautiful, talented people, all making creative and meaningful contributions to our communities. Stephen is a gifted musician, writer, editor, and teacher; Kate is a mental health professional serving some of our most vulnerable populations. Matt and Kris are doing it all! They are accomplished academics, both teaching, researching, and directing programs in the Department of Psychology at the University of Alabama. They also are the parents of Elliot, age nine, and Evan, age five. On family visits—birthdays, holidays, or just about any time since we're retired—I marvel at their parenting and how they seamlessly juggle the competing and equally important demands of work and family, seemingly with a consistent sense of emotional equilibrium toward each other and especially toward their children.

At an adults-only dinner last summer, I caught myself saying to Matt and Kris, "You guys are amazing."

They looked at each other and then at me and said, "Thank you."

"No, really, I mean it. I get to watch and participate in your family and to see up close what good parenting looks like. You so clearly unconditionally love and support your kids. You lift them up, catching them when they are doing the right thing while also disciplining them and setting limits. You consistently model good behavior and communicate openly and lovingly with them. And the kids get it! Really, it's amazing. It's a big deal."

Matt and Kris shot each other another look.

"You know, I'm working on this book project and revisiting how things were in my early life, so to see how well you love your children and how they love you is very healing for me," I added, with a burr in my throat. "I didn't have much of what you have. I remember the first time Elliot asked me to come and read him a bedtime story. I was terrified! I didn't grow up with books or the experience of bedtime stories, and I *still* get really nervous reading out loud. It was just a kids' book, but my nerves were jangled. Really," I said, half embarrassed and with a tear in my eye.

I looked down at the table and fiddled with my napkin. "I want to thank both of you, really. You're the real deal and you're helping me to heal my past."

Mary Ellen reached for my hand and gave it a squeeze. As I looked up, I saw Kris mouth to Matt, *"I love you."*

In the few moments during which this exchange of words and emotions took place, I realized that these simple moments are the rewards of doing the difficult work to heal past traumas. My understanding of trauma has matured. I now accept the idea that trauma is not what happened to me in my external world—poverty, neglect, abuse, hunger—but rather what happened to me internally as a result of these things. Deep emotional, mental, physical, and spiritual wounds hardened over time, making me rigid and reactive toward myself, my world, and those in it. I threw myself fully into an addiction to drugs and alcohol that only temporarily soothed my dysphoria. As every alcoholic and addict knows, there are not enough substances in the world to ever get *that* job done.

Healing trauma is a long game. It is a spiritual awakening to our true selves; to our joy, our pleasure, our peace of mind, our bonds with others, love, belonging, happiness, forgiveness, purpose, and meaning. It is not a science, but rather the intuitive art of wooing and bringing forth what is inherently ours: our spiritual essence. For me, this process has involved making a walk back to myself by revisiting those places in me and in my life that I had long abandoned—my lost, addicted young woman; my confused and sullen adolescent; and my lonely, neglected, yet resilient and brave child. I continue on this path into my spiritual essence, accompanied today by the rewards of making this journey—joy, happiness, vulnerability, belonging, and all the rest. This is my birthright. It is a journey to a prize of which I am worthy. It is my birthright and it is yours too.

I write to share a story told from the perspective of a woman who has worked long and hard through various traditional and non-traditional therapeutic mechanisms to integrate my affective, cognitive, behavioral, and even physiological systems—the healing and embrace—within myself. Secondly, I write to be of service to my readers. The purpose of this book is to be of service and value to others—trauma survivors, those caught in the throes of addiction, those in recovery, and those who treat them and love them.

I believe that healing can take place in the interactive space between the reader and the writer. Though our lived experiences may not be exactly the same, anyone who has experienced trauma—and I happen to believe that if you are breathing, you have experienced trauma at some point in your life—has experienced the fracturing of spirit that occurs because of it. In this way, we are all the same. By sharing the most intimate accounts of my life, I invite the reader to recognize our shared humanity so that we can understand one another better. My lived experiences may be different than those of my readers, but pain is pain. My life was messy, flawed, and complicated, but by owning and sharing my pain and my healing, I hope to inspire others to own their stories, too.

We are living in a time of great social, political, economic, and environmental turmoil. It is a traumatic time. People feel a lack of connection—being seen, being heard, being valued. I understand this. That is why I have revealed my vulnerabilities in this book, seeing that gesture as an instrument of public service, believing that societies evolve and mature to the extent that individuals do.

Behind God's Back can be read, discussed, and used as an instrument of change in a variety of settings: in book clubs, among those living with and healing from trauma and addiction, in multimodal treatment programs by survivors and the professionals who work with them, and by family members who love and support those who are struggling with addiction or already in recovery. With the use of categorically developed study guides—child development, social work, psychiatry, community organizing—the book can also be used to educate present and future students training in these disciplines to learn through my story and "see the universal in the specific."

In the end, my goal is to express love, joy, grief, shame, despair, heartache, fear, desire, ambition, hope, and healing, reminding us that we all are a part of a human family with far more similarities than distinctions.

ON TRAUMATIC MEMORIES

The nature and impact of trauma co-occurring in mental and physiological systems is a complex and complicated issue for survivors and treatment providers.

When I look back on the years of my own healing, treatment seems to have had an intuitive art to it but was not supported by science. For me, the retrieval, recollection, and processing of traumatic memories came in horrifying and extreme waves of physical, cognitive, and emotional experiences. Nightmares, flashbacks, emotional swings, and intense somatic experiences occurred at times with acute vividness and other times without.

Now, the treatment of trauma is aided by science. Researchers studying trauma now can show what actually happens—in the brain and in the nervous system—during and after traumatic events. Today, studies in neuropsychology, neuroscience, and evolutionary and cognitive psychology work together to inform potential new intervention strategies for trauma survivors.

In writing this book, I trudged along the difficult road of retrieving and processing traumatic memories, organizing them, and expressing them in written form. The book is based on actual events in my life as truthfully as my recollection permits. Where I could, details have been verified through interviews with family and friends or are supported by independent personal documentation. Occasionally, dialogue consistent with my character or nature of the person speaking has been supplemented. In most cases, characters are actual individuals, and some names of people who appear in the story have been changed to protect their privacy.

PHOTO CREDITS

COVER
Foreground: Circa 1960, Miller personal photo collection
Background: © 2020 MLive Media Group. All rights reserved.
Used with permission.

PAGE 13
Circa 1950, Miller personal photo collection

PAGE 20
Circa 1950, Miller personal photo collection

PAGE 31
Circa 1951, Miller personal photo collection

PAGE 33
Circa 1959, Miller personal photo collection

PAGE 38
1995, Miller personal photo collection

PAGE 39
1955, Miller personal photo collection

PAGE 41
Circa 1959, Miller personal photo collection

PAGE 42
Circa 1963, Miller personal photo collection

PAGE 52
Miller personal photo collection

PAGE 56
Circa 1960, Miller personal photo collection

PAGE 62
Top and bottom: 1966, Miller personal photo collection

PAGE 66
Top: 1966, Miller personal photo collection
Bottom: 1967, Miller personal photo collection

PAGE 69
Circa 1957, Miller personal photo collection

PAGE 70
Circa 1970, Miller personal photo collection

PAGE 82

PAGE 83
2016, Miller personal photo collection, photo by Mary Ellen Trenga

PAGE 86
2015, Wikimedia Commons

PAGE 123
Undated, Gateway Rehabilitation Center. Used with permission.

PAGE 145
Undated, Brotha Ash Productions. Used with permission.

PAGE 149
Undated, Brotha Ash Productions. Used with permission

PAGE 159
2011, Institute of Politics Archives. Used with permission.

PAGE 161
Undated, Institute of Politics Archives. Used with permission.

PAGE 221
1991, Miller personal photo collection

PAGE 222
Top and bottom: 1991, Miller personal photo collection

PAGE 235
Top and bottom: 1994, Miller personal photo collection

PAGE 238
Circa 1955, Miller personal photo collection

PAGE 245
2012, Institute of Politics Archives. Used with permission.

PAGE 249
Top: 2015, Institute of Politics Archives. Used with permission.
Bottom: Undated, Institute of Politics Archives. Used with permission.

PAGE 250
Circa 2006, Institute of Politics Archives. Used with permission.

PAGE 251
Circa 2007, Miller personal photo collection

PAGE 267

ABOUT THE AUTHOR

"My work is anchored in the belief that healing can take place in the interactive space between the reader and the writer."

Terry Miller is director emerita of the University of Pittsburgh Institute of Politics, currently living in Milton, Delaware, where she writes, practices Zen Buddhism, and works to support human service agencies. She is an award-winning author, visionary consultant, and advocate working to address social, economic, and racial inequality issues.

Miller grew up in 1950s Pittsburgh, Pennsylvania, where "the black and gritty smoke from the steel works was as dark and biting as some of the characters I encountered in this mid-century mill town." Her family lived in the city's Arlington Heights Projects, and, with her two brothers, she was raised by a single mother in a strife-filled home. But the cycle of poverty, abuse, and addiction that characterized her life was broken when—at age thirty—Miller finally went to college. She attended the University of Pittsburgh, training as a social worker and community organizer, earning both bachelor's and master's degrees in social work. She led a university-based policy center for twenty-five years, founded nonprofit organizations dedicated to recovery and at-risk populations, and won numerous accolades.

In 2021, Miller won the Established Individual Artist Award for Nonfiction from the Delaware Division of the Arts, in partnership with the National Endowment for the Arts, for her work in *Behind God's Back: Finding Hope in Hardship*. She was also a 2016 finalist for a Western Pennsylvania Press Club Golden Quill Award. In 2015, her writing was published in the *Pittsburgh Quarterly Magazine*.

Miller is an inspirational speaker and has presented at national, state, and local conferences on issues related to healing trauma. A true visionary whose personal life is a testimony to the human spirit, her compelling story inspires audiences to look at the big picture of their own lives, encouraging them to aspire to be the best possible versions of themselves.

CPSIA information can be obtained
at www.ICGtesting.com
Printed in the USA
BVHW041934090122
625831BV00014B/1372